More Than 100 Recipes
from Food Network's Ultimate Cooking Challenge

BOBBY FLAY'S
THROWDOWN!

BOBBY FLAY WITH STEPHANIE BANYAS AND MIRIAM GARRON

CLARKSON POTTER/PUBLISHERS
NEW YORK

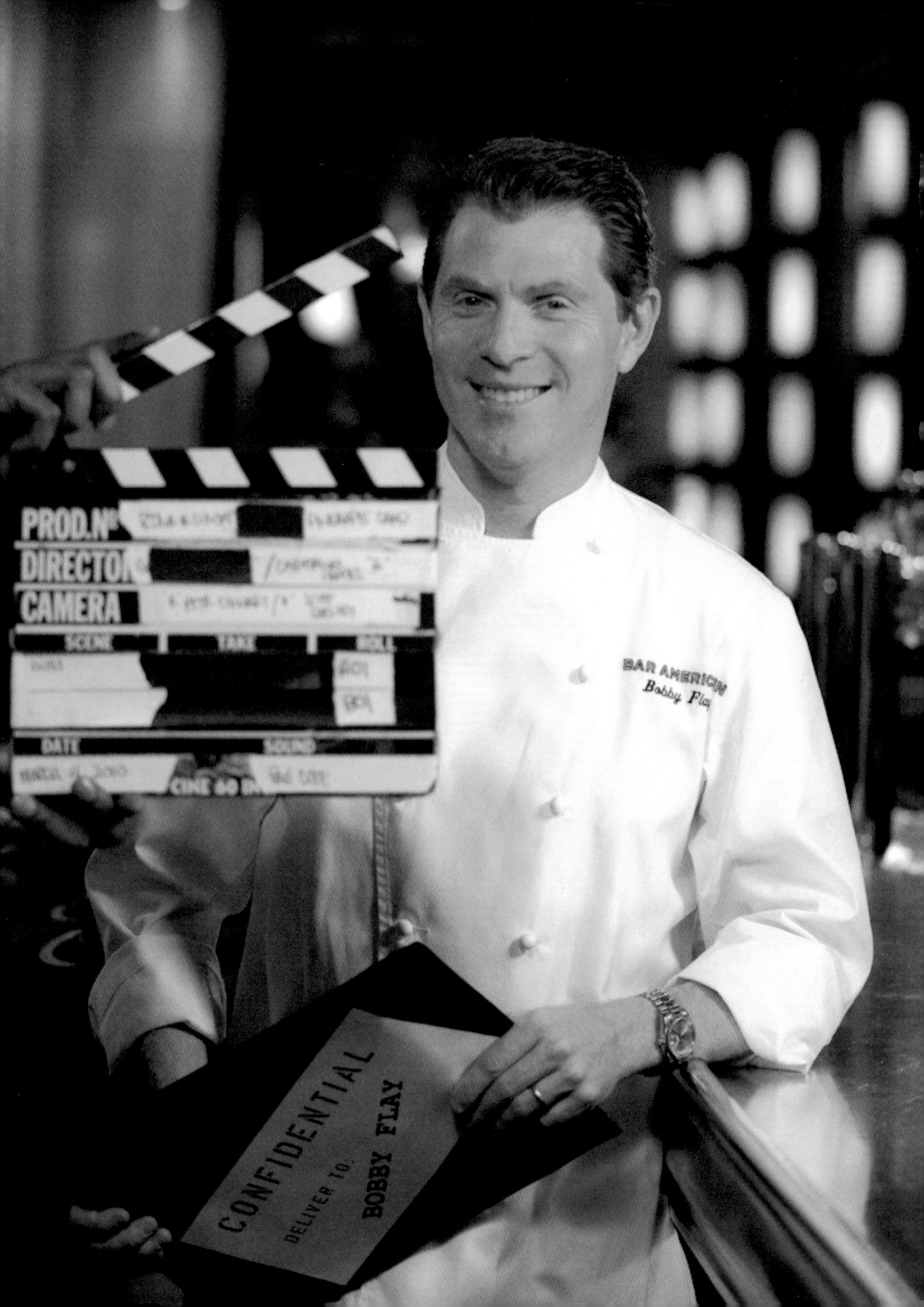
PROD.Nº
CAMERA
CONFIDENTIAL
DELIVER TO:
BOBBY FLAY

CONTENTS

Acknowledgments

Stephanie Banyas, Miriam Garron, Sally Jackson, Renee Forsberg, Lauren Bailey, Ben Fink, Barb Fritz, Jennifer Baum, Kay Lindsay, Chris Langley, Brooke Vecchio, Eliza Whipple

At Clarkson Potter, Rica Allannic, Marysarah Quinn, Ashley Phillips, Kate Tyler, Jill Browning, Donna Passannante, Christine Tanigawa, Joan Denman, Lauren Shakely

At Food Network, Brooke Johnson, Bob Tuschman, Bruce Seidel, Susie Fogelson, Kim Williamson, Susan Stockton, Jill Novatt, Danielle LaRosa, Katie Rubel, Susan Vu, Ivee Stephens, Liz Tarpy, Carrie Welch, Lisa Kreuger, Amanda Melnick, Katie Ilch, Lynda Chen, Mory Thomas, Santos Loo, Jay Brooks, Morgan Hass, Erik Pinkston, M. J. McNamara, Anastasiya McNearey Barabanova, Katie Carey, Gracielle Caces, Emilia Fonda, Gabriela Grande,

Joo Sang Jeong, Jamie Tulchin, Jonathan Piereth, Loan Nguyen, Vince Camillo, Young Sun Huh, Jacob Schiffman, Rob Bleifer, Marina Spau

At Rock Shrimp Productions, Kim Martin, Fran Alswang, Rebecca Bregman, F. Stone Roberts, Eve Schenk, S.B., Abigail Bahret, Bjorn Bellenbaum, Emily Benson, Jeanne Bernard, Darin Bresnitz, P.C., P.C., Donna Clapp, Kathryn Cooper, John Dias, J.F., R.F., Brian Falk, Stephanie Feder, Anthony Fitzgerald, Adam Fleishhacker, Michele Friedman, Courtney Fuglein, Kate Gibson, Adam Hall, Robin Held, Alejandra Huerta, A.J., J.K., Grace Kim, Rachel Knobelman, Debbie Levin, Vanessa Moreno, Ninja, Drew Oberholtzer, Philip Opere, C.P., D.P., Jessica Pantzer, Grace Ramirez, Matt Reynolds, Luke Riffle, C.S., S.S., Michael Sellers, Sam Shinn, L.T., Henry Tenney, D.W., Dahlia Warner, David Wheir, David Wilson

Introduction

Throwdown . . . It sounds like a brutal death match between two wrestlers or an Ultimate Fighting Championship cage fight. But in fact, a Throwdown is a friendly surprise competition and the best part about it is the ending, when we all get to eat some seriously delicious food.

The genesis for Throwdown! was pretty simple. When I had taped close to one hundred episodes of a show called Food Nation for Food Network a few years ago, I realized that by traveling around the country I had been privileged to meet so many wonderful people who were cooking, smoking, deep-frying, steaming, and baking these amazing regional dishes. Filming the show across America had really opened my eyes to how incredibly rich our country is when it comes to our food and the people who cook it.

Couple that with the fact that I have always felt that good cooks are at their best when they are not overthinking what they're doing—but instead making their particular specialties—and the germ of the idea for Throwdown! was born. What if I assembled a group of covert researchers to find the best cooks in America—those so known for a single dish that they have become celebrities in their own community, local heroes who have won their neighbors' hearts with the dishes they are passionate about?

And that's how it all started. The setup, which does involve a few white lies so we can keep our cover, goes something like this: We find someone terrific and tell them that Food Network wants to shoot a special with them. We tell them that over the next few days we want to see what they do in terms of shopping and prepping the food, and that we'd like to meet their friends and family because we want to hear great things about them that they can't say about themselves. While all of this is going on, I'm practicing and strategizing with my two trusted assistants, Stephanie and Miriam, to make a version of what our guest chef is making. At some point the production team asks the star to create a small party to celebrate their special on Food Network.

Then comes the moment of truth. Just when everything is going along swimmingly, I crash the party and politely challenge our star to a Throwdown, right then and there. For me, this is both the most exciting and the most nerve-racking moment of the show. The same questions run through my mind every time: Will they accept the Throwdown and be into it or will they show me the door? Do they know what the show is or am I going to have to explain it to them in the heat of excitement? And do they even know who I am? (Trust me, several people have not.)

So far, I have to say we have had wonderful success with people being incredibly gracious and receptive, despite our little white lie—OK, big fat lie. It's always a good time and a win-win situation for everyone. I get to meet some of the nicest people, travel to some of the best places in this country, and, most important, eat absolutely great food. Also, I can honestly say that I learn something valuable at every Throwdown, including how to make the perfect puffy taco shell with Diana Barrios Treviño in San Antonio; award-winning Texas chili with Cindy Reed Wilkins in Houston; truly crispy fish and chips with Mat Arnfeld, a British national who now resides in New York City; the most delicious, rich, gooey sticky buns with Joanne Chang in Boston; and how to become a certified pitmaster cranking out perfectly barbecued and smoked pulled pork sandwiches with Lee Ann Whippen in Virginia.

And the competitors? They get national exposure for themselves and their food on one of the top-rated shows on Food Network, where they will be seen by millions of people over and over again. Food Network fans are loyal and curious and I'm thrilled that they've been so supportive of the small businesses that we've featured on Throwdown!

In the end, it's not about who wins or loses. In fact—a little behind-the-scenes info—when I initially pitched the show idea to Food Network, I specifically spelled out that there would <u>not</u> be a formal panel of judges. My idea was to just have a bunch of clips of people eating both dishes and giving their comments so that viewers could decide for themselves who "won." Then we'd fade to black, almost like at the end of a good movie that doesn't quite wrap everything up and leaves you thinking about what might have happened—or what happens next. In the end it was decided that there would be a formal judging at each Throwdown to determine a winner. My record is not very good in terms of wins, but that is OK with me. <u>Throwdown!</u> is much more than just a show to me. Ultimately, it's about the people we meet and the food they teach us to love.

Ironically, I get challenged a couple dozen times a day: on the subway, in my restaurants, on the street, on an airplane . . . everywhere. But it doesn't work that way. We have to find you. If you challenge me, you'll know I'm coming and that ruins part of the fun.

If you want my best advice on how to become a competitor on <u>Throwdown!</u> here it is: Be the best at what you do, do it with passion, and do it with a smile. I have three full-time researchers constantly on the lookout for amazing food and the people who make it. They have their ears to the ground and are listening to what people are saying about folks cooking around the country. If you are good, we will find you.

So to all of you awesome cooks out there, keep doing what you do, but ask yourself this: Are you ready for a Throwdown?

Bobby Flay

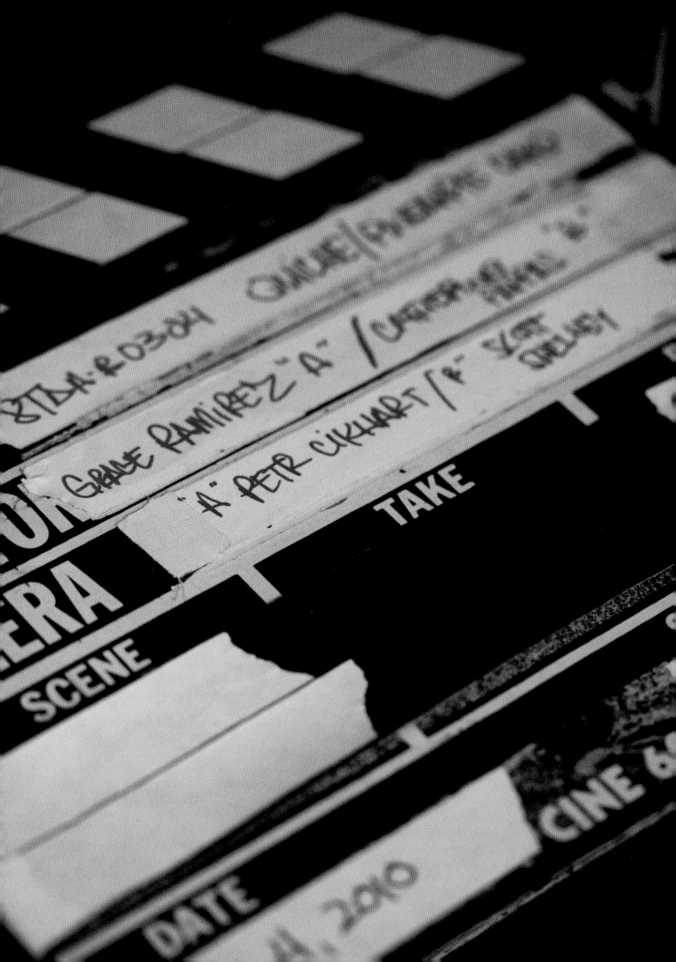

EPISODE GUIDE

Season 1

Pilot. Barbecue	Butch Lupinetti	Mount Laurel, NJ
1. Chowder	Ben Sargent	Brooklyn, NY
2. Wedding Cake	Michelle Doll	Brooklyn, NY
3. Red Chili	Cindy Reed Wilkins	Houston, TX
4. Jerk Chicken	Angela Shelf Medearis	Austin, TX
5. Steak	Eric Dominijanni	Twentynine Palms, CA
6. Breakfast	Lynn Winter	Louisville, KY
7. Burgers	Susan Mello	Queens, NY
8. Jambalaya	Emile Stieffel	New Orleans, LA
9. Cocktails	Tobin Ellis	Las Vegas, NV
10. Doughnuts	Mark Isreal	New York City, NY
11. Cheesesteak	Tony Luke Jr.	Philadelphia, PA
12. Ice Cream	Jeff Sommers	Saint Paul, MN
13. Fried Chicken	Jasper Alexander	Saratoga Springs, NY
14. Pizza	Giorgio Giove	Staten Island, NY

Season 2

1. Chocolate	Fritz Knipschildt	Norwalk, CT
2. Chicken Cacciatore	Keith Young	Freeport, Long Island, NY
3. Meatloaf	Jack and Rocco Collucci	Hyannis, MA
4. Mac 'n' Cheese	Delilah Winder	Philadelphia, PA
5. Fish and Chips	Mat Arnfeld	New York City, NY
6. Cheesecake	Alan Rosen	Brooklyn, NY
7. Cuban Roast Pork	Roberto Guerra	Miami, FL
8. BBQ Spare Ribs	Buz Grossberg	Richmond, VA
9. Cupcakes	Terri Wahl	Los Angeles, CA
10. Hot Dogs	Richard, Gloria, and Beverly Pink	Hollywood, CA
11. Buffalo Wings	Drew Cerza	Buffalo, NY
12. Sticky Buns	Joanne Chang	Boston, MA
13. Hot Browns	Joe and John Castro	Louisville, KY

Season 3

1. Crêpes	Andrea Day-Boykin and Nessa Higgins	Austin, TX
2. Puffy Tacos	Diana Barrios Treviño	San Antonio, TX
3. Jerk Steak	Nigel Spence	Mount Vernon, NY
4. Chicken Fried Steak	Paula Deen	Savannah, GA
5. Fruit Pie	Janet LaPosta and Ally Taylor	Rockland, ME
6. Crab Cakes	Mitch Weiss	Boothbay Harbor, ME
7. Muffuletta	Mike and Jack Serio	New Orleans, LA
8. Blondies	Tom Finney and Mark Ballard	Columbus, OH
9. Meatballs	Mike Maroni	Northport, NY
10. Ice Cream Sundaes	Julia Reynolds	Greenwich, NY
11. Lasagna	Mark Bove	Burlington, VT
12. Turkey and Dressing	Renee Ferguson	Geneva, IL
13. Gingerbread	Johanna Rosson	Macomb, IL

Season 4

1. Biscuits and Jam	Carol Fay	Nashville, TN
2. Ice Pops	Norma and Irma Paz	Nashville, TN
3. Chocolate Chip Cookies	Pam Weekes and Connie McDonals	New York City, NY
4. Eggplant Parmesan	David Greco	Bronx, NY
5. Chicken and Waffles	Melba Wilson	New York City, NY
6. Pretzels	The Pretzel Boys	Philadelphia, PA
7. Arroz con Pollo	Jorge Ayala	New York City, NY
8. Grilled Cheese	Connie and Bill Fisher	Collingswood, NJ
9. Dumplings	Sohui Kim	Brooklyn, NY
10. Pulled Pork	Lee Ann Whippen	Chesapeake, VA
11. Arepas	Maribel Araujo and Aristides Barrios	New York City, NY
12. Rematch on the Grill	Butch Lupinetti, Delilah Winder, Nigel Spence, and Tobin Ellis	Miami, FL

Season 5

1. Coconut Cake	Robert Carter	Charleston, SC
2. Moules Frites	Teddy Folkman	Washington, DC
3. Seafood Gumbo	Poppy Tooker	New Orleans, LA
4. Paella	Gerard Nebesky	Occidental, CA
5. Chiles Rellenos	Ramiro Arvizu and Jaime Martin Del Campo	Bell, CA
6. Brown Bag Apple Pie	Dan Scheel and John Bauer	Mukwonago, WI
7. Red Velvet Cake	Raven Dennis	Brooklyn, NY
8. Bûche de Noël	François Payard	New York City, NY
9. Deep Dish Pizza	Marc Malnati	Chicago, IL
10. Falafel	Einat Admony	New York City, NY
11. Chocolate Bread Pudding	Jerome Chang and Chris Chen	New York City, NY
12. Cioppino	Phil DiGirolamo	Moss Landing, CA
13. Sushi	Philip Yi	Los Angeles, CA

Season 6

1. Pad Thai	Nongkran Daks	Chantilly, VA
2. Ravioli	Robert Durso Sr. and Robert "Bobby" Durso Jr.	Flushing, NY
3. Chicken Pot Pie	Sandy Pollock and Crystal Cook	Austin, TX
4. Blueberry Pancakes	Neil Kleinberg and DeDe Lahman	New York City, NY
5. Matzoh Ball Soup	Jeff Nathan	New York City, NY
6. Shrimp and Grits	Joe Barnett	Washington, GA
7. North Carolina Ribs and Beans	Ed Mitchell	Raleigh, NC
8. German Chocolate Cake	Aliyyah Baylor	New York City, NY
9. Fried Fish Escovitch	Sheron Barnes	New York City, NY
10. Country Captain Chicken	Matt and Ted Lee	Charleston, SC, and New York City, NY
11. Fish Tacos	Cesar Gonzales	San Diego, CA
12. Green Chile Cheeseburger	Bob Olguin	San Antonio, NM
13. Sloppy Joes	Andrew and John Schnipper	New York City, NY

Season 7

1. Steak Fajitas — Father Leo Patalinghug — Emmitsburg, MD
2. Barbecue Chicken and Potato Salad — Brad Turner — Fort Lee, VA
3. Lobster Club Sandwich — Lynn Archer — Rockland, ME
4. Pumpkin Pie — Michele Albano — Norwalk, CT
5. Feast of Seven Fishes — Pellegrino family — New York City, NY
6. Manhattan Fish Chowder — John Addis — Brooklyn, NY
7. Liège Belgian Waffles — Thomas DeGeest — New York City, NY
8. Chocolate Brownies — Shawna Lidsky and Katherine Hayward — South Hero, VT
9. Burritos — Victor and Miguel Escobedo — San Francisco, CA
10. Omelets — Misty Young — Truckee, CA
11. Stuffed French Toast — Omar Giner — Hoboken, NJ
12. Cuban Sandwich — Nick Vazquez — Jersey City, NJ

BARBECUE

One of the two original pilots we shot before the show was picked up by Food Network, this episode documents the birth of <u>Throwdown!</u> The next time you watch it, you'll notice the absence of Stephanie and Miriam in the test kitchen as well as a few other differences (for example, there was only one judge instead of two). When we taped this show, <u>Throwdown!</u> was in no way a part of the American or even the Food Network vernacular, and when I showed up to challenge Butch, he honestly had absolutely no idea what was happening. Today it is becoming progressively more difficult to surprise my challengers because more and more people are familiar with the show.

ON THIS EPISODE OF THROWDOWN!...

I faced off with national BBQ champion Butch Lupinetti. His barbecue is some of the world's best—which he thought had earned him bragging rights to a role in an upcoming Food Network barbecue special. What Butch didn't know was that I would be rolling into his backyard to take him on. Fire up the ribs and rubs for the ultimate barbecue battle!

"I was completely and utterly surprised when Bobby showed up in my yard. I didn't know what to do, so I gave him a big bear hug. Bobby spent his Sunday afternoon talking to my friends as if he had known us all of his life. What a great guy."
—BUTCH LUPINETTI

Name: Butch Lupinetti
Hometown: Mount Laurel, New Jersey
Website: www.smackyourlipsbbq.com

The Garden State was never known for barbecue, or at least it wasn't until Butch came along. This New Jersey native's claim to fame? He has won more than 400 awards for his barbecue in the past fifteen years, spending six months out of the year on the road participating in competitions. Butch's winning philosophy: "Cook it low, cook it slow. Serve no swine before its time." His highest honor came in 2005 when he won the Super Bowl of barbecue, taking first place at the Best in the West Nugget Rib Cook-off in Sparks, Nevada. Looking for your own taste of Butch's barbecue? This "lover, looker, and BBQ cooker" has his own line of barbecue rubs and sauces that you can purchase on his website.

Butch planned on pulling out all the stops for his Food Network special and invited more than 100 guests to his backyard for a party celebrating his daughter's birthday. This is a guy who goes all out, and he prepared brisket, pulled pork, grilled chicken, a whole roasted pig, his prize-winning ribs, of course, and sides of cornbread and baked beans. Phew! Butch was too busy cooking to have a clue that I was about to turn his party into a Throwdown.

I certainly had my work cut out for me. Butch has the experience, the recipes, and the equipment (did you see his rig?!)—plus, I love his attitude. I am pretty confident in my grilling abilities but barbecue is a whole other game, so I got to work in the test kitchen. I tested a recipe for ribs, first baking them in the oven and then finishing them on the grill. I changed my game plan at the Throwdown, however, and prepared ribs *and* pulled pork, smoked chicken, coleslaw, grilled corn with Cotija cheese and lime, and a lobster potato salad. I wasn't messing around; I was out to win.

We cooked and cooked and cooked some more. There was enough food to feed everyone in the crowd—twice—and the crowd kept filling their plates. I was getting some rave reviews, but Butch definitely had the home team advantage. I mean, his backyard was filled with his family and friends! Could I receive a fair chance? I was doubtful, but that's why we called in Mount Laurel town official and barbecue lover John Drinkard to pick a reigning pit master. Butch and I each selected one dish for the judging; he chose his ribs and I went for my smoked chicken. My chicken scored a 9.6—nice! But Butch's ribs got a 9.8. John loved both dishes, but I was edged out by the master.

This Throwdown was an unbelievable experience. Butch is a man who lives his craft every single day of his life. You can tell from his exuberance how much he loves what he does, and it shows in his food. I got to eat amazing barbecue and to spend the day with one of the nicest guys you could ever have the pleasure of meeting. And Butch, the pleasure was all mine.

I couldn't wait to see the look on Butch's face when I finished my two-hour drive to his Mount Laurel, New Jersey, party and issued him my challenge. It was worth it—he was completely shocked and I was treated to one of the warmest welcomes in Throwdown history. He may not have known what was going on at first, but once he did, he took the challenge like a seasoned pro.

THE SECRET TO COOKING GREAT RIBS
BY BUTCH LUPINETTI

I like my ribs lean, tender, and beautiful. Select lean ribs and cut off the visible fat. Lay the ribs out and put your seasoning rub on them. Let them sit for at least 30 minutes and up to 24 hours in the refrigerator. Overnight really is best.

Just lay the ribs on your grill real nice. You'll want them on the side that doesn't have the fire under it, the "not" in what we call the "hot and not." Place the ribs on a rack over a pan of water (about 1 inch of water). Fire up the other side of your grill. Set the temperature to 225°F. It is important to know where 225°F is on your grill or pit. A small oven thermometer will do just fine.

Take a piece of heavy-duty aluminum foil, add soaked and drained wood chips (we like hickory), wrap them up real good, poke some holes in the top of the foil, and then put them on the fire or coals. Now you're smokin'! Close your lid and leave them be. Don't be peeking. Just let them smoke.

When the ribs are tender and pull back from the bone a touch (2 pounds will take about 4½ hours), then, and only then, is when you sauce them. Move the ribs to the hot side. Sauce them real good, bone side down first.

When your ribs get bubbly but not burnt, flip them. Sauce the other side until it bubbles. This should take 3 to 5 minutes total. Remove from the grill and enjoy!

CHOWDER

ON THIS EPISODE OF THROWDOWN!...

I took on the "Brooklyn Chowder Surfer" Ben Sargent and his Island-inspired Bahamian chowder. Notorious for his questionable surfing style, his incredible seafood soups, and his willingness to do almost anything in the pursuit of a great wave and even better food, Ben has become a bit of an East Coast legend. ◯ First schooled in the art of chowder-making by his grandfather at the tender age of five, Ben has devoted most of his life to embracing the ocean, both by riding its waves and by creating delicious soups with its bounty. Once the proprietor of Hurricane Hopeful Chowder Bar, Ben has spun his Food Network debut into an appearance on the *Martha Stewart Show* and his own web series documenting his ocean-centric travels and the dishes he finds on them. Ben is still chasing his dream of getting his famous chowder onto supermarket shelves across the country, and I would have to say he's got the skills to ride the wave of that dream all the way.

Name: Ben Sargent
Hometown: Brooklyn, New York
Website: www.brooklynchowdersurfer.com

Ben and I have the same philosophy when it comes to chowder: we want to avoid being conventional (read: boring) without jeopardizing the integrity and history of this classic American dish. Once considered "poor man's food," chowder began as a hearty meal of odds and ends collected by the fishermen of seafaring communities to sustain them on their long stretches at sea. The local ingredients and preferences of those communities led to there being not one definitive chowder recipe, though most chowders are a variation on the same theme. All chowder should be chock-full of fresh seafood and flavor with a rich, silky consistency that is neither too thick nor too thin—you know, just right! As long as you adhere to those principles, the sky is your limit!

Preparing to take on the Brooklyn Chowder Surfer, I took to the test kitchen to get my chowder pot rolling. We whipped up two different versions, the first being a fairly classic sweet potato clam chowder that has been on the menu at my restaurant Bar Americain since its opening in 2005. For a slightly less traditional option, I also tried my hand with a lobster corn chowder. Lobster makes this chowder decidedly upscale (though you could certainly substitute less expensive shrimp), and this is a dish worth pulling out for special occasions. Corn not only adds incredible flavor and a natural sweetness, it also acts as a natural thickener that eliminates the need for flour (an ingredient Ben and I agree on skipping). Lobster, corn, chiles . . . it may not be the standard, but this is definitely an all-American chowder.

I had thought all along that I would submit the sweet potato chowder to the judge's table, but once I arrived at the Throwdown and learned that Ben would be going all out with his Bahamian monkfish chowder with plantains, coconut milk, and curry, I decided to go with my flashier dish, the lobster corn chowder. Our chowders couldn't have looked or tasted any more different than they did, but they had one thing in common: they were both flat-out delicious. Our judge had a difficult decision to make. Ultimately, she went with my version for the simple reason that she liked the ingredients better. Food tastes are totally subjective—we eat what we like, and why we like what we do is anyone's guess. That doesn't mean that one individual ingredient or dish is better or worse than the other; it just is what it is. On this day, this particular judge preferred lobster and corn to monkfish and plantains. As for me, I was pleased with the win, but I'd be happy to eat Ben Sargent's chowder any day of the week.

WINNER!

Bobby Flay's
Lobster and Green Chile Chowder
with Roasted Corn Salsa
SERVES 6 TO 8

4 (1½-pound) lobsters, steamed

3 tablespoons unsalted butter

1 medium Spanish onion, finely chopped

3 cloves garlic, finely chopped

1 cup dry white wine

6 ears fresh corn, roasted (see Notes), kernels
   removed from the cobs (2 cups), cobs halved

4 cups lobster stock (see Sources, page 269),
   low-sodium chicken broth, or vegetable broth,
   or more if needed

3 poblano chiles, roasted, peeled, seeded
   (see Notes), and diced

3 cups heavy cream

Kosher salt and freshly ground black pepper

¼ cup finely chopped fresh cilantro leaves,
   plus whole leaves for garnish

Roasted Corn and Green Chile Relish (recipe
   follows)

1. Remove the claws from the lobsters. Carefully crack the claws, and remove the meat in one piece if you can. Remove the tail meat and chop it into 1-inch chunks. Set the lobster aside in the refrigerator. Coarsely chop the shells and reserve.

2. Melt the butter in a large pot over medium-high heat. Add the onion and cook until soft, about 4 minutes. Add the garlic and cook for 30 seconds. Raise the heat to high, add the wine, lobster shells, and corncobs, and cook until the wine has completely reduced. Add the 4 cups lobster stock and bring to a boil. Reduce the heat and simmer for 15 minutes. Strain the broth into a bowl, discard the shells and corncobs, and return the broth to the pot.

3. Add 1 cup of the roasted corn kernels and cook until the corn is just tender, 15 minutes. Transfer the soup to a blender, in batches, and puree until smooth. Strain into a clean saucepan and bring to a simmer. Stir in the remaining 1 cup roasted corn kernels, and the chiles, and cook for 5 minutes.

4. Meanwhile, put the heavy cream in a medium saucepan, bring it to a simmer over medium heat, and cook until reduced by half, about 10 minutes.

5. Add the reduced cream to the chowder and simmer for 5 minutes. If the chowder appears too thick, add additional stock or water to thin it slightly.

6. Add the reserved chopped lobster meat, season with salt and pepper, and stir in the chopped cilantro. Ladle the chowder into bowls and top each one with a few tablespoons of the relish, a lobster claw, and a few fresh cilantro leaves.

(recipe continues)

Roasted Corn and Green Chile Relish

6 ears fresh corn, roasted (see Notes), kernels
    removed from the cobs (2 cups)

1 poblano chile, roasted, peeled, seeded
    (see Notes), and finely diced

½ small red onion, finely diced

Juice of 2 limes

2 teaspoons honey

2 tablespoons canola oil

Kosher salt and freshly ground black pepper

Combine the corn, poblano, onion, lime juice, honey, and oil in a medium bowl and season with salt and pepper. Let the relish sit at room temperature for at least 30 minutes to allow the flavors to meld.

NOTES

To roast corn: Preheat the oven to 425°F. Remove the silks from the corn, but leave the husks on. Soak in cold water for 10 minutes. Drain the corn, place on baking sheets, and roast in the oven until tender and slightly charred, 15 to 20 minutes. Let cool slightly; then remove the husks and slice off the kernels, letting them fall into a bowl.

To roast chiles: Preheat the oven to 400°F. Brush the chiles with canola oil and season them with salt and pepper. Place them on a rimmed baking sheet and roast in the oven, rotating them occasionally, until charred on all sides, about 30 minutes. Remove from the oven. Transfer to a bowl, cover with plastic wrap, and let sit for 15 minutes to allow the skin to loosen. Then peel, halve, and seed.

Ben Sargent's
Bahamian Seafood Chowder

SERVES 10

2 tablespoons unsalted butter

1½ pounds conch (see Note), pounded to
⅛-inch thickness and cut into ½-inch-wide
strips

1 large Spanish onion, halved and thinly sliced

Kosher salt and freshly ground black pepper

2 red bell peppers, diced

2 green bell peppers, diced

3 tablespoons Jamaican curry powder

½ teaspoon cayenne pepper

Pinch of sweet paprika

1 bay leaf

1 quart heavy cream

3 cups fish stock (see Sources, page 269),
bottled clam juice, or vegetable stock

1 (28.5-ounce) can peeled tomatoes, crushed
by hand, with juices

2 (13-ounce) cans coconut milk

¼ cup cream of coconut, such as Coco Lopez

3 pounds russet or other baking potatoes,
peeled and diced

3 large carrots, peeled and diced

2 large green plantains, peeled, quartered
lengthwise, and diced

2 yellow plantains, peeled, halved lengthwise,
and diced

1 pound firm-fleshed white fish, such as
mahimahi, cut into ½-inch pieces

¼ cup chopped fresh flat-leaf parsley leaves

Hot sauce, for serving

1. Melt the butter in a large heavy-bottomed pot over medium heat. Add the conch and onion, season with salt and pepper, and cook, stirring occasionally, until the onion is translucent, about 10 minutes. Add the red and green bell peppers and cook until soft, about 8 minutes. Stir in the curry powder, cayenne, paprika, bay leaf, and salt to taste, and cook until fragrant, about 4 minutes.
2. Stir in the heavy cream, fish stock, tomatoes and their juices, coconut milk, cream of coconut, potatoes, carrots, and green and yellow plantains. Bring to a brisk simmer and cook, stirring occasionally, until the conch and green plantains are tender, about 1 hour. Taste, and season with salt and pepper.
3. Add the mahimahi and parsley, and simmer until the fish is just cooked through, about 5 minutes. Discard the bay leaf, and serve with hot sauce on the side.

NOTE
Conch is generally available frozen. It must be trimmed and then pounded. Use a paring knife to trim off any silver skin or yellow patches, which will remain tough no matter how long they are pounded or cooked. Then put the conch pieces between sheets of plastic wrap and pound with a meat mallet.

RED CHILI

ON THIS EPISODE OF THROWDOWN!...

It was all about the official dish of Texas, red chili. I headed to Houston to challenge chili queen Cindy Reed Wilkins to a bowl o' red competition . . . and perhaps a little Texas two-step. ○ The only back-to-back winner of the CASI International Chili Championship, Cindy Reed Wilkins won more than fifteen first-place awards before retiring from the competition circuit to develop her own line of chili seasonings called "Cin Chili." Since deciding to share her award-winning recipe with the world at large, she has expanded her customer base and sells her products to more than 300 grocery and specialty food stores around the world. ◎ Texas chili is not the chili con carne, made of ground beef and red kidney beans, that most of us grew up on. Rather, the dish (considered by Texans to be the one "true" chili, of course) is all about the meat and the gravy. Chuck is the meat of choice and it is always cubed, never ground. Deep russet in color and with a silklike consistency, the gravy should be well balanced with heat that hits both the front and then the back of the mouth. This dish has a lot of rules, so you know that Cindy had her game on to win as many competitions as she did.

"Three years later, we are growing and expanding our business by leaps and bounds! Thanks, Bobby!"
—CINDY REED WILKINS

Name: Cindy Reed Wilkins
Hometown: Houston, Texas
Website: www.cinchili.com

CASE FILE: 1.3

I cook southwestern food every day, but I rarely make chili, so I took to the test kitchen to practice my recipe. I had heard that the secret to competition chili is to pack as much intense flavor into each spoonful as possible, so my strategy was to create layer upon layer of flavor with a twelve-chile chili. I know what you must be thinking: *twelve* chiles? Isn't that overkill? No way! The more the merrier! All the chiles work together in unison to give this dish incredible flavor. The gravy's base is a combination of dried red chiles, fresh green chiles, onions, garlic, tomatoes, and spices, pureed until smooth. For the beef, I went for a flavorful bottom round cut, diced into small cubes, seared off until golden brown, then cooked in the gravy until tender.

Upon our arrival in Houston, Stephanie wondered aloud what the crowd would have to say when a bunch of New York city slickers stepped out of the car to challenge an award-winning Texas chili queen to a Throwdown. Yeah, it was a little gutsy. Seasoned champ Cindy accepted the challenge in stride, though Stephanie had been right—the crowd did question our abilities.

One taste of Cindy's chili told me why she'd done as well as she had on the road. Her meat was perfectly tender and her sauce, made with just the right amount of spice, had an amazingly silky quality. As much as I liked Cindy's chili, I really liked mine, too, and was eager to hear what a true chili champion would have to say about it. Cindy tasted it and said she loved the front and back heat—coming from her, that's high praise!

We brought in former chili champions Joe and Shirley Stewart to do a blind tasting. My chili had great heat and a nicely balanced sweetness as well as tender beef. They called Cindy's a classic Texas chili full of great flavor. This decision wasn't proving to be an easy one. While Cindy and I differed on a couple of points, such as the size of the cubes of beef and fresh as opposed to ground chiles, we both agreed that each of our chilis was award-winning. And so did the judges—they couldn't come to a clear conclusion and declared this Throwdown a tie! (This was the first and last time that ever happened on a Throwdown. After this match, we decided that there had to be a clear-cut winner at the end of every show, even if it took all night to pick one.) I was happy with the tie. It was a great afternoon spent enjoying good food, a spirited crowd, and the work of a talented and passionate champion. Any time I can tie with someone as great as Cindy, you know I'm taking it.

Bobby Flay's
Twelve-Chile Chili
SERVES 8

1 (32-ounce) can plum tomatoes with juices

2 ancho chiles, soaked, stemmed, and seeded

2 pasilla chiles, soaked, stemmed, and seeded

2 New Mexican red chiles, soaked, stemmed, and seeded

2 cascabel chiles, soaked, stemmed, and seeded

1 guajillo chile, soaked, stemmed, and seeded

2 cayenne chiles, soaked, stemmed, and seeded, or ½ teaspoon cayenne powder

1 chipotle chile in adobo, chopped

2 jalapeño chiles, chopped

1 poblano chile, chopped

1 serrano chile, chopped

1 habanero chile, chopped

¼ cup canola oil

2½ pounds bottom round, placed in the freezer for 30 minutes and cut into ½-inch dice

Kosher salt and freshly ground black pepper

2 medium Spanish onions, finely diced

4 cloves garlic, finely chopped

1 tablespoon ground cumin

½ teaspoon chile de árbol powder

2 cups homemade chicken stock (see page 220) or canned low-sodium chicken broth

2 tablespoons clover honey

2 tablespoons pure maple syrup

1 ounce bittersweet chocolate, melted

Toasted Cumin Crema (recipe follows)

1. Put the tomatoes and their juices and all of the soaked and fresh chiles in a food processor and process until very smooth. (If using cayenne powder, add with the chile de árbol in step 3.)

2. Heat the oil in a large Dutch oven over high heat until it begins to shimmer. Season the beef with salt and pepper, and sear in batches until golden brown on all sides. Remove the beef to a large platter with a slotted spoon.

3. Remove all but 2 tablespoons of the fat from the pan. Add the onions and cook until soft, 4 to 5 minutes. Add the garlic and cook for 1 minute. Add the cumin and chile de árbol powder, and cook for 30 seconds. Return the beef to the pan, and add the tomato mixture and the chicken stock. Bring to a boil, reduce the heat to medium-low, cover, and simmer until the beef is fork-tender, 1¼ to 1½ hours.

4. Stir in the honey, maple syrup, and bittersweet chocolate, and season with salt and pepper. Ladle into bowls and top each one with a dollop of Toasted Cumin Crema.

Toasted Cumin Crema

1 tablespoon whole cumin seeds, toasted, cooled, and ground in a coffee or spice grinder

1½ cups Mexican crema, crème fraîche, or sour cream

Kosher salt and freshly ground black pepper

Whisk the cumin and crema together in a small bowl, and season with salt and pepper. Cover and refrigerate for at least 30 minutes before serving.

Cindy Reed Wilkins's Cin Chili

SERVES 4 TO 6

1 teaspoon vegetable oil

2 pounds beef chuck, cut into ³/₈-inch cubes

Seasoned salt

1 (14½-ounce) can low-sodium beef broth

1 (8-ounce) can no-sodium tomato sauce

1 teaspoon or 1 cube chicken bouillon

1 teaspoon or 1 cube beef bouillon

2½ teaspoons onion powder

2½ teaspoons garlic powder

6 tablespoons plus 2 teaspoons chili powder

½ teaspoon jalapeño powder

¼ teaspoon ground white pepper

2 serrano chiles, roasted, peeled, and seeded
    (see Notes, page 22)

¼ teaspoon plus ⅛ teaspoon cayenne pepper

3½ teaspoons ground cumin

¼ teaspoon brown sugar

1. In a heavy 4-quart saucepan over medium-high heat, heat the oil until smoking hot. Add the beef chuck cubes and 1 teaspoon seasoned salt, and cook until the beef is browned on all sides.

2. Add the beef broth and tomato sauce, and bring to a slight boil. Add the chicken bouillon, beef bouillon, 2 teaspoons of the onion powder, 1 teaspoon of the garlic powder, 1 tablespoon of the chili powder, the jalapeño powder, and the white pepper. Return to a boil; then reduce the heat and simmer for 1 hour.

3. Add the serrano chiles, 1 teaspoon of the garlic powder, 5 tablespoons of the chili powder, ¼ teaspoon of the cayenne pepper, 2 teaspoons of the cumin, and the brown sugar. Bring to a boil over medium-high heat; then reduce the heat and simmer for 30 minutes. If the mixture seems dry, add some water. Taste, and add additional seasoned salt if desired. Remove the serrano peppers.

4. Add the remaining ½ teaspoon onion powder, ½ teaspoon garlic powder, 2 teaspoons chili powder, ⅛ teaspoon cayenne, and 1½ teaspoons cumin. Simmer, stirring occasionally, for 30 minutes.

STEAK

ON THIS EPISODE OF THROWDOWN!...

I faced off in a desert duel against U.S. Marine Captain and steak-making champion Eric Dominijanni, a.k.a. "Captain D." Set on his turf at the Twentynine Palms Marine Base in California's Mojave Desert, it was a sizzling combination of sun, sand, and steak—the perfect recipe for a Throwdown. ◉ Captain D, who also answers to "Disco," knows what it is like to improvise a meal and has done so all over the world, from Japan to Iraq. Captain D leads a company of 250 marines and every chance he gets, he likes to treat his marines to a homemade meal. Born and raised in Forest Hills, Queens, this captain is also one serious competitor . . . *ooh-rah!* His Captain D's Disco Hot and Tangy Steak—chuck marinated in cola, orange peel, ginger, teriyaki sauce, and habanero chiles, then grilled to perfection—won him a regional title.

"I had a few advantages: (1) I was able to marinate my food overnight so the flavor really seeped into the steak, while Mr. Flay had to prep his steaks on the spot. (2) I was used to the desert and 100°-plus heat, while Mr. Flay was beet-red despite the sunblock 300. (3) I had a company of Marines with rifles who would have come after me or Mr. Flay if I did not win!"
—ERIC DOMINIJANNI

Name: Eric Dominijanni
Hometown: Queens, New York
Occupation: United States Marine

This tough marine thought it was his skill on the grill that had landed him front and center in a national competition in New York City as well as his own profile on a Food Network special. He'd get competition and airtime all right—just not the way he had planned.

In the test kitchen, I decide on filet mignon with a cooked ancho chile–tomato salsa, with crispy garlic chips and torched goat cheese. I was happily plotting my approach in the air-conditioned comfort of the Food Network kitchen, but little did I know that I would have to come up with a whole other plan of attack when I arrived at the Marine Base, where the temperature was 120°F in the shade. Ouch.

Throwdown day brought us to the Mojave Desert, where we found Captain D preparing to break ranks and putting on a barbecue for his well-deserving men. Before he could serve up his honored hot and tangy steak to the troops, he got a surprise visit from this civilian. The heat proved to be a problem in more ways than one for this freckle-faced Irish boy. My original plan to do a cooked salsa with melted goat cheese disappeared like a desert mirage. I knew I had to change my strategy. Luckily, I never travel without backup. I whipped up a new, uncooked glaze from molasses, mustard, red chiles, and horseradish. (I had to nix the goat cheese altogether because it had actually melted in the coolers!) While I was at it, I also swapped the filet mignon for my favorite cut, the rib eye.

Captain D's hungry men had been eyeing our steaks all afternoon and now it was time for them to eat. We had battled the desert heat and both of our steaks had passed the Marine Corps taste test. But whose steak is good enough to win the Throwdown? Our judge, Jamie Purviance, had just traveled all the way from San Francisco and he was ready to eat. The author of Weber grilling cookbooks judges steak competitions all over the country. Jamie tucked into our steaks and judged them on their tenderness and depth of flavor. He awarded us both high marks in each category, but by a slim margin, chose Captain D's steak.

I can't even put into words what this Throwdown meant to me. Getting to feed the brave, amazing men and women of the United States Marine Corps and to compete against Captain D—a talented cook and heroic man who has dedicated his life to keeping you, me, and this entire country safe—was one of the biggest honors of my life.

Bobby Flay's
Grilled Rib Eye with Molasses-Mustard Glaze

SERVES 4

2 (1½-inch-thick) bone-in rib-eye steaks

½ cup molasses

2 heaping tablespoons Dijon mustard

2 heaping tablespoons prepared horseradish, drained

1 teaspoon ancho chile powder

Kosher salt and freshly ground black pepper

Canola oil

1. Remove the steaks from the refrigerator 30 minutes before grilling.

2. Whisk the molasses, mustard, horseradish, and ancho powder together in a small bowl, and season with salt and pepper. Let the glaze sit at room temperature for at least 30 minutes before using, to allow the flavors to meld.

3. Heat your grill to high, or heat a cast-iron grill pan over high heat until it just begins to smoke. Brush both sides of the steaks lightly with canola oil and season them liberally with salt and pepper. Place the steaks on the grill or grill pan, and cook until golden brown and slightly charred, 4 to 5 minutes.

4. Turn the steaks over, brush the tops liberally with some of the glaze, reduce the heat to medium, and continue grilling until the bottom is golden brown and slightly charred and the center is medium-rare, 6 to 7 minutes.

5. Remove the steaks to a cutting board, brush with more of the glaze, and let rest for 5 minutes before slicing.

WINNER!

Eric Dominijanni's
Disco's Hot and Tangy New York Strip Steaks
SERVES 4

1 (12-ounce) can cola

½ cup soy sauce

½ cup garlic teriyaki sauce

1 habanero chile, with seeds, finely chopped

1 tablespoon grated orange zest

1 tablespoon grated fresh ginger

1 tablespoon extra virgin olive oil, plus more for
   brushing the steaks

1 teaspoon freshly ground black pepper

¾ teaspoon fresh lemon juice

⅛ teaspoon kosher salt

4 (8-ounce) New York strip steaks, each ¾ inch
   thick

1. Mix all the ingredients except the strip steaks in a medium bowl.

2. Place the steaks in a large resealable plastic bag and pour in the marinade. Press out the air, seal the bag, and turn several times to coat the meat. Set the bag in a bowl and refrigerate for 4 to 6 hours, turning the bag occasionally.

3. Let the steaks (still in the bag) stand at room temperature for 20 to 30 minutes before grilling.

4. Remove the steaks from the bag and set them aside. Pour the marinade into a small saucepan, bring to a boil, and cook for about 10 seconds. Pour half of the marinade into a small bowl to use for basting the steaks. Reduce the heat under the saucepan and simmer the remaining marinade, stirring occasionally, until it has reduced to the consistency of a dipping sauce, 5 to 10 minutes.

5. Preheat your grill to high.

6. Pat the steaks dry with paper towels. Lightly coat the steaks with the oil. Grill the steaks over direct high heat, turning them once and basting frequently with the marinade, for 3 to 4 minutes per side for medium-rare (or to your desired doneness). Remove from the grill and let rest for 2 to 3 minutes. Serve warm, with the dipping sauce on the side.

BREAKFAST

ON THIS EPISODE OF THROWDOWN!...

It was the early birds' fight for the worm with a battle of the breakfasts. I would have to be up at the crack of dawn in order to stand a chance against Kentucky's morning meal master, Lynn Winter. ○ Lynn began her career not as a restaurateur, but as a custom woodworker plying her trade in Kentucky and northern California. In 1991, ready to leave her life of furniture-making behind, Lynn sold her woodworking tools and set up a new kind of shop—her very own restaurant, Lynn's Paradise Café, in Louisville, Kentucky. From the ever-changing interior to the revolving displays of artwork, there is always something happening at Lynn's. In the two decades since Lynn first opened her café's doors, she's managed to wrangle numerous awards and honors such as Ernst and Young's "Entrepreneur of the Year," the "Tower Award for Women Leaders," and the National Restaurant Association's "Chairman's Award for Grassroots Leadership." Clearly, opening the café was the right move.

"Was I surprised?! I didn't have any idea that I was being punked. But once I found out, I loved the challenge of it all! Bobby was tough to beat but a real gentleman. I'm not sure what won me the contest, the food or my four-inch stiletto heels. We're hoping the food."
—LYNN WINTER

Name: Lynn Winter
Establishment: Lynn's Paradise Café
Hometown: Louisville, Kentucky
Website: www.lynnsparadisecafe.com
Phone: (502) 583-3447

Lynn is a born and raised southerner complete with a sweet spot for breakfast. She may not have known it before I showed up with a Throwdown in hand, but her outrageous scrambled eggs, laden with creamy Jarlsberg cheese and country ham, were known as her signature dish—the one her customers craved, the one that made Food Network come knocking—and I just had to try my hand at outdoing this country morning dream.

If I've said it once, I've said it a million times: I love breakfast foods. I could eat breakfast morning, noon, and night. The one thing I like as much as eating breakfast? Well, that might just be preparing it. However, unlike Lynn, I don't prepare 3,000 breakfasts a week, so I really had my work cut out for me with this one. Could my Mexican-inspired chilaquiles trump Lynn's country-style Kentucky Farmhouse Scramble?

There are hundreds of ways to prepare eggs, but my recipe for chilaquiles might just be my favorite. It's creamy scrambled eggs layered between crispy blue corn tortillas with cheddar cheese and a spicy tomatillo sauce—sort of a free-form egg lasagna, if you will. Chilaquiles has been on my brunch menu at Mesa Grill since it opened, and to this day it continues to be one of our most popular brunch dishes. Just as Lynn stayed true to the food and flavorings she knew best, so did I with this southwestern take on eggs.

The judging was close—who doesn't love a great breakfast?—but in the end, top honors went to country ham and onion rings. Early-bird Lynn took the win, and sadly this breakfast time was over.

Bobby Flay's
Scrambled Eggs Chilaquiles
SERVES 4

2 cups canola oil

12 (6-inch) blue corn tortillas

Kosher salt

8 tablespoons (1 stick) unsalted butter

12 large eggs, lightly beaten

Freshly ground black pepper

Roasted Tomatillo Sauce (recipe follows)

½ cup plus 4 teaspoons crema, crème fraîche,
   or sour cream

1½ cups (6 ounces) grated white cheddar
   cheese

4 tablespoons chopped fresh cilantro leaves

1. Heat the oil in a medium saucepan over medium heat until it reaches 350°F on a deep-frying thermometer.

2. Fry the tortillas, one at a time, in the hot oil until just crispy, 20 to 30 seconds. Remove to a plate lined with paper towels and season lightly with salt.

3. Heat the butter in a large skillet over low heat. Add the eggs, and season with salt and pepper. Cook slowly, stirring constantly with a wooden spoon, until soft curds form.

4. To serve, ladle some of the tomatillo sauce into 4 shallow bowls and top each with a fried tortilla. Spread 1 tablespoon of the crema and a few tablespoons of the sauce evenly over each tortilla. Top each with some of the eggs and then 2 tablespoons of the cheddar cheese. Top with another tortilla, repeat, and then top with a final tortilla. Spoon the remaining eggs and cheese on top and garnish each serving with a tablespoon of the chopped cilantro leaves.

Roasted Tomatillo Sauce

12 tomatillos, peeled, rinsed, and halved

1 large red onion, quartered

4 cloves garlic

¾ cup plus 3 tablespoons olive oil

Kosher salt and freshly ground black pepper

1 cup fresh spinach leaves

1 tablespoon pureed chipotle chile in adobo

¼ cup fresh lime juice

3 tablespoons honey

1. Preheat the oven to 375°F.

2. In a small roasting pan, toss the tomatillos, onion, and garlic with the 3 tablespoons olive oil, and season with salt and pepper. Roast in the oven until the vegetables are soft and golden brown, 20 to 25 minutes.

3. Meanwhile, bring a medium pot of salted water to a boil. Set up an ice bath in a medium bowl. Blanch the spinach in the boiling water for 30 seconds, then drain and transfer to the ice water. Drain the spinach well and squeeze out the excess water between your hands.

4. Transfer the tomatillos, onion, and garlic to a food processor, and add the chipotle, lime juice, and spinach. Process until smooth. With the motor running, slowly add the ¾ cup olive oil until emulsified. Season with the honey and salt and pepper to taste. Serve warm.

WINNER!

Lynn Winter's
Kentucky Farmhouse Scramble
SERVES 4

1 tablespoon unsalted butter

1 tablespoon canola oil

8 ounces boneless country ham, diced

1 small red bell pepper, roasted (see Notes,
    page 22) and diced

12 large eggs, beaten

1 cup (4 ounces) grated Jarlsberg cheese

Freshly ground black pepper

1. Heat a 12-inch nonstick sauté pan over
medium-high heat. Add the butter and oil and
swirl around the pan until the butter melts.
Add the country ham and cook until it begins
to brown, about 3 minutes.

2. Turn the heat to medium-low. Stir in the
roasted red bell pepper and beaten eggs. After
the eggs begin to set, stir slowly from edge to
edge with a heat-resistant rubber spatula until
large curds form. This will take anywhere from
5 to 8 minutes. If they are setting too quickly,
reduce the heat to low. While the eggs are still
moist and slightly runny, fold in the grated
cheese and season with pepper.

COCKTAILS

ON THIS EPISODE OF THROWDOWN!...

I paid a visit to America's favorite city for sinning, Las Vegas, to place my bet against the house favorite, mixologist Toby Ellis. I love cocktails and was willing to gamble that I could win this Throwdown, even though deep down I thought I didn't have a "shot." **O** BarMagic principal Toby Ellis has two decades' worth of bartending, hospitality, and nightlife experience under his belt. In his years behind the bar, he has held the titles of cofounder and president of the Flair Bartenders' Association, head bartender for Caesars Palace Las Vegas, and new store opening bar trainer for TGI Friday's. This onetime New York and Washington, D.C.–based ad man has both organized and judged all styles of bartending competitions since 1997, as well as serving as a technical advisor and on-air judge for television programming on channels from A&E to NBC and even our very own Food Network. He not only does the judging; he's also been judged and is a three-time mixology champion and a nine-time world finalist in competitions including Legends, Best in the West, and Cayman Masters.

Name: Tobin Ellis
Hometown: Las Vegas, Nevada
Website: www.barmagic.com

When I caught up with him, Toby was wowing the crowd at the elite nightclub Pure in Caesars Palace, right across from my Mesa Grill restaurant. Yes, it's safe to say I've seen what cocktail magic Toby is capable of weaving! One of his favorite concoctions (and the one he chose to highlight for Food Network and, unwittingly, this Throwdown) is a fragrant blend of basil, lemons, brown sugar, and South African cane rum. This is a man as passionate about cocktails as I am about food. Toby is a stalwart believer in the importance of fresh ingredients and adding flair to his bartending arsenal—two key ingredients in increasing the quality (and price) of the cocktail.

I know how to make a basic cocktail, but for something a bit more elaborate I needed a little help, so I treated myself to a lesson from master mixologist Dale DeGroff. This cocktail king shared his rules for a perfect cocktail with me: First and foremost, go fresh—no premade mixes allowed. Second, you want to achieve that perfect balance of sweet and sour. Finally, technique is key. Shaking on ice—hard!—for 10 seconds would help load my deck for a winning cocktail. It was time to belly up to the test-kitchen bar and see what I could do on my own.

I quickly came to the realization that I wouldn't be winning this one with flair, so I relied on my chef skills, hoping to take Toby on with flavor. My cocktail started out as the Deconstructed Asian Colada. After some eye-rolling and laughter from Stephanie and Miriam, it became known simply as The Throwdown. I muddled limes with Thai basil, sugar, and ginger-infused simple syrup, threw in some fresh pineapple and golden rum, shook with ice, and topped it all with a sweetened coconut milk floater. Delicious, if I do say so myself. And with that, this Throwdown team was Las Vegas–bound.

Toby willingly accepted my Throwdown and prepared his awesome Serengeti cocktail for the occasion. You couldn't let that smile fool you— Toby was all business and a true competitor. The judging criteria were presentation, taste, and marketing potential. The judges thought my cocktail was clean, refreshing, and citrusy, and very marketable. It seemed that luck was on my side, and this time, I pulled a winning hand. Winner or not, I'd raise my drink to Toby's master mixology any day. Cheers!

WINNER!

Bobby Flay's
The Throwdown Cocktail

SERVES 2

2 lime wedges

¼ cup finely diced fresh pineapple

6 fresh mint leaves, plus whole sprigs for
   garnish

4 fresh Thai basil leaves, plus whole sprigs
   for garnish

1 tablespoon sugar

2 tablespoons Ginger Simple Syrup (recipe
   follows)

3 ounces golden rum

Ice cubes

2 tablespoons cream of coconut, such as
   Coco Lopez

1. Combine the lime, pineapple, mint leaves,
Thai basil leaves, sugar, and simple syrup in
a cocktail shaker and muddle well. Add the
rum and shake for 10 seconds.

2. Fill 2 rocks glasses with ice, pour the drink
over the ice, and float 1 tablespoon of the
cream of coconut over each drink. Garnish
with mint and Thai basil sprigs.

Ginger Simple Syrup

½ cup sugar

1 (4-inch) piece fresh ginger, peeled and sliced

Combine the sugar, ½ cup water, and the
ginger in a small saucepan. Bring to a boil
and cook until the sugar has dissolved, about
2 minutes. Remove from the heat and let cool.
Strain out the ginger, cover, and refrigerate
until cold, at least 30 minutes.

Tobin Ellis's
Serengeti
SERVES 1

½ lemon, cubed

4 fresh basil leaves, plus more for serving

1 tablespoon light brown sugar

1½ ounces Leblon cachaça

¾ ounce Domaine de Canton ginger liqueur
   or homemade ginger syrup

2 dashes Angostura bitters

Ice cubes

Crushed ice

Candied ginger and fresh basil leaves wrapped
   in a lemon twist, for garnish (optional)

1. Muddle the lemon, basil leaves, and brown sugar in a mixing glass. Add the Leblon cachaça, Domaine de Canton liqueur, and Angostura bitters, and shake with ice cubes.
2. Layer crushed ice and basil leaves in a collins glass. Strain the mixture through a fine-mesh strainer into the glass. Garnish with the ginger-basil twist if desired, and serve.

CHEESESTEAK

ON THIS EPISODE OF THROWDOWN!...

It was time to take on two Philly icons: cheesesteak and its king, Tony Luke. Could my gourmet twist on the Philly classic be enough to topple tradition? Would I get some brotherly love? Forgetaboutit! ○ The only place cheesesteaks taste good is in Philadelphia. That's where they were born in the 1930s, and the competition among the local sandwich shops, each wanting to claim their version as the best, keeps the bar for excellence set high. You'd be hard-pressed to find a Philly native who isn't fiercely loyal to their favorite cheesesteak and ready to fight to the death to prove it. There's Pat's, Geno's, and then my fave, Tony Luke's. ○ Tony Luke opened his now-famous cheesesteak shop in 1992 with his sons Nick and Tony. This is a family business; as Tony Jr. says, he was "born with a silver spatula in hand." Tony Luke's cheesesteaks were voted the Best of Philly in 1994, 1999, and 2004. They use only fresh ingredients, making each of the 2,000 sandwiches they sell a day to order. They also bake their own bread, and not just once a day, but every hour!

"I was terrified when Bobby challenged me to a Throwdown. You have to remember I live in Philadelphia; this is a town where if one of our sports personalities is responsible for losing a championship game, he doesn't just get booed—he gets run out of town. And the only thing Philadelphia loves as much as their sports teams is the cheesesteak. Now that's pressure! Bobby was great to work with; he is a true competitor and genuinely a good man. Doing the Throwdown took me from local to national recognition. Thank you, Bobby, and thank you, Food Network."

—TONY LUKE JR.

Name: Tony Luke Jr.
Establishment: Tony Luke's
Hometown: Philadelphia, Pennsylvania
Website: www.tonylukes.com
Phone: (215) 551-5725

An authentic Philly cheesesteak is a sandwich of thinly sliced beef (Tony Luke uses rib eye) that is cooked on a griddle with onions and cheese and served on a soft Italian roll. All flavors should marry, with no one component standing out. The classic has no mushrooms or peppers. There are a couple of basic questions to answer when ordering a Philly cheesesteak: You can get it either "wit or witout" the onions, and then there's the question of the cheese—provolone, which has great flavor, or Cheez Whiz, which has the perfect melting consistency and becomes totally integrated with the steak.

I know Tony, so I knew my work would be cut out for me. This time, Steph and Miriam offered no real help in the test kitchen. Miriam had never eaten a Philly cheesesteak in her life, and Stephanie, who was born and raised in western Pennsylvania, wasn't a fan simply on principle (there's no love lost between Pittsburgh and Philadelphia). I had to come up with my own strategy, and that was to make a cheesesteak with more refined flavors.

I started with the cheese, opting to make my own aged provolone sauce, which has a pronounced flavor but also the creamy texture of the Whiz for the best of both worlds. As for the with or without, I went all in, cooking my beef with cubano peppers, caramelized onions, and sautéed mushrooms. I chose sirloin for its tenderness, and while I normally wouldn't take any steak past medium-rare, I did follow this Philly rule: all steak is cooked through.

This Throwdown day had a rocky start. Stephanie was under the weather and couldn't make the trip to Philly, so I made a 4 a.m. phone call to my trusty ex-sous-chef Christine Sanchez, who agreed to fill in. Tony may have been surprised at first, but he gave us a warm welcome. I thought he would be making his classic cheesesteak, but he changed plans, pulled out all the stops, and switched his entry to "The Italian": steak dressed up with broccoli rabe, Italian red hot peppers, fried onions, and slices of aged sharp provolone.

A little something I picked up from Tony and his Philly crowd is the proper way to eat a cheesesteak, and this is it: Stick your butt out, bend over slightly, and go for it. A good sandwich is going to drip, but this way when it does, it drips on the ground, not on your shirt. Maybe. But now it was the judges' turn to do the eating. April White, then food editor of *Philadelphia* magazine, and Ben Franklin (the one, but not the only) both said that Tony's cheesesteak was perfectly balanced with juicy meat, wonderful cheese, a soft roll, and Philly attitude. They loved mine too, especially the cheese sauce. But the entry with the slight edge was revealed to be Tony's and this Throwdown was his. There can be only one town for cheesesteaks, and that's Philadelphia, and in that town, Tony Luke's should be your stop.

Bobby Flay's Philly Cheesesteak

SERVES 6 TO 8

3 tablespoons unsalted butter

1 tablespoon canola oil

3 large Spanish onions, halved and thinly sliced

Kosher salt and freshly ground black pepper

4 tablespoons olive oil, plus more for cooking
   the steak

2 poblano chiles, thinly sliced

2 cubano chiles, thinly sliced

1½ pounds mushrooms, such as a mix of
   cremini and shiitake, coarsely chopped

3 tablespoons finely chopped fresh parsley
   leaves

1 (2-pound) New York strip loin, placed in the
   freezer for 30 minutes, then very thinly sliced

6 to 8 soft hoagie rolls

Provolone Sauce (recipe follows)

1. Heat 2 tablespoons of the butter and the canola oil in a large sauté pan over medium heat. Add the onions, season with salt and pepper, and cook slowly, stirring occasionally, until golden brown and caramelized, 35 to 40 minutes.

2. Heat 2 tablespoons of the olive oil in a medium sauté pan over high heat. Add the chiles and cook until soft, about 5 mintues. Season with salt and pepper.

3. Heat the remaining 1 tablespoon butter and 2 tablespoons olive oil in a large sauté pan over high heat. Add the mushrooms and cook until they are golden brown, about 8 minutes. Stir in the parsley and season with salt and pepper.

4. Heat a griddle over high heat and drizzle with a little olive oil. Season the meat with salt and pepper and cook, in batches, until just cooked through, about 45 seconds per side.

5. Place several slices of the meat on the bottom half of each roll, spoon some of the cheese sauce over the meat, and top with any combination of the mushrooms, onions, and peppers.

Provolone Sauce

1 tablespoon unsalted butter

1 tablespoon all-purpose flour

2 cups whole milk, hot

2 cups (8 ounces) grated aged provolone cheese

¼ cup freshly grated Parmesan cheese

1 teaspoon kosher salt

¼ teaspoon freshly ground black pepper

Melt the butter in a medium saucepan over medium heat. Whisk in the flour and cook for 1 minute. Slowly whisk in the hot milk, increase the temperature to high, and cook, whisking constantly, until thickened, 4 to 5 minutes. Remove from the heat and whisk in the provolone, Parmesan, salt, and pepper. Serve warm.

WINNER!

Tony Luke's
Traditional Philly-Style Cheesesteak
SERVES 2 TO 4

4 tablespoons canola oil

1 small white onion, diced

Kosher salt and freshly ground black pepper

1 pound very thinly sliced rib-eye steak

6 slices white American cheese, or

    4 tablespoons Cheez Whiz

2 (9-inch) Italian rolls

1. Heat a griddle over medium heat. Add 2 tablespoons of the canola oil and heat it. Add the onion and cook, stirring, until translucent. Do not brown the onion. Season with salt and pepper. Transfer to a plate and set aside.

2. Add the remaining 2 tablespoons oil to the griddle. Add the steak, spreading it out and moving it around frequently. When there isn't any red in the meat, season with salt and pepper. The steak will be cooked but not browned.

3. If using American cheese, put it on top of the meat, reduce the heat to low, and cook until the cheese melts. If using Whiz, spread it on the insides of your rolls. With a spatula, take your steak and carefully place it in the rolls. Top it with the onion, and enjoy.

FRIED CHICKEN

ON THIS EPISODE OF THROWDOWN!...

I was winging it against Jasper Alexander in a Throwdown that brought me to New York State's horse-racing hotspot, Saratoga. ○ Jasper first fell in love with cooking while in college on the West Coast. After fronting a one-man catering endeavor, he went east to attend the celebrated Culinary Institute of America. From there, he spent time in the kitchen of three of the most highly esteemed New York City restaurants: Gotham Bar and Grill, Gramercy Tavern, and Aureole. These are swanky places, but it was at Hattie's where Jasper found his home.

"Bobby is somewhat a fixture here in Saratoga Springs during the six-week horse race meet and, more important, a regular customer when in town. I knew that Bobby had horses racing on the same day that we were going to be filming at the track so in the back of my mind I had hoped that he might drop by the shoot to give the show a little star power. When he did show up, I thought to myself: fantastic, this should really help make sure the show actually makes it on Food Network. After Bobby delivered the 'Are you ready for a Throwdown?' line, I immediately turned to my camera guy and asked, 'What the heck is a Throwdown?'

"Being involved in the show was a great experience and has been tremendous for business. Every time the show airs we see a new group of people who say they came because they saw the Throwdown."

—JASPER ALEXANDER

Name: Jasper Alexander
Establishment: Hattie's Restaurant
Hometown: Saratoga Springs, New York
Website: www.hattiesrestaurant.com
Phone: (518) 584-4790

It's been seven years since executive chef Jasper Alexander took over the reins of Hattie's restaurant, but Hattie's history stretches back far longer than that. Louisiana born and raised Hattie first came to Saratoga as a cook for a Chicago family who spent their summers in cool upstate New York. That job gave her the means to open her eponymous restaurant in 1938. Her legendary southern cuisine made the restaurant a Saratoga landmark famous for its delectable fried chicken. Jasper has put a few spins on Hattie's seventy-year-old recipe since he jumped in the saddle, but much has remained the same—namely, the use of fresh, seasonal ingredients from local farmers. It's just as Hattie wanted it: fresh from the farm, straight to the plate. Salt and black pepper season Hattie's—now Jasper's—fried chicken while a single dipping in straight flour creates its light and crispy crust. Befitting his equine haven of a location, Jasper thought that he—and his restaurant, Hattie's—was throwing a racetrack reception for Food Network's winning circle.

When it comes to the perfect fried chicken, Jasper and I agree on a couple of key factors: the importance of fresh and well-seasoned chicken pieces, and oil that is heated to (and maintained at) just the right temperature. But as Stephanie and Miriam discovered in the test kitchen, that's where our similarities end. I tenderize my chicken in a tangy bath of buttermilk laced with cayenne or hot sauce before dipping it not once, but twice in flour seasoned with salt, pepper, onion powder, and garlic powder. It's not just a crunchy crust I'm after, but layer upon layer of savory flavor. For my money, if there's fried chicken, there's got to be some honey somewhere, so I serve mine with a drizzle of honey mixed with Tabasco sauce.

Jasper had no problem accepting my Throwdown challenge at the Sarasota Springs racetrack. He said if he could take care of 300 covers with a few cooks and a few burners each night at Hattie's, then this would be nothing for him.

While the crowd seemed to like my chicken, I can't help but think they were biased toward the hometown favorite. The judges assessed our plates on the fried chicken's crispiness, juiciness, and overall flavor. They liked Jasper's large portion but thought that mine looked better (darker and crispier). All three judges thought that both were great and we almost tied. But in the end, they went with Jasper's, saying it was lighter and less greasy. Miss Hattie's chicken—now in the hands of Jasper Alexander—retained its legendary status. If you are ever in Saratoga, remember that there's more to do than watch the races; make the time to try Miss Hattie's Throwdown-winning fried chicken. It's always a shoo-in.

Bobby Flay's Fried Chicken with Tabasco Honey

Bobby Flay's
Fried Chicken with Tabasco Honey

SERVES 4 TO 6

1 quart plus 2 cups buttermilk

Kosher salt

2 teaspoons chile de árbol powder, or
  2 tablespoons hot sauce

2 small chickens (3 to 4 pounds total), each cut
  up into 8 pieces (breasts halved)

3 cups all-purpose flour

1 tablespoon garlic powder

1 tablespoon onion powder

1 tablespoon sweet Spanish paprika

2 teaspoons cayenne pepper

Freshly ground black pepper

Canola oil, for deep-frying

Tabasco Honey (recipe follows)

Fresh flat-leaf parsley leaves, for garnish

1. *To prepare the chicken,* whisk together
1 quart of the buttermilk, 2 tablespoons salt,
and the chile de árbol powder in a large bowl.
Add the chicken, turn to coat, cover, and refrigerate for at least 4 hours or overnight.

2. Stir the flour, garlic and onion powders,
paprika, and cayenne together in a large bowl.
Divide the flour mixture between 2 shallow
platters and season generously with salt and
pepper. Pour the remaining 2 cups buttermilk
into a bowl. Drain the chicken in a colander
and pat it dry. Dredge the pieces, a few at a
time, in the flour mixture and pat off any
excess. Then dip in the buttermilk and allow
the excess to drain off. Dredge the pieces in
the second plate of flour and pat off the
excess. Put the chicken pieces on a baking
rack set over a baking sheet and set aside
while the oil heats.

3. Pour about 3 inches of oil into a deep cast-
iron skillet; the oil should not come more than
halfway up the sides of the skillet. Put the skillet over medium-high heat and heat the oil to
375°F on a deep-frying thermometer. Working
in batches, add a few chicken pieces to the hot
oil and fry, turning occasionally, until evenly
golden brown and cooked through, about
20 minutes. Remove from the oil with a slotted
spoon and transfer to a rack to drain. Serve on
a platter, drizzled with Tabasco Honey and
garnished with parsley.

Tabasco Honey

1 cup honey

3 tablespoons Tabasco sauce

Kosher salt

Whisk together the honey, Tabasco, and salt to
taste in a bowl. Serve with the chicken.

WINNER!

Jasper Alexander's
Hattie's Southern Fried Chicken
SERVES 4

1 (3½-pound) chicken, cut into 8 pieces, rinsed,
   and patted dry

1 tablespoon kosher salt

½ tablespoon freshly ground black pepper

Vegetable oil, for frying

3 cups all-purpose flour

1. Put the chicken in a large baking dish and sprinkle with the salt and pepper. Refrigerate for 1 hour.

2. In a large cast-iron skillet, heat enough oil to come about halfway up the pieces of chicken to 325°F. Put the flour in a large, sturdy plastic bag. Add the chicken, a few pieces at a time, and shake to coat; shake off any excess flour. Working in batches, add the chicken pieces to the hot oil and fry, turning the chicken and adjusting the heat as necessary, until the skin is golden and a meat thermometer inserted into the chicken registers 160°F, 20 to 25 minutes.

CHICKEN CACCIATORE

ON THIS EPISODE OF THROWDOWN!...

I turned up the heat with New York City firefighter Keith Young. Keith thought that he was showing off his firehouse favorite chicken cacciatore for the Food Network special "Real Men Cook," but I had something else in mind. At 6 feet 6 inches and 250 pounds, Keith Young was an impressive opponent. This member of Ladder 158 in Brooklyn is also a volunteer firefighter in the Long Island town of Freeport, where he lives with his wife and children. Just like fighting fire, food is a passion for Keith. Before he joined the FDNY, Keith earned a Bachelor of Science degree from the prestigious Johnson & Wales culinary school and worked in a half dozen restaurants from New York to Lake Tahoe. His previous career has served him and his coworkers well—they are guaranteed an outstanding meal when he's in the kitchen, and he's freed from dish-washing duty. In 2003 Keith published *Cooking with the Firehouse Chef,* a cookbook full of his favorite recipes and anecdotes from one of the "hottest" kitchens in the world. That book led to television appearances from the *Today* show, to Wayne Brady, and of course, to Food Network.

"We kept busting Bobby's chops because he had everything prepped, he had four burners working, and he had a woman behind a curtain, like the Wizard of Oz, handing him any pot or pan that he needed. You never see her on camera. We were an hour behind Bobby when it came to service. Stressful, definitely, but the cold beers seemed to make it all go away!"

—KEITH YOUNG

Name: Keith Young
Hometown: Freeport, Long Island, New York
Occupation: Firefighter

Keith needs to do more than make food that's deliciously satisfying; he also has to be frugal because there is no such thing as a free meal at the firehouse. Firefighters pay for their own meals, and Keith has become the master of cooking on a tight budget; typically each meal costs no more than $8.00 a head. This Throwdown brought me a challenge of my own: I had to work within the same budget of $280 for 35 people. I enlisted NYC firefighter and award-winning chef Tom Sullivan to help me keep my wallet in check. With his help and his calculator, I met my goal and filled my shopping carts with bread, pasta, chicken, and produce for $273.21. (By the way, Keith had me beat on that one—his total came to $270.78.)

Before I could surprise Keith and the troops at the New York City Fire Museum, I went to the test kitchen. It had been years since I had prepared chicken cacciatore (Italian translation: hunter's-style chicken) and I wasn't about to mess with a classic. My strategy was to stay true to the integrity of the dish. Stephanie and Miriam battled with me to add fresh rosemary and thyme, something I thought could overpower the dish, but in the end, I went along with them. I learned long ago that sometimes it's easier just to give in (especially to those two!).

My version is quite similar to Keith's: full of sliced peppers, onions, garlic, mushrooms, tomatoes, chicken stock, and wine. Capers add a bit of briny flavor, red pepper flakes bring heat, and a touch of honey curbs the natural acidity of the tomatoes. Keith uses white wine in his dish because he thinks it goes well with the chicken's white meat; I opted for a red wine, which I felt paired well with the tomatoes. He also flours his chicken, which I didn't do, to give it a great crust and to help thicken the sauce. I browned my chicken slowly, rendering the fat and crisping its exterior, while allowing the sauce to thicken naturally, reducing it over high heat on the stove once the chicken was done.

As I prepared to issue my challenge, I had to wonder . . . could I beat the heat or would I go up in flames? Keith had none of my qualms. Upon tasting my dish, which he likened to a Bolognese, he said that he liked it but was still confident that he would smoke me. The judges enjoyed both dishes; each sauce's consistency was excellent and they loved our presentations. But there was just one dish that brought Grandma to mind and reminded them of a classic chicken cacciatore—and that was Keith's.

He watches our backs and keeps his crew going strong so that they can do the same. No question about it, Keith Young is a guy who deserves the win.

Bobby Flay's
Chicken Cacciatore
SERVES 4 TO 6

4 tablespoons olive oil

1 (3½- to 4-pound) chicken, cut into 8 pieces (breasts halved)

Kosher salt and freshly ground black pepper

1 pound cremini mushrooms, quartered

1 large red onion, halved and thinly sliced

1 large yellow bell pepper, thinly sliced

1 serrano or jalapeño chile, finely diced

3 cloves garlic, thinly sliced

¼ teaspoon red pepper flakes

1 cup dry red wine

2 cups homemade chicken stock (see page 220) or canned low-sodium chicken broth

1 (28-ounce) can plum tomatoes, with juices, pureed

3 sprigs fresh rosemary

3 sprigs fresh thyme

Honey

2 tablespoons brined capers, drained

¼ cup chopped fresh basil leaves, plus whole leaves for garnish

1 pound spaghetti, cooked al dente

Thinly shaved Parmesan cheese

1. Heat 2 tablespoons of the oil in a large Dutch oven over high heat. Season the chicken pieces on both sides with salt and pepper. Working in batches, place the chicken in the pan, skin side down, and cook until golden brown, 3 to 4 minutes. Turn the chicken over and cook until golden brown, 2 to 3 minutes. Remove the chicken to a large plate.

2. Add another tablespoon of the oil to the pan and heat until almost smoking. Add the mushrooms, season with salt and pepper, and cook, stirring occasionally, until they are golden brown and their liquid has evaporated, about 10 minutes. Remove to a plate.

3. Add the remaining 1 tablespoon oil, the onion, and the bell pepper to the pan and cook until soft, about 4 minutes. Add the serrano chile, garlic, and red pepper flakes, and cook for 1 minute. Stir in the wine and cook until almost completely reduced. Add the chicken stock, tomatoes, rosemary, and thyme, and bring to a simmer. Return the dark meat and the mushrooms to the pan, reduce the heat to medium-low, cover the pan, and cook for 30 minutes.

4. Add the white meat to the pan, cover, and continue cooking for 10 minutes. Remove the chicken with a slotted spoon to a large shallow bowl and tent it loosely with foil.

5. Raise the heat under the pan to high and cook the liquid, stirring occasionally, until thickened to a sauce consistency, about 15 minutes.

6. Season with salt, pepper, and honey to taste. Stir in the capers and basil, and pour the sauce over the chicken. Garnish with fresh basil sprigs. Serve over the spaghetti, and top with shaved Parmesan.

WINNER!

Keith Young's
Chicken Cacciatore
SERVES 6 TO 8

¾ cup all-purpose flour

Kosher salt and freshly ground black pepper

1 cup olive oil

2 (3- to 3½-pound) chickens, cut into 8 pieces
(breasts halved)

6 cloves garlic, halved

10 ounces white mushrooms, sliced

1 large onion, halved and cut into
½-inch-thick slices

2 green bell peppers, cut into ½-inch-wide slices

2 red bell peppers, cut into ½-inch-wide slices

1 cup dry white wine

3 tablespoons tomato paste

1 (28-ounce) can whole tomatoes, with
juices, crushed

1 teaspoon red pepper flakes

1 teaspoon dried oregano

12 fresh basil leaves, chopped

1. Stir the flour, 2 tablespoons salt, and 1 tablespoon pepper together in a shallow dish. Heat the oil in a pot over medium-high heat. Working in batches so you don't crowd the pan, toss the chicken in the flour to coat, shaking off any excess. Fry until golden brown all over, about 5 minutes per side, removing the chicken to a plate as it is done.

2. Reduce the heat to medium, add the garlic to the pot, and cook, stirring, until it turns golden brown. Transfer the garlic to the plate with the chicken.

3. Raise the heat to medium-high, add the mushrooms, and cook until they release most of their liquid, about 5 minutes. Add the onion and green and red bell peppers, and cook until soft, about 7 minutes.

4. Add the wine and simmer until reduced by about half. Stir in the tomato paste, then the tomatoes, red pepper flakes, oregano, and salt to taste. Return the chicken, garlic, and any juices on the plate to the pot, cover, and reduce the heat so that the mixture simmers. Simmer for 15 minutes.

5. Uncover the pot and simmer until the chicken is cooked through, 15 minutes. Stir in the fresh basil just before serving.

MEATLOAF

ON THIS EPISODE OF THROWDOWN!...

It's an American classic: meatloaf. I stepped into the ring with Cape Codders Jack and Rocco Collucci, some serious trash-talking meatloaf makers. ○ The Colluccis are fourth-generation restaurateurs who were serving up fantastic food with extreme hospitality in the friendly environment of the Collucci Brothers Diner. Both their characters and their cuisine are larger than life and have earned them rave reviews in Cape Cod's papers. Their aim: gourmet food served diner-style. Comfort food may fill their menu, but these good-natured brothers have another, not so soft side: both have a fierce competitive edge, at least when it comes to their food. Jack and Rocco were perfect *Throwdown!* material.

"People ask us, 'What's Bobby Flay really like?' He is the genuine article and extremely kind with his time. I can't count how many pictures he posed for and never once even looked like maybe he'd had enough. He's a Yankee fan, and of course we're all Red Sox here. Our people gave him hell for it. Man, he took a lot from that crowd! My favorite part was listening to him and Rocco talking shop during the breaks, like they were just two chefs talking about the business. That was very cool."
—JACK COLLUCCI

Names: Jack and Rocco Collucci
Establishment: 4 Bros. Bistro
Hometown: West Yarmouth, Massachusetts
Website: www.colluccibros.com,
www.4brosbistro.com
Phone: (508) 771-0799

Their diner's menu had all the classics—omelets, colossal sandwiches, burgers—but the specialty was meatloaf. Jack ran the front of the house while Rocco handled the kitchen. Jack said that as soon as he tasted the meatloaf that Rocco and their father developed, he knew they had their signature dish. Packed with rich flavor, their tender, moist version is sure to comfort any hungry soul.

In the test kitchen, I learned that, unlike most people, Stephanie and Miriam don't have fond childhood memories of meatloaf. Miriam's mom cooked it only once and it was so bad she never made it again. Stephanie's mom made a great meatloaf but it was one of the few meals that Stephanie refused to eat. I liked this challenge—I enjoy taking American classics and giving them a dynamic twist. Meatloaf would be no exception. I gave the meatloaf lots of natural moistness by adding sautéed zucchini, onions, and peppers and went light on the bread crumbs. Balsamic vinegar, grated Parmesan cheese, lots of garlic, fresh parsley, and thyme pump up the meatloaf's flavor profile even more. The Collucci brothers and I agree that great meatloaf needs to have a good amount of moisture, flavor (it can't just taste like hamburger), and a great outside texture. Much as you would for tasty and tender Italian meatballs,

we used a blend of ground beef, pork, and veal. We found the best way to get a good crust is to shape the loaf and bake it on a baking sheet, not in a deeper pan. This way the meat doesn't steam in the pan's confines and the oven's direct heat can brown its total surface.

Cape Cod can be somewhat desolate in the off-season, but the Collucci Brothers Diner stayed hot all year long. We made our trek mid-winter, and while we almost didn't make it (an ice storm canceled our flight, forcing us into a cab, onto the train to Boston, culminating in a midnight icy drive to our hotel—phew!), we found the Collucci family's celebration in full swing. (They threw a sixty-fifth birthday party for their father to coincide with their Food Network "special.")

The Colluccis' meatloaf was an instant trip down memory lane, and while my souped-up version got a warm reception, the judges went with the good-time guys' old-time favorite.

Postscript: The Collucci brothers closed their diner in Hyannis when their lease ended but have moved on to bigger and better things—Colluccis' 4 Bros. Bistro in West Yarmouth, Massachusetts. Have no fear: their "Throwdown Meatloaf" has a place of honor on their new menu.

Bobby Flay's
Roasted Vegetable Meatloaf
with Balsamic Glaze

SERVES 6

3 tablespoons olive oil

1 large zucchini, finely diced

1 red bell pepper, finely diced

1 yellow bell pepper, finely diced

1 small onion, finely diced

Kosher salt and freshly ground black pepper

5 cloves garlic, finely chopped

½ teaspoon red pepper flakes

2 large eggs, lightly beaten

¼ cup chopped fresh parsley leaves

1 tablespoon finely chopped fresh thyme leaves

8 ounces ground pork

8 ounces ground veal

1 pound ground beef chuck

1 cup panko (Japanese) bread crumbs

½ cup freshly grated Pecorino Romano cheese

1 cup ketchup

¼ cup plus 2 tablespoons balsamic vinegar

1. Preheat the oven to 425°F.

2. Heat the oil in a large sauté pan over high heat. Add the zucchini, red and yellow bell peppers, onion, and salt and pepper to taste, and cook until almost soft, 5 minutes. Stir in the garlic and ¼ teaspoon of the red pepper flakes, and cook for 30 seconds. Remove from the heat and let cool.

3. Whisk the eggs, parsley, and thyme together in a large bowl. Add the pork, veal, beef, bread crumbs, cheese, ½ cup of the ketchup, the 2 tablespoons balsamic vinegar, and the cooled vegetables, and mix until just combined. Mold the meatloaf into a 12-inch-long, 6-inch-wide loaf on a baking sheet lined with parchment paper.

4. Whisk the remaining ½ cup ketchup, ¼ cup balsamic vinegar, and ¼ teaspoon red pepper flakes together in a small bowl, and then brush the mixture over the entire loaf. Bake the meatloaf for 1 to 1¼ hours, until cooked through. Remove from the oven and let rest for 10 minutes before slicing.

WINNER!

Jack and Rocco Collucci's
Collucci Brothers' Meatloaf
SERVES 4 TO 6

2 tablespoons vegetable oil

2 celery stalks, finely chopped

1 medium onion, finely chopped

2 pounds 80/20 ground beef

2 large eggs, lightly beaten

Dash of hot sauce, preferably Tabasco

Dash of Worcestershire sauce

Kosher salt and freshly ground black pepper

3 slices white bread, torn into small pieces and
   soaked in cold water

½ cup Italian-seasoned dry bread crumbs

½ cup ketchup

1. Preheat the oven to 375°F.

2. Heat the oil in a medium sauté pan over medium-high heat. Add the celery and onion, and sauté until tender, about 7 minutes. Set aside to cool.

3. In a large bowl, combine the celery mixture, ground beef, eggs, hot sauce, and Worcestershire sauce, and season with salt and pepper. Squeeze the water out of the bread, add the bread to the bowl, and combine. Mix in the dry bread crumbs. Shape into a firm 9 × 6-inch loaf on a rimmed baking sheet. Spread the ketchup over the top, and bake in the oven until cooked through, 45 to 55 minutes.

MAC 'N' CHEESE

ON THIS EPISODE OF THROWDOWN!...

I went to Philadelphia so I could go cheese to cheese with mac 'n' cheese queen Delilah Winder. Delilah thought that she had been chosen for a television special entitled "America's Favorite Food" and that Food Network was throwing her a cookbook release party. She had no idea that she would be sharing her spotlight with this surprise guest. ○ Delilah owns four Delilah's Southern Cuisine stands in Philly and has built an empire on her soul food dishes, especially that mac and cheese. She combines the traditions of her grandmothers with the artisanal ingredients of a modern chef to create her incredible seven-cheese macaroni and cheese. A local legend in Philadelphia, Delilah and her warm smile, boisterous personality, and delicious soul food grabbed national attention when Oprah Winfrey named her mac and cheese the best in the country. Delilah parlayed that fame into her own cookbook, *Delilah's Everyday Soul: Southern Cooking with Style.*

"The experience was over the top, especially to have the opportunity to interact with someone in the industry whom I have adored from afar. And each and every time the segment runs, fans line up for mac and cheese as though it is the last food on the planet. Thanks, Throwdown!, for a once-in-a-lifetime experience."
— DELILAH WINDER

Name: Delilah Winder
Establishment: Delilah's Southern Cuisine
Hometown: Philadelphia, Pennsylvania
Website: www.delilahwinder.com
Phone: (856) 528-4133

Delilah's mac and cheese is not just outrageously good; it's flat-out outrageous. The recipe calls for seven cheeses (and that's not including the Velveeta), a dozen eggs, half a pound of butter, and 6 cups of half-and-half. According to her calculations, each serving weighs in at almost 2,000 calories! She doesn't fear the fat in the slightest, noting that her grandparents lived on the food she now so lovingly prepares, and they lived well into their nineties.

I started my quest for the perfect macaroni and cheese at *the* place to shop for cheese in the Big Apple: Murray's Cheese. I made my selections: slightly aged fontina, a great-tasting melting cheese; creamy Asiago, which also melts really well; Irish cheddar, for good luck; and sharp American cheddar and imported Parmesan cheese, for lots of flavor.

I take my mac and cheese pretty seriously and brought my game face with me to the test kitchen. Most people's childhood memories of this dish start and end with elbows and one kind of cheese, typically cheddar or Colby. (And that's if it didn't come from a box!) Our macaroni and cheese is decidedly more upscale. Taking my cue from Italian carbonara, my dish is chock-full of pancetta, garlic, and parsley in a five-cheese sauce enriched with egg yolks. I'm putting my five cheeses up against Delilah's seven. Stephanie, Miriam, and I had just one disagreement this time: I like my macaroni overcooked in my mac and cheese, but Stephanie and Miriam would have none of it. As far as they're concerned, pasta—no matter how it's served—should always be cooked al dente.

The delightful Delilah took my challenge, and the mac and cheese battle began. She certainly won over her hometown crowd! Our secret judges—Patrice Rames, chef-owner of Bistro St. Tropez, which specializes in comfort food, and Kevin Washington, owner of Ron's Ribs, the oldest African American–owned restaurant in Philadelphia—had a hard time deciding; these were two very different styles of mac and cheese. While they loved Delilah's, they fell for my presentation and crust and just felt mine had more cheese flavor . . . go figure. This Throwdown win might have been mine, but at the end of the day, we all know that the Mac 'n' Cheese Queen belongs on her well-deserved throne.

NOTE

We cut the yield and ingredients of Delilah's recipe in half for home cooks, but the delicious proportions remain the same.

Bobby Flay's Macaroni and
Cheese Carbonara

WINNER!

Bobby Flay's
Macaroni and Cheese Carbonara
SERVES 4

Unsalted butter, for the baking dish

1 tablespoon olive oil

1 (1-inch-thick) slice pancetta, cut into
   small dice

4 cloves garlic, finely chopped

3 tablespoons all-purpose flour

5 cups whole milk, or more if needed, hot

4 large egg yolks, lightly whisked

2 teaspoons finely chopped fresh thyme leaves

½ teaspoon cayenne pepper

2 cups (8 ounces) grated Asiago cheese, plus
   more for the top

1½ cups (6 ounces) grated Irish white cheddar,
   plus more for the top

1½ cups (6 ounces) grated American cheddar,
   such as Goot Essa Mountain Valley, plus more
   for the top

1 cup (4 ounces) grated aged fontina cheese,
   plus more for the top

½ cup freshly grated Parmesan cheese, plus
   more for the top

Kosher salt and freshly ground black pepper

1 pound elbow macaroni, cooked just under
   al dente

½ cup coarsely chopped fresh flat-leaf parsley
   leaves

1. Preheat the oven to 375°F. Butter the bottom and sides of a 10 × 10 × 2-inch baking dish and set it aside.

2. Heat the oil in a large sauté pan over medium heat. Add the pancetta and cook until golden brown on all sides, about 8 minutes. Remove with a slotted spoon to a plate lined with paper towels.

3. Add the garlic to the fat in the pan and cook until light golden brown, 1 minute. Whisk in the flour and cook for 1 to 2 minutes. Whisk in the hot milk, raise the heat to high, and cook, whisking constantly, until thickened, about 5 minutes. Whisk in the eggs until incorporated and let cook for 1 to 2 minutes. Remove from the heat and whisk in the thyme, cayenne, and all the different cheeses until completely melted. Season with salt and pepper. If the mixture appears too thick, add additional warm milk, ¼ cup at a time.

4. Put the cooked macaroni in a large bowl, add the cheese sauce, reserved pancetta, and the parsley, and stir until combined. Transfer to the prepared baking dish.

5. Combine an additional ¼ cup each of Asiago, cheddars, fontina, and Parmesan in a bowl, and sprinkle evenly over the top. Bake until the dish is heated through and the top is a light golden brown, 12 to 15 minutes. Remove from the oven and let rest for 10 minutes before serving.

Delilah Winder's
Seven-Cheese Mac and Cheese
SERVES 8

Unsalted butter, for the baking dish

1 pound elbow macaroni

6 large eggs, at room temperature

8 tablespoons (1 stick) unsalted butter, melted

½ cup (4 ounces) cubed Velveeta cheese

3 cups half-and-half, at room temperature

2½ cups (10 ounces) grated sharp yellow
cheddar cheese

1 cup (4 ounces) grated extra-sharp white
cheddar cheese

¾ cup (3 ounces) shredded mozzarella cheese

½ cup (2 ounces) grated Asiago cheese

½ cup (2 ounces) grated Gruyère cheese

½ cup (2 ounces) grated Monterey Jack cheese

½ cup (2 ounces) grated Muenster cheese

Pinch of kosher salt, or to taste

1½ teaspoons freshly ground black pepper

1. Preheat the oven to 325°F. Lightly butter a 4-quart rectangular baking dish.

2. Bring a large saucepan of salted water to a boil. Add the macaroni and cook until slightly al dente, about 7 minutes. Drain and set aside to keep warm.

3. Whisk the eggs in a large bowl until frothy. Add the butter, Velveeta, and 1 cup of the half-and-half. Add the warm macaroni and toss until the Velveeta has melted and the mixture is smooth. Add the remaining 2 cups half-and-half, 1½ cups of the yellow cheddar, the remaining cheeses, the salt, and the pepper. Toss until completely combined.

4. Pour the mixture into the prepared dish, and bake for 30 minutes. Sprinkle with the remaining 1 cup yellow cheddar and bake until golden brown on top, about 30 minutes. Serve hot.

FISH AND CHIPS

ON THIS EPISODE OF THROWDOWN!...

It was a taste of England with Mat Arnfeld and his award-winning fish and chips. The catch of the day? A Throwdown, of course! ⭕ New York City's Greenwich Avenue is home to a growing ex-pat British population that craves the tastes of their old homeland. Ready to feed that craving with the best fish and chips outside of the U.K. is one of the most popular joints on the block, the restaurant A Salt & Battery. People are hooked on chef/owner Mat Arnfeld's classic fish and chips because they are the "reel" deal. ⭕ Mat started flipping fish and chopping potatoes when he was just a kid back at his father's chip shop in northern England. He has had plenty of years to develop his perfectly crispy battered and fried fish accompanied by tasty golden chips. (Yes, we'd call those chips French fries, but *don't* do that at A Salt & Battery! To the Brits, they are chips. Period.) The batter is Mat's secret to success; the combination of ingredients fry up to a crispy coating that retains its texture with every bite and stays crispy even when heaped with the preferred condiments of vinegar and Mat's homemade tartar sauce.

Name: Mat Arnfeld
Establishment: A Salt & Battery
Hometown: New York, New York
Website: www.asaltandbattery.com
Phone: (212) 691-2713

I had never made a classic fish and chips before, so I went to get some pointers from some guys who know a thing or two about them—the Gotham Knights rugby players, many of whom were born and raised in the U.K. and all of whom have great appetites. Their tips: The fish should be mild-flavored and fresh, and the batter should be crispy but not too thick. Chips are thicker than American fries, more like a steak fry than a French fry. Tartar sauce and malt vinegar are must-have accompaniments. Instructions in mind, I headed to the test kitchen to get things rolling.

Sadly, my batter failed miserably. It just wasn't crisp enough for my liking. In my mind, the culprits were the flour and eggs. I like a lighter, crisper batter and decided to buck tradition and use the batter that has been a mainstay at Mesa Grill for years, a tempura batter of rice flour and water. Its one downfall is that, since it contains no eggs, it doesn't get very brown when fried. So I turned to another Mesa Grill staple, ancho chile powder, which not only gives a great color to the batter but also adds a nice hint of spice.

Ready to turn up the heat some more, I spiked my vinegar with serrano chiles and added habaneros to my lemony tartar sauce. Even though I know that proper English-style chips should be thick-cut, I decided to stick with what I know best, and as an American, that meant French fries. Once Mat accepted my challenge, we got cooking. But things weren't going too swimmingly for me at this Throwdown—I had my batter set but my fryers failed. Facing a restless crowd hungry for their promised fish and chips, I had to think fast. I asked the staff at the nearby Chelsea Brewing Company if I could borrow their fryers, and finally we were ready to feed the masses.

The judges, both British and American to make a level playing field, were looking for perfectly cooked fish with a light, crisp batter and crisp chips. I received high marks on all points, but ultimately Mat's traditional recipe took the win. This may not have been a triumph for the New World, but luckily we can share in the prize of A Salt & Battery's jolly good fish and chips.

Bobby Flay's
Fish and Chips
SERVES 4 TO 6

Canola or peanut oil

3 large Idaho potatoes, peeled, cut into
   ¼-inch-thick fries, and soaked in cold water

3 cups rice flour

Kosher salt and freshly ground black pepper

2 tablespoons plus 1 teaspoon ancho chile
   powder

2½ pounds fresh cod, cut into 8 pieces

¼ cup chopped fresh cilantro leaves

Lemon-Habanero Tartar Sauce (recipe follows)

Serrano Vinegar (recipe follows)

1. Preheat the oven to 325°F. Fill a deep-fryer or a deep pot halfway with oil, and preheat to 325°F.

2. Drain the fries in batches on paper towels. Fry each batch until a pale blond color, 3 to 4 minutes, and remove to a baking sheet lined with paper towels.

3. Raise the oil temperature to 365°F.

4. Whisk 2 cups of the rice flour with 1 cup cold water in a medium bowl, and season with salt, pepper, and the 1 teaspoon ancho chile powder.

5. Put the remaining 1 cup flour on a large plate and season with salt and pepper. Season the fish fillets on each side with salt and pepper, and lightly dredge them in the seasoned flour, tapping off any excess. Working in batches, dip the fish in the batter and fry until golden brown on both sides and just cooked through, about 5 minutes total. Remove the fish with a slotted spoon to a plate lined with paper towels. Then transfer to a baking sheet and keep warm in the oven until ready to serve.

6. Raise the oil temperature to 375°F. Combine the remaining 2 tablespoons ancho chile powder with 1 tablespoon salt in a small bowl.

7. Fry the potatoes again, in batches, until golden brown, 3 to 4 minutes. Remove to a baking sheet lined with paper towels, and season with the chile mixture and the cilantro.

8. Serve the fish and chips in baskets, with the tartar sauce and vinegar on the side.

Lemon-Habanero Tartar Sauce

3 cups fresh lemon juice

2 tablespoons honey

1½ cups mayonnaise

3 anchovy fillets in oil, patted dry and chopped

1 habanero chile, chopped

6 cornichons, finely diced

2 tablespoons brined capers, drained

Kosher salt and freshly ground black pepper

1. Bring the lemon juice to a boil in a small saucepan over high heat and cook, stirring occasionally, until reduced to ¼ cup, about 20 minutes. Whisk in the honey and let cool.

2. Combine the reduced lemon juice, mayonnaise, anchovies, and habanero in a food processor and process until smooth. Scrape the mixture into a medium bowl, and stir in the cornichons and capers. Season with salt and pepper. Cover and refrigerate for at least 1 hour before serving.

Serrano Vinegar

2 cups white wine vinegar

8 serrano chiles, pricked with a fork

1 tablespoon kosher salt

Bring the vinegar to a simmer in a small saucepan. Add the chiles and salt, remove from the heat, and transfer to a glass bottle or jar. Let sit at room temperature for 8 hours before refrigerating.

WINNER!

Mat Arnfeld's
Fish and Chips
SERVES 4

2 cups all-purpose flour, sifted, plus more as
    needed

Kosher salt

1 pint brown ale

Vegetable oil, for deep-frying

8 large Idaho potatoes, peeled and sliced
    ½ inch thick

4 (6-ounce) cod, haddock, or halibut fillets,
    about 1 inch thick

Malt vinegar, for serving

1. Put 1½ cups of the flour and a pinch of salt in a medium bowl. Whisk in the ale until smooth. (For a lighter batter, use a handheld immersion blender to combine.) The batter should have the consistency of heavy cream; if it is too thin, whisk in a little more flour. Cover and refrigerate for 1 hour.

2. Fill a deep-fryer or heavy pot halfway with oil, and heat to 300°F. Add your chips carefully, so as not to excite the oil, and cook for about 3 minutes; they shouldn't color. Transfer to a paper-towel-lined baking sheet and let cool.

3. Raise the oil temperature to 350°F. Put your chips in the oil and fry until golden brown, 3 to 4 minutes. Drain on a paper-towel-lined baking sheet and sprinkle with salt.

4. Raise the oil temperature to 375°F.

5. Put the remaining ½ cup flour in a baking dish. Season the fish generously with salt; then dredge in the flour, shaking off any excess. Give the batter a stir and dip the fish in the batter, shaking off any excess. Fry the fish, flipping once and adjusting the heat as necessary, until golden brown and cooked through, 4 to 5 minutes. Transfer to a plate lined with paper towels, and season with salt. Serve with the chips and malt vinegar.

CHEESECAKE

ON THIS EPISODE OF THROWDOWN!...

It's a New York classic: cheesecake. I am going slice against slice versus Alan Rosen and Junior's restaurant, where his family has been serving their legendary cheesecake since 1957. After all this time, Alan still makes it the way his grandfather did almost sixty years ago. This is about more than cheesecake; for Alan, it's a labor of love. ○ Alan thinks the reason behind the film crews is a special called "Then and Now." Will my one cheesecake be enough to topple this maker of millions? Alan has been at this long enough to have garnered some serious respect. Junior's cheesecake is a part of Alan Rosen's family legacy, so I know he's got the "Then" covered. If I'm going to have a shot at winning, my best bet is to try for the "Now" with a more modern take on New York's second-most-famous slice. ○ I'm the first to admit that baking isn't really my thing, so I went off to get a lesson from another New York

City cheesecake legend, Eileen of Eileen's Special Cheesecake in SoHo. A cheesecake crust is typically a simple one of graham crackers and butter. The batter consists of cream cheese, sour cream, vanilla, lemon juice, and eggs. Elaine showed me how she separates her eggs, adding the yolks directly to the batter and then folding in the whites, which she has beaten into soft peaks. This step gives her cake an almost mousselike consistency. There are a couple of "don'ts" to be aware of to keep the cake from cracking: don't overbake and don't overbeat. Cooking the cheesecake in a water bath is another way to keep its top smooth and unbroken.

Name: Alan Rosen
Establishment: Junior's
Hometown: Brooklyn, New York
Website: www.juniorscheesecake.com
Phone: (800) 4JUNIOR or (718) 852-5257

I took what I had learned from Eileen and headed to the test kitchen to work on my cake with Stephanie and Miriam. I decided to meld the basic cheesecake with another American classic dessert, caramel apple pie, and combined soft, warm caramelized apples with a warm caramel sauce to pour over the cold, creamy cheesecake. (Alan does something along the same wavelength by combining his cheesecake with another American classic, devil's food cake.) As much as I loved Eileen's cake, I decided that I wanted mine to have a slightly denser consistency, so I used whole eggs in the batter. I tweaked my graham cracker crust by adding some ground toasted walnuts for additional flavor and crunch. The apples were sautéed in a light caramel glaze made from thickened apple juice, butter, a vanilla bean, and sugar. A rich caramel sauce made from sugar, heavy cream, and a healthy dose of Calvados (an apple brandy) put the dish over the top.

I made my way to Junior's with a Throwdown challenge in hand, and we were met by a New York crowd that was passionate about their cheesecake. Obviously Alan had his steadfast devotees cheering him on, though I managed to win over a good portion of the crowd. But it was up to our judges, food critic Arthur Schwartz and Ruthy's Cheesecake & Rugelach Bakery owner Patricia Alessi. They were grading us on flavor, texture, and creativity.

What a difficult decision! Both had great flavor and were smooth and creamy. In fact, Alan might have even had an edge over me on those points. In the end, the judges went for the apples over the chocolate. I knew my cheesecake was good, but good enough to beat a New York legend like Junior's? Maybe I should rethink my stance on baking, but I definitely haven't changed my mind about Junior's cheesecake— it's a New York City landmark.

WINNER!

Bobby Flay's Caramel Apple Cheesecake
SERVES 8 TO 10

Cheesecake

Cooking spray

8 whole graham crackers

1 cup lightly toasted walnuts, coarsely chopped

2 tablespoons light brown sugar

5 tablespoons unsalted butter, melted

½ cup plus 2 tablespoons granulated sugar

1 tablespoon grated orange zest

3 (8-ounce) packages Philadelphia cream cheese, at room temperature

½ cup plus 2 tablespoons finely packed light muscovado sugar

4 large eggs, at room temperature

1 large vanilla bean, seeds scraped out, seeds and pods reserved

1 teaspoon pure vanilla extract

½ teaspoon fine salt

½ cup heavy cream

(recipe continues)

Apples

2 cups apple juice

¼ cup granulated sugar

1 tablespoon unsalted butter, cold

3 Granny Smith apples, peeled, cored, and thinly sliced

3 Fuji apples, peeled, cored, and thinly sliced

¼ cup Calvados or other apple brandy

½ cup crème fraîche

Apple-Caramel Sauce (recipe follows)

1. *To make the cheesecake,* preheat the oven to 350°F. Spray the bottom and sides of a 9-inch springform pan with cooking spray.

2. Combine the graham crackers, ½ cup of the walnuts, and the brown sugar in a food processor and process until finely ground. With the motor running, add the butter through the feed tube and process until the mixture just comes together. Pat the mixture evenly into the prepared pan, place it on a baking sheet, and bake in the oven until light golden brown and just set, about 8 minutes. Cool completely on a wire rack.

3. Combine ¼ cup of the granulated sugar and the orange zest in a food processor, and process until combined.

4. Put the cream cheese in the bowl of a stand mixer fitted with the paddle attachment, and beat until light and fluffy, 3 to 4 minutes. Add the orange sugar, remaining ¼ cup plus 2 tablespoons granulated sugar, and the muscovado sugar, and beat until the sugar is incorporated and the mixture is light and fluffy. Add the eggs, one at a time, and mix until just incorporated, scraping the sides and bottom of the bowl. Add the vanilla seeds (save the pod for the apples), vanilla extract, and salt, and beat until combined. Add the heavy cream and mix until just combined.

5. Scrape the mixture into the cooled crust. Set the springform pan on a large piece of heavy-duty aluminum foil, and fold the foil up the sides to surround it. Set the pan in a large roasting pan. Pour hot tap water into the roasting pan until it reaches about halfway up the sides of the springform pan (the foil will keep the water from seeping into the cheesecake). Bake until the edges of the cake are slightly puffed and set and the center still jiggles, about 55 minutes.

6. Turn off the heat, prop the oven door open with a wooden spoon, and leave the cheesecake in the water bath in the oven for 1 hour.

7. Remove the springform from the water bath, place it on a wire rack, and cool to room temperature, 2 hours. Then cover the pan and refrigerate until the cheesecake is chilled through, at least 4 hours and up to 24 hours.

8. *To cook the apples,* bring the apple juice, sugar, and reserved vanilla bean pod to a boil in a large sauté pan over high heat. Cook until slightly thickened and reduced to ½ cup, 10 minutes. Remove the vanilla bean pod and discard.

9. Stir in the butter until melted. Add the apples and cook, stirring occasionally, until lightly caramelized and soft, 8 to 10 minutes. Add the Calvados and simmer until reduced by half. Transfer the apples to a plate and let cool slightly.

10. *To serve,* remove the foil and sides from the springform pan. Spread the crème fraîche over the cheesecake. Top with the warm apple topping, drizzle liberally with the caramel sauce, and sprinkle with the remaining ½ cup chopped walnuts. Serve additional caramel sauce on the side.

Apple-Caramel Sauce

1½ cups granulated sugar

¾ cup heavy cream, hot

Pinch of fine salt

3 tablespoons Calvados or other apple brandy

½ teaspoon pure vanilla extract

1. Combine the sugar and ¼ cup water in a medium saucepan and bring to a boil over high heat. Cook, swirling the pot occasionally to even out the color, until amber, 10 to 12 minutes.

2. Slowly add the heavy cream and salt to the caramel. Whisk until smooth. Remove from the heat, and stir in the Calvados and vanilla extract. Serve warm.

Alan Rosen's
Junior's Devil's Food Cheesecake
SERVES 8 TO 10

Cheesecake

Cooking spray

3 (8-ounce) packages cream cheese, at room
temperature

1⅓ cups sugar

3 tablespoons cornstarch

1 tablespoon pure vanilla extract

2 extra-large eggs

⅔ cup heavy cream

Chocolate Cake

2¼ cups sifted cake flour

2 teaspoons baking powder

½ teaspoon fine salt

12 tablespoons (1½ sticks) unsalted butter,
at room temperature

1 cup granulated sugar

½ cup firmly packed dark brown sugar

3 extra-large eggs, separated

4 ounces bittersweet or semisweet chocolate,
melted and cooled

1 tablespoon pure vanilla extract

1½ cups whole milk

½ teaspoon cream of tartar

Dark Fudge Frosting

6 cups (1½ pounds) sifted confectioners' sugar

½ cup unsweetened cocoa powder

½ teaspoon fine salt

1½ cups (3 sticks) unsalted butter, at room
temperature

6 ounces bittersweet or semisweet chocolate,
melted and cooled

2 tablespoons dark corn syrup

2 tablespoons pure vanilla extract

½ cup heavy cream, or more if needed

2 ounces bittersweet or semisweet chocolate,
shaved to form chocolate curls

1. *To make the cheesecake layer,* preheat the oven to 350°F and generously grease with nonstick cooking spray the bottom and sides of a 9-inch springform pan, preferably nonstick. Wrap the outside with aluminum foil, covering the bottom and extending all the way up the sides.

2. Place 1 package of the cream cheese, ⅓ cup of the sugar, and the cornstarch in a large bowl and beat with an electric mixer on low speed until creamy, about 3 minutes, scraping the bowl down a couple of times. Blend in the remaining 2 packages cream cheese, 1 package at a time, scraping the bowl down after each. Raise the mixer speed to medium and beat in the remaining 1 cup sugar, and then the vanilla. Blend in the eggs, one at a time, beating well after adding each. Beat in the cream just until it's completely blended. Do not overmix.

3. Pour the batter into the prepared pan and place it in a large shallow pan. Add hot water to reach about 1 inch up the sides of the springform. Bake until the edges are light golden brown and the top is light golden tan, about 1¼ hours.

4. Remove the springform from the water bath, transfer it to a wire rack, and cool for 2 hours. Then cover the pan with plastic wrap and refrigerate until completely cold, about 4 hours. Place in the freezer until ready to assemble the cake.

5. *To make the chocolate layer,* preheat the oven to 350°F if necessary. Butter and flour or generously grease with nonstick cooking spray the bottom and sides of three 9-inch round cake pans. Line the bottom of each pan with a round of parchment or waxed paper.

6. Sift the flour, baking powder, and salt together into a medium bowl. In a large bowl, beat the butter and both sugars together with an electric mixer on medium speed until light yellow and creamy. Add the egg yolks, one at a time, beating well after each. Beat in the melted chocolate and the vanilla. Using a wooden spoon, stir in the flour mixture, alternating with the milk, mixing well after each until blended.

7. Put the egg whites and cream of tartar in a clean bowl and beat on high speed until stiff (but not dry) peaks form. Fold about one-third of the whites into the chocolate batter; then gently fold in the remaining whites. Don't worry if you still see a few white specks—they'll disappear during baking.

8. Divide the batter evenly among the prepared cake pans. Bake until a toothpick inserted in the center comes out with moist crumbs clinging to it, about 30 minutes. Cool the cakes in the pans on a wire rack for 15 minutes. Then remove the cakes from the pans and gently peel off the paper liners. Let cool completely, about 2 hours. Then cover with plastic wrap and refrigerate overnight or until ready to assemble the cake.

9. *To make the frosting,* sift the confectioners' sugar, cocoa powder, and salt together into a large bowl. In another large bowl, beat the butter with an electric mixer on high speed until light yellow and slightly thickened, about 3 minutes. With the mixer still running, beat in the chocolate, corn syrup, and vanilla. Reduce the mixer speed to low and beat in the sugar-cocoa mixture in two additions, beating well after each. Blend in the cream until the frosting has a spreading consistency, adding a little more cream if needed. Whip the frosting on high speed until light and creamy, about 2 minutes.

10. Remove the cheesecake from the freezer and let stand at room temperature for 10 minutes. Place 1 layer of devil's food cake, top side down, on a cake plate and spread some of the frosting over the top. Release and remove the ring of the springform; then remove the frozen cheesecake from the bottom of the pan. Place the cheesecake, top side down, on the frosted cake layer and spread some frosting over it. Top with the second devil's food layer, top side down. Spread with more frosting and cover with the third devil's food layer, top side up. Frost the sides and top of the cake with the remaining frosting. Decorate with the chocolate curls. Refrigerate for at least 2 hours to allow the cheesecake to thaw enough to slice easily.

11. Use a sharp straight-edge knife, not a serrated one, to cut into slices.

CUBAN ROAST PORK

ON THIS EPISODE OF THROWDOWN!...

I headed to Miami Beach for some legendary Cuban roast pork with Roberto Guerra, the King of the Caja China. Roberto calls the Caja China a "roasting pit on wheels," and he ought to know. He and his father designed it based on similar insulated cooking boxes that his father saw while growing up in Cuba. (The ingenious cooking system was first brought to Cuba in the early 1900s by Chinese workers—ergo its name.) The wooden box, which in English translates to "China box," is an insulated vehicle for cooking traditionally long-cooking items quickly. But I just call it the "magic box" because of its powers to produce the most succulent roast pork around.

Roberto's specialty is Cuban-flavored roasted whole pig, but for what he thought was a slot on Food Network's special on the cuisine of Cuba, he prepared a pork shoulder. He marinated the pork in a mojo, a mixture of sour orange juice, bay leaves, garlic, salt, and pepper.

"What's funny is that the Sunday night before the taping, my wife and I were watching the Food Network and a <u>Throwdown!</u> show was airing. I turned around to my wife and said, 'Wouldn't it be nice if Bobby Flay would do a Throwdown with me and La Caja China?' So imagine how I felt when Bobby showed up at the National Hotel—it was a dream come true. Thanks to the Throwdown, our business has increased substantially."
—ROBERTO GUERRA

Name: Roberto Guerra
Hometown: Miami, Florida
Website: www.lacajachina.com
Phone: (305) 888-1323

Roberto then stuffed the pork with ham, prunes, bacon, and guava shells, and glazed it with a mixture of brown sugar and malta, a Cuban soft drink brewed from barley, hops, and water, much like beer. However, unlike beer, malta is nonalcoholic. It is similar in color to stout (dark brown) but very sweet, with a molasses-like flavor. Roberto was all set to show off his magical prowess with the Caja China at a party in Miami for friends, family, and the Food Network's film crew.

I was really excited as I headed to the test kitchen. My mission was to create a roast pork that celebrates the flavors of Cuba using the Caja China. As I couldn't use the box inside the test kitchen—for ventilation reasons, it has to be used outdoors—I instead focused on my flavors for the pork and cooked it in the oven. I didn't want to marinate my pork in a sugar-based marinade because I believed the high heat would burn the outside of the meat. (However, I was to learn at the Throwdown that that really isn't the case, as Roberto roasts his in malta, brown sugar, and sour oranges and achieves spectacular results.)

I started by scoring the skin of the pork to allow the fat to render and yield a crisper exterior. I marinated it in garlic, oil, and fresh oregano before roasting. I began the pork shoulder in a 425°F oven for an hour before turning the oven temperature down to 350°F. The pork roasted in the oven for another 2 hours until the skin was super-crispy and the interior registered 175°F. But those 3 hours were in the oven—in the Caja China, because of the intense heat and insulated interior, it would take about half that time. Once the long wait was up, I removed the pork and marveled at its incredibly crisp skin and tender meat. I shredded the pork into big pieces, then drizzled the shredded meat with a "sour orange" sauce made from orange juice, lime juice, serrano chile, cilantro, garlic, and olive oil.

It was a beautiful sunny day and Roberto was busy getting ready for his party at the National Hotel in Miami's South Beach. Stephanie, Miriam, and I were down the block assembling our Caja Chinas and prepping our pork so that it would be ready to serve at the Throwdown. My lack of patience when setting up the Caja China came back to haunt me at the Throwdown when I realized I hadn't put the racks in the box. Without the racks in place, my pork would sit in its juices, thereby preventing it from getting a super-crispy skin.

As I snuck up on Roberto, I found him happily making another Cuban specialty, the Mojito. Drink in hand, he readily accepted my Throwdown and the battle of the Cuban barbecue began. Judge Maria Vasquez, who runs www.cuban foodmarket.com, an online store for Cuban food specialties, commented on my pork first, saying it was good but needed a little more salt. Our other judge, Chef Pepin, who has been cooking on Spanish TV since 1988 and considers himself to be an expert on pork, thought it was only so-so. Both Maria and Chef Pepin loved the crispy exterior and soft interior of Roberto's pork, as well as its sweetness. Chef Pepin did come around, and both he and Maria said that they honestly thought both dishes were fantastic, but as for a winner, Roberto took the prize.

Bobby Flay's
Cuban Pork with Sour Orange Sauce

SERVES 8

1 bone-in pork shoulder (about 4 pounds),
trimmed of excess fat

12 cloves garlic, coarsely chopped

½ cup olive oil

¼ cup plus 2 tablespoons finely chopped fresh
oregano leaves

3½ cups fresh orange juice

1¼ cups fresh lime juice

Grated zest of 1 orange

Grated zest of 1 lime

Kosher salt and freshly ground black pepper

Mojo Dipping Sauce (recipe follows)

1. Using a paring knife, make small slits over the entire surface of the pork. Set aside 1 teaspoon of the garlic for the sauce, and rub the rest into the slashes. Whisk together the oil and the ¼ cup oregano in a large roasting pan. Add the pork, turn to coat, cover, and let marinate in the refrigerator for at least 8 and up to 24 hours.

2. Remove the pork from the refrigerator 30 minutes before roasting.

3. Preheat the oven to 425°F.

4. Combine 3 cups of the orange juice, 1 cup of the lime juice, and the orange and lime zests in a large saucepan over high heat. Boil to reduce to 2 cups. Remove from the heat and stir in the remaining ½ cup orange juice, ¼ cup lime juice, reserved 1 teaspoon chopped garlic, and remaining 2 tablespoons oregano. Let the sour orange sauce cool to room temperature.

5. Season the pork with salt and pepper, transfer the roasting pan to the oven, and roast for 30 minutes.

6. Reduce the oven temperature to 350°F and continue roasting until the pork is golden brown and a thermometer inserted into the center reaches 180°F, about 2 hours. Baste the pork with the sour orange sauce during the last 30 minutes of cooking.

7. Remove the pork from the oven, baste it with any remaining sauce, tent it loosely with foil, and let it rest for 15 minutes before slicing. Serve slices drizzled with a little of the Mojo Dipping Sauce.

Mojo Dipping Sauce

4 cloves garlic

1 serrano chile, chopped

3 tablespoons fresh cilantro leaves

Kosher salt

¾ cup fresh orange juice

¼ cup fresh lime juice

¼ cup extra virgin olive oil

1 tablespoon clover honey

Using a mortar and pestle, mash the garlic, serrano, cilantro, and a few pinches of salt until it becomes a paste. Add the orange juice, lime juice, oil, and honey, and stir to combine.

WINNER!

Roberto Guerra's Stuffed Pork Shoulder
SERVES 8 TO 10

1 (6- to 7-pound) boneless pork shoulder, butt
   end, flattened so that it can be rolled

¼ cup sour orange juice, or ¼ cup fresh orange
   juice plus 2 tablespoons fresh lime juice

6 bay leaves

4 cloves garlic, chopped

2 tablespoons kosher salt

2 tablespoons freshly ground black pepper

8 ounces thinly sliced ham

8 slices bacon

1 cup pitted prunes

1 cup canned guava shells in syrup, drained

2 cups firmly packed dark brown sugar

1 (12-ounce) bottle malta

1. Score the fat on the pork shoulder well. Combine the sour orange juice, bay leaves, garlic, salt, and pepper in a large resealable bag or plastic container, add the pork, and marinate for at least 12 and up to 24 hours.

2. Preheat the oven to 325°F.

3. Put the meat, fat side down, on a cutting board with a shorter end toward you. Line the meat with the ham slices, then the bacon slices, prunes, and guava shells. Roll the meat up, starting at the end toward you, working carefully to keep the filling inside the roll. Every few inches, tie the roll firmly with butcher's twine. Place it, fat side down, in a roasting pan.

4. Whisk the brown sugar with the malta, and pour half of the mixture over the pork. Roast the pork for about 2 hours, basting occasionally.

5. Turn the meat fat side up, pour the remaining malta mixture over it, and cook until the pork reaches an internal temperature of 180°F on an instant-read thermometer, 2 to 3 hours.

6. Allow to cool slightly before cutting into thin slices. Skim the fat from the drippings, and then pour the drippings over the sliced meat.

CUPCAKES

ON THIS EPISODE OF THROWDOWN!...

It was a childhood favorite: cupcakes. But there was nothing child-size about my opponent's cupcakes; Terri Wahl's cupcakes are big enough for two with flavor to match. ⬤ Terri is the chef and owner of Auntie Em's Kitchen in Los Angeles, California, where she dishes out gourmet comfort food to a venerable list of Hollywood's A-list . . . who deem her cupcakes the best in town. She bakes 250 cupcakes a day and up to 700 on holidays, with flavors such as coconut cream, tangy lemon, and what will be her Throwdown cupcake, decadent red velvet with cream cheese frosting. Auntie Em's cupcakes are super-moist, and Terri knows the importance of having a good cake-to-frosting ratio. Each of her cupcakes is actually a full cup, and while they are big enough to share, it would be hard to find someone willing to do so after that first bite. ⬤ Food may be Terri's current passion, but she has another: music. She spent years on the road, playing guitar for the all-girl punk rock band The Red Aunts. While Terri eventually put down her guitar and picked up a whisk, she never stopped rocking. The *Los Angeles Times, Variety,* and *Los Angeles* magazine all agree: Terri's cupcakes rock!

Name: Terri Wahl
Establishment: Auntie Em's Kitchen
Hometown: Los Angeles, California
Website: www.auntieemskitchen.com
Phone: (323) 255-0800

There are two parts to a cupcake: the icing and the cake. Both have to work on their own, but the combination of the two is important in crafting a cupcake that both looks and tastes great. In the test kitchen, we went off the beaten path and dreamed up a new cupcake combo: gingerbread cake with caramelized mango buttercream. We used butter in the test kitchen, but we later tweaked the recipe to replace some of it with oil to make the cake moister. (Terri agrees that butter makes a drier cake and uses only oil in her cupcakes.) The combination gave me the best of both worlds: flavor from the butter and moistness from the oil.

Terri thought that she was taking part in a Food Network special on our nation's current obsession with cupcakes. But when we arrived on the scene, she quickly figured out what was up and jumped to challenge me to a Throwdown. She was the first ever to beat me to the punch before I could issue my challenge. She talked a good game, even rolling her eyes at our flavor combinations, but hey, I like confidence. Terri feels that what people want is good old-fashioned cupcakes, not crazy kooky ones, but I've always been known for stepping out of the box when it comes to flavors.

Candace Nelson of Sprinkles Cupcakes and *Hey There, Cupcake!* author Clare Crespo came in to do the judging honors. They both found Terri's cupcake super-moist and the flavor of its frosting, as well as the combination of cake and frosting, to be lovely, though they would have liked a little more cocoa flavor in the cake. Was I at a disadvantage for serving a normal-size cupcake, unlike Terri's "more is more" offering? It turned out not to matter: they loved the flavor of the cake and while they couldn't quite figure out the flavor of my frosting, they were into it. Candace and Clare had a tough time with this one and conferred for quite a while before they had their winner . . . and that was me. Typically *Throwdown!*'s audience and judges seem to veer toward the familiar, more traditional entries, but not this time. The judges loved the uniqueness of our cupcake. It doesn't happen often, so we took our win with pride.

WINNER!

Bobby Flay's
Gingerbread Cupcakes
with Caramelized Mango Buttercream

MAKES 12 CUPCAKES

Cupcakes

¾ cup granulated sugar

1 (3-inch) piece fresh ginger, peeled and
    coarsely chopped

Cooking spray

1¾ cups all-purpose flour

1 teaspoon baking powder

¾ teaspoon baking soda

¼ teaspoon fine salt

1 tablespoon ground ginger

2 teaspoons ground cinnamon

¼ teaspoon ground cloves

3 tablespoons unsalted butter, melted

3 tablespoons vegetable oil

¾ cup firmly packed dark brown sugar

2 large eggs

6 tablespoons molasses

Caramelized Mango Buttercream

2 cups (4 sticks) plus 2 tablespoons unsalted
    butter, slightly softened but still cool, cut into
    small pieces

2 ripe mangos, coarsely chopped

6 large egg yolks

Cooking spray

¾ cup sugar

½ cup light corn syrup

1 tablespoon pure vanilla extract

¼ cup finely diced candied ginger, for garnish

(recipe continues)

1. *To make the cupcakes,* combine the granulated sugar, fresh ginger, and ¾ cup water in a small saucepan and bring to a boil over high heat. Cook until the sugar has melted and the mixture thickens slightly, about 2 minutes. Remove from the heat and let infuse for 30 minutes. Then strain the ginger syrup before using.

2. Meanwhile, preheat the oven to 350°F. Line 12 muffin cups with paper liners and spray the liners with cooking spray.

3. Sift together the flour, baking powder, baking soda, salt, ground ginger, cinnamon, and cloves into a medium bowl.

4. Whisk the melted butter, oil, brown sugar, eggs, and molasses together in a large bowl. Add the dry ingredients and stir until the batter is smooth.

5. Fill each paper liner with ⅓ cup of the batter, to come about ¼ inch below the top of the liner. Bake just until the tops feel firm and a toothpick inserted into the center comes out with a few moist crumbs attached, 12 to 15 minutes. Remove from the oven and brush the tops liberally with the ginger syrup. Let sit in the pan for 5 minutes before removing. Let cool completely on a wire rack before frosting.

6. *To make the frosting,* heat the 2 tablespoons butter in a large sauté pan over high heat. Add the mangos and cook until caramelized and soft, about 10 minutes. Transfer to a food processor and process until smooth. Pass the mixture through a medium-mesh strainer into a bowl. Discard the solids.

7. In the bowl of a stand mixer fitted with the whisk attachment, beat the egg yolks on high speed until creamy and pale yellow, about 5 minutes.

8. Spray a heatproof measuring cup with cooking spray. Combine the sugar and corn syrup in a saucepan and bring to a full rolling boil over medium-high heat. Cook without stirring until the syrup reaches the soft-ball stage, 238° to 242°F on a candy thermometer. Immediately pour it into the measuring cup to halt the cooking.

9. Add a small amount of the syrup to the beaten egg yolks, turn the mixer on to high speed, and beat for about 5 seconds. Continue stopping the mixer, adding syrup, and beating in the same manner until all of the syrup is incorporated. Beat the mixture until it is completely cool.

10. Add the remaining 2 cups butter, a few pieces at a time, beating until incorporated before adding the next pieces. When all of the butter has been blended in, add the vanilla and the mango puree and beat until combined.

11. Frost the top of each cupcake liberally with the buttercream, and garnish with the candied ginger.

Terri Wahl's
Red Velvet Cupcakes
MAKES 12 JUMBO CUPCAKES

Cupcakes

3½ cups all-purpose flour

1¼ teaspoons baking soda

1¼ teaspoons fine salt

1¼ teaspoons unsweetened cocoa powder

3 cups sugar

1½ cups vegetable oil

1¼ cups buttermilk

3 large eggs

2 tablespoons plus 2 teaspoons red food coloring

1¼ teaspoons distilled white or apple cider vinegar

1¼ teaspoons pure vanilla extract

Cream Cheese Frosting

1 cup (2 sticks) unsalted butter, at room temperature

1½ (8-ounce) packages cream cheese, at room temperature

1 pound confectioners' sugar, sifted

1½ teaspoons pure vanilla extract

1. *To make the cupcakes,* preheat the oven to 350°F. Line 12 jumbo muffin cups with paper liners.

2. Sift the flour, baking soda, salt, and cocoa powder into a bowl and set aside.

3. In an electric mixer fitted with the paddle attachment, mix the sugar, oil, and buttermilk on medium speed until combined. Add the eggs, food coloring, vinegar, vanilla, and 2 tablespoons water, and mix well. Turn the mixer to low and add the dry ingredients a little bit at a time, scraping down the sides occasionally, beating until combined. Be sure not to overmix, or the cupcakes will be tough.

4. Fill the muffin cups about three-quarters full with batter. Bake until a toothpick inserted into the center comes out clean, 30 to 35 minutes. Set aside to cool.

5. *To make the frosting,* beat the butter and cream cheese together in an electric mixer fitted with the paddle attachment until smooth. Gradually add the confectioners' sugar, scraping the bowl down as needed. Beat in the vanilla. If too soft, chill briefly. Divide the frosting among the cupcakes; then smooth with a small offset spatula.

BUFFALO WINGS

ON THIS EPISODE OF THROWDOWN!...

I headed to Buffalo, New York, birthplace of the buffalo chicken wing, to take on Wing King Drew Cerza. ○ Drew Cerza is the founder of the National Buffalo Wing Festival, the "Super Bowl" of the wing industry, where more than half a million people from across the country have sampled more than 100 different varieties of wings . . . oh yeah, that's over 1 million wings. Along the way, Drew's festival has raised over $100,000 for Buffalo-area charities. He deserves his crown. ○ Always thrilled to help promote his hometown and its wings, Drew happily agreed to be a part of a special highlighting the country's best spicy foods, Food Network's "Hall of Flame." He planned a party at the historic Anchor Bar in Buffalo for his segment and had no idea that I would be heating things up with a surprise of my own.

"It was Take Your Daughter to Work Day, which my twelve-year-old, Nicole, and I have participated in for years. So that day Nicole was by my side and a big part of the show. It was a very special bonding moment for us. And she became a superstar to her friends in school when the show came out."
            —DREW CERZA

Name: Drew Cerza
Hometown: Buffalo, New York
Website: www.buffalowing.com
Phone: (716) 565-4141, ext. 12

The key to good chicken wings is not to overcook them; the texture should be nice and crispy on the outside with a perfectly cooked, juicy interior. They need heat—just the right amount of burn—and a touch of sweetness for balance. Drew has hundreds of wing variations up his sleeve, and the one he brings out for this occasion is his Bourbon Street Buffalo Wings. The sweet and tangy sauce is made with chili sauce, ancho chile, barbecue sauce, and bourbon. I had to get my own wing down, so it was off to the test kitchen.

In the test kitchen, I sprinkled my wings with salt and pepper and then dredged them in ancho-seasoned flour before their bath in the deep-fryer. Everyone knows that the key to hot wings is the hot sauce, so I set to work on mine: chipotle, mustard, more ancho powder, vinegar, and a little honey to cut the acidity. The hot sauce is added to melted butter, and the wings, hot out of the fryer, are tossed in the mixture. The classic dip is typically a mixture of mayonnaise, sour cream, and a domestic blue cheese. My dip is a riff on that, made instead with thick and tangy Greek yogurt, a little grated red onion, cilantro, and my favorite blue cheese, a Spanish Cabrales. Crisp jicama sticks stand in for celery.

Recipe in hand, I went up to Buffalo to find Drew. Now, this challenge was in the early days of *Throwdown!* when many people weren't familiar with the show, and I definitely threw Drew for a loop. It took him a few moments to get his head around what was going on. But after a few phone calls and consultations with friends, he was on board and ready to battle! We began working on our dishes and Drew came over to check out my ingredients for himself. He liked my combination of sweet and heat, calling the mustard a nice addition. Once the wings were cooked and sauced, we each got to try the other's wings. Drew has one word for mine: "awesome." He said it was the crispiest wing he had ever had that wasn't dried out—and that is high praise coming from the Wing King. But I have to give it to the King: his wing is perfectly cooked and I loved its sweet sauce.

Dave Botticelli of Duff's Famous Wings in Amherst, New York, and Syracuse student and chicken–wing lover Greg Bacorn sat down to judge our wings on flavor, texture, and creativity. Mine were crispy, crunchy, and juicy with a subtle heat that built with time. But they didn't love my presentation and found the jicama a little confusing. Drew's wings were moist and had a smooth, balanced flavor. These wings had two totally different tastes and the judges had a hard time deciding on a winner. In the end, they gave Drew the win, saying his wings were juicier and loving his sauce and celery sticks.

When you go up against someone referred to as the "Wing King," there is always a chance that you just might lose. And I did. But Drew is truly one of the nicest and probably one of the most respectful competitors that I have gone up against. Hats off to the Wing King.

Bobby Flay's
Hot Wings with Blue Cheese–Yogurt Sauce

SERVES 4 TO 6

Blue Cheese–Yogurt Sauce

1¼ cups Greek yogurt

½ cup crumbled blue cheese, preferably Cabrales

2 tablespoons finely grated red onion

2 tablespoons finely chopped fresh cilantro leaves

Kosher salt and freshly ground black pepper

Hot Wings

Canola oil, for deep-frying

2 cups all-purpose flour

Kosher salt and freshly ground black pepper

3 tablespoons ancho chile powder

1½ teaspoons garlic powder

3 pounds chicken wings, split at the joint, wing tips removed and discarded

¾ cup red wine vinegar

2 tablespoons pureed chipotle chile in adobo

¼ teaspoon chile de árbol powder or cayenne pepper

1 heaping tablespoon Dijon mustard

8 tablespoons (1 stick) unsalted butter

1 to 2 tablespoons honey, to taste

3 tablespoons finely chopped fresh cilantro leaves

Jicama sticks, for serving

1. *To make the sauce,* stir together the yogurt, blue cheese, red onion, cilantro, and salt and pepper to taste in a bowl. Refrigerate for at least 30 minutes before serving.

2. *To cook the wings,* heat 2 inches of canola oil in a large deep pot until it reaches 365°F on a deep-frying thermometer.

3. Stir the flour, 2 teaspoons salt, 1 teaspoon pepper, 1 tablespoon of the ancho powder, and the garlic powder together in a large shallow bowl. Season the wings with salt and pepper, and add the wings, in batches, to the flour mixture to lightly coat; tap off any excess flour. Add the wings, in batches, to the hot oil and cook until golden brown and cooked through, 8 to 10 minutes. Remove with a slotted spoon and place on a plate lined with paper towels to drain for a few minutes; then transfer to a large bowl.

4. Whisk the vinegar, chipotle puree, remaining 2 tablespoons ancho chile powder, chile de árbol powder, and mustard together in a small bowl.

5. Melt the butter in a large sauté pan over low heat. Add the vinegar mixture, bring to a simmer, and cook for 30 seconds. Season with salt, pepper, and honey to taste. Pour the sauce over the wings and toss well to coat. Transfer the wings to a platter and sprinkle with the cilantro. Serve with jicama sticks and the blue cheese sauce on the side.

WINNER!

Drew Cerza's
Bourbon Street Buffalo Wings
SERVES 8 TO 10

2 tablespoons unsalted butter

1 large shallot, chopped

2 cloves garlic, chopped

¼ cup bourbon, plus more for serving

½ cup firmly packed light brown sugar

½ cup honey

1 tablespoon ancho chile powder

1 cup chili sauce

1 cup barbecue sauce

⅓ cup prepared buffalo wing sauce, such as
  Texas Pete or Frank's

Vegetable oil, for deep-frying

3 pounds chicken wings, split at the joint, wing
  tips removed and discarded

Kosher salt

Prepared blue cheese dressing, for serving

1. Melt the butter in a medium saucepan over medium heat. Add the shallot and garlic and cook, stirring occasionally, until softened and fragrant, 2 to 3 minutes. Stir in the bourbon, brown sugar, and honey and heat through, 2 minutes.

2. Whisk in the ancho chile powder, chili sauce, barbecue sauce, and wing sauce. Bring to a simmer and cook, stirring occasionally, for 2 minutes. Keep warm while you fry the wings.

3. Heat 4 inches of oil to 350°F in a deep heavy-bottomed saucepan or a deep-fryer.

4. Season the chicken wings with salt. Fry, in batches, until golden brown on both sides and cooked through, about 15 minutes. Remove the wings from the oil and drain on a platter lined with paper towels.

5. Put the wings in a large mixing bowl, add the sauce, and toss well to coat. Serve with blue cheese dressing and half shots of bourbon, on the side, for adults to sip.

STICKY BUNS

ON THIS EPISODE OF THROWDOWN!...

It was a battle of the buns in Boston when I took on bakery owner Joanne Chang and her "sticky sticky" buns. It was an old-school bake-off, where a man or woman could only be as good as his or her glaze. ◉ Chef/owner Joanne Chang opened her bakery and café, Flour, in Boston's South End in 2000, and the accolades and awards have been rolling her way ever since. It was a simple concept—provide amazing pastries and food with friendly service that encourages customers to linger over their treats—and it works. Flour's patrons always leave with a smile, especially if they've managed to get their hands on one of Joanne's scrumptious pecan-filled brioche sticky buns before they sell out on any weekend morning. Topped with a sinful mixture of brown sugar, cream, and lots of butter ("icing" wouldn't do it justice—this is Joanne's special "goo"), these buns are delectable.

"I'm sure you are aware of this already, but appearing on Throwdown! pretty much changed our lives at Flour. In fact for a while we had a Bobby Flay shrine up in the kitchen (it was cute, not creepy, I promise!) to acknowledge the amazing effect being on your show had on all of us. We went from making a very humble 10 to 12 sticky buns a day to making literally 20 times that amount . . . and still that wasn't enough. I'm opening a third location and I've also written a baking book. So, Bobby, thank you."

—JOANNE CHANG

Name: Joanne Chang
Establishment: Flour Bakery
Hometown: Boston, Massachusetts
Website: www.flourbakery.com
Phone: (617) 267-4300

Joanne's path to Flour did not follow a standard trajectory—far from it. This math whiz graduated from Harvard University with an honors degree in applied mathematics and economics before venturing into corporate America. But after two years and a lot of soul-searching, she knew it was time for a change of plans; it was time to do something she loved. Luckily for Boston's sweet-toothed residents, that something was cooking.

It's not easy to fool her, but we managed to convince Joanne that she had earned a starring role on a Food Network special called "The Science of Sweets." *My* mission was to master both the art and the science of baking in order to balance the equation and win this Throwdown. Since I'm not the baking scholar, I took a quick lesson from NYC's Amy's Bread owner Amy Scherber. Her bakery is one of my favorite places in the city for bread and sticky buns, and my lesson gave me a needed boost of confidence.

I headed to the test kitchen to see about bringing some unexpected flavors to my sticky bun. I started with an egg and butter–rich brioche-like dough, which I spread with butter and sprinkled with cinnamon before rolling it up and cutting it into rolls. My topping was an orange-caramel glaze of butter, brown sugar, honey, orange juice, and orange zest. Classically sticky buns are all about pecans, but I wanted to try something a little different, so I added sliced almonds and pine nuts to the mix. The pine nuts didn't add much flavor or crunch, so I ended up ditching them. I had my bun.

Up in Boston, Joanne was sharing her sticky bun secrets with a group of Harvard students at her bakery, clueless that I was just moments away. I arrived with my challenge, and like most bakers I face on *Throwdown!*, she didn't break a sweat. Instead she burst out laughing and told me to bring it! Immediately I learned that my dough was nothing like hers; she uses a lot of eggs and butter in her dough and referred to mine as "lean" because of its minimal amount of fat.

The crowd put our sticky buns to the test but left the final call to judges Martin Breslin, a Harvard chef, and Dan Andelman, of Boston's Phantom Gourmet. They judged our entries on their texture, the gooeyness of the glaze, and the overall taste. They were surprised by my use of almonds, but thought the nuts brought a nice change of pace. And they immediately got the orange flavor. Martin and Dan loved the appearance of Joanne's buns and her incredible glaze, though they would have preferred just a touch less of it. It wasn't a big surprise when they pronounced Joanne the winner.

So we lost—but actually, I was proud to lose to someone as great as Joanne. Her sticky buns are flat-out amazing and probably the best I've ever eaten. Going to Beantown? Make it "Buntown" with a trip to Flour.

Bobby Flay's Sticky Buns with Orange–Honey–Brown Sugar Glaze and Toasted Almonds

Bobby Flay's
Sticky Buns with Orange–Honey–Brown Sugar Glaze and Toasted Almonds
MAKES 8 TO 10 BUNS

Dough

1 package active dry yeast

¼ cup plus a pinch of granulated sugar

1 cup milk, warm (about 110°F)

4 tablespoons (½ stick) unsalted butter, plus
   more, melted, for brushing the dough

1½ teaspoons pure vanilla extract

1 large egg yolk

2¾ cups all-purpose flour

¾ teaspoon fine salt

Glaze

1 cup packed light muscovado sugar

8 tablespoons (1 stick) unsalted butter, cut in
   half, plus extra for the baking pan

½ cup fresh orange juice

Grated zest of 1 orange

¼ cup honey

1½ cups sliced almonds, lightly toasted

Filling

4 tablespoons (½ stick) unsalted butter, at room
   temperature

¼ cup packed light muscovado sugar

¼ cup granulated sugar

1 tablespoon ground cinnamon

1. *To make the dough,* sprinkle the yeast and the pinch of granulated sugar over the warm milk in a small bowl; set aside until foamy, about 5 minutes.

2. Melt the butter in a small saucepan. Whisk the butter, vanilla, and egg yolk into the yeast.

3. Whisk the flour, remaining ¼ cup granulated sugar, and the salt together in a large bowl. Stir in the yeast mixture to make a sticky dough. Knead the dough on a floured work surface until it is soft and elastic, 6 to 8 minutes. Shape it into a ball and brush it with a little melted butter. Place in a bowl, cover, and let rise until doubled in size, about 1½ hours.

4. Remove the dough from the bowl and gently knead for a few minutes to deflate. Re-form it into a ball. Return it to the bowl, cover with buttered plastic wrap, and refrigerate for 4 hours.

5. *To make the glaze,* generously butter a 9 × 13-inch baking pan. Combine the muscovado sugar, butter, orange juice, zest, and honey in a medium saucepan and bring to a boil over high heat. Stir occasionally until the mixture thickens and the sugar dissolves, about 5 minutes. Carefully pour the glaze mixture into the buttered pan, evening it out by tilting the pan. Sprinkle the almonds over the top. Set aside to cool slightly while you prepare the buns.

6. Roll the dough into a 10 × 18-inch rectangle with a long edge facing you. *To make the filling,* spread the 4 tablespoons butter over the surface. Combine the muscovado sugar, granulated sugar, and cinnamon in a small bowl, and scatter the mixture over the butter. Roll the dough into a long tight cylinder; pinch the long edge to seal. Using fine string or dental floss, cut the cylinder into 1½-inch-thick rolls. Evenly space the rolls, cut side up, on top of the caramel mixture in the pan. Cover, and let rise in a warm spot until doubled in size, about 1½ hours.

7. Preheat the oven to 350°F.

8. Place the baking pan in the oven and bake the buns until golden, 30 to 35 minutes.

9. Remove the pan from the oven and let rest for 5 minutes before inverting the buns onto a large platter. Serve warm.

WINNER!

Joanne Chang's
Sticky Sticky Buns
MAKES 8 BUNS

Brioche Dough

1¼ cups all-purpose flour, plus more if needed

1 cup plus 2 tablespoons bread flour

1½ teaspoons plus ⅛ teaspoon active dry yeast,
   or ½ ounce fresh cake yeast

3 tablespoons granulated sugar

1½ teaspoons kosher salt

3 large eggs

11 tablespoons unsalted butter, cut into
   12 pieces, at cool room temperature

Goo

12 tablespoons (1½ sticks) unsalted butter

1½ cups firmly packed light brown sugar

⅓ cup clover honey

⅓ cup heavy cream

¼ teaspoon kosher salt

½ cup chopped pecans, toasted

Filling

¼ cup granulated sugar

¼ cup firmly packed light brown sugar

⅛ teaspoon ground cinnamon

½ cup chopped pecans, toasted

1. *To make the dough,* combine the flours, yeast, granulated sugar, salt, ¼ cup cold water, and the eggs in the bowl of a stand mixer fitted with the dough hook attachment. Beat on low speed until all the ingredients come together, about 4 minutes, stopping the mixer as needed to scrape the sides and bottom of the bowl. Once the dough has come together, beat on low speed for another 4 minutes. The dough will be stiff and will seem quite dry.

2. With the mixer on low speed, begin to add the butter one piece at a time, mixing well after each addition until it disappears into the dough. Once all the butter has been added, continue to mix on low speed, stopping the mixer occasionally to scrape the sides and bottom of the bowl, until all the butter is incorporated into the dough, about 5 minutes. Increase the speed to medium and beat until the dough becomes sticky, soft, and somewhat shiny, about 10 minutes. Test the dough by pulling at it; it should stretch a bit and have a little give. If the dough seems wet and more like a batter than a dough, add additional all-purpose flour, a tablespoon at a time, and mix until it comes together.

3. Transfer the dough to a lightly floured flat surface and knead gently for a few moments. Shape the dough into a ball and place it in a large bowl. Cover the dough with plastic wrap, pressing the wrap directly onto the surface of the dough. Let the dough proof in the refrigerator for at least 6 or up to 12 hours.

(recipe continues)

4. *To make the goo,* 30 minutes before you are ready to roll out your dough, melt the butter in a medium saucepan over high heat. Add the brown sugar and whisk until smooth. Remove from the heat and whisk in the honey, cream, ⅓ cup water, and the salt until smooth. Pour the goo into a 9 × 13-inch baking dish, covering the bottom evenly. Sprinkle the pecans evenly over the surface and let cool slightly (about 20 minutes) before adding the buns.

5. *To make the filling,* combine the granulated sugar, light brown sugar, cinnamon, and pecans in a small bowl.

6. Remove the dough from the refrigerator (it will be the consistency of cold, damp Play-Doh) and transfer it to a floured surface. Roll it out into a 12 × 16-inch rectangle that's ¼ inch thick. Sprinkle the cinnamon-sugar filling evenly over the surface. Starting from a short side, roll up the rectangle tightly like a jelly roll. Trim about ¼ inch from each end to even them.

7. Use a chef's knife to cut the roll into 8 equal pieces, each about 1½ inches wide. Place the buns, evenly spaced, cut side up, on top of the goo in the baking dish. Cover with plastic wrap and let rise in a warm spot until almost tripled in size, 2 to 3 hours.

8. Position a rack in the center of the oven and preheat the oven to 350°F.

9. Place the baking dish in the oven and bake until the buns are golden brown and the goo is bubbly, 30 to 40 minutes. Let the dish cool on a wire rack for 15 minutes. Then invert the buns, one at a time, onto a serving platter, and spoon any extra goo and pecans from the dish over the top.

CRÊPES

ON THIS EPISODE OF THROWDOWN!...

It was all about crêpes. Craypes . . . crehps . . . however you say it, my mission was clear: I had to take on the ladies of Flip Happy Crêpes for the best crêpes this side of France. Owners Andrea Day-Boykin and Nessa Higgins thought they were to be featured in a Food Network special called "Crêpe Expectations." Those expectations would be shattered when I showed up. Would they be ready to go griddle to griddle with me? The real question was, would I be ready for them? ○ Fun, laid-back, and chock-full of old-school charm, Flip Happy Crêpes makes its home in a souped-up vintage Airstream trailer in Austin, Texas. Andrea and Nessa's slogan is "Made from scratch, with love," and the scores of happy patrons filling the picnic tables are testament to its truth. Longtime friends and partners since they opened their crêperie in 2006, Andrea and Nessa share a passion for good food. Artfully thin enough to let their intrinsic flavor shine while still thick enough to cradle the ingredients, their crêpes run the gamut from savory roasted chicken, mushrooms, white cheddar, and caramelized onions to sweet and delicate lemon curd with blueberry dressing. ○ I went to the test kitchen to practice my technique—or lack thereof. I just couldn't get the hang of the professional crêpe griddle, so I played it safe with a nonstick pan and set about making my blue corn crêpe with a spicy barbecued duck and shiitake mushroom filling. The crêpe batter is typical up until the addition of blue cornmeal for color and a touch of nutty sweetness. I made the filling by shredding duck breasts that had been braised in chicken stock flavored with my barbecue sauce until the meat was fall-off-the-bone tender. I have been serving a version of this dish at Mesa Grill since it opened more than a decade ago and had total faith in my flavors, but would that make up for what I lacked in technique?

Names: Andrea Day-Boykin and Nessa Higgins
Establishment: Flip Happy Crêpes
Hometown: Austin, Texas
Website: www.fliphappycrepes.com
Phone: (512) 552-9034

Andrea and Nessa were hosting their "Crêpe Expectations" party for family and friends outdoors. Or at least that's what they thought until I rolled up with some style of my own—that's right, it was crêpe to crêpe and Airstream to Airstream! Nessa and Andrea were up for the change of plans and they flipped, filled, and handed out their Cuban-style crêpes, stuffed with shredded pork, pepper jack cheese, pickles, and hot sauce.

After a long afternoon of throwing down crêpes, Texas-style, it was time to put our dishes to the test at the judges' table. Pastry chef Philip Speer and restaurateur Terry Wilson did the honors, critiquing our crêpes on texture, their combination of flavors, and overall satisfaction. Andrea and Nessa's Cuban crêpe got high marks for its first-rate filling chock-full of pork. Their crêpe itself was perfectly cooked, with a great crisp outer texture and fluffy interior. My crêpe didn't fare quite as well; Philip and Terry said it wasn't as crispy as it should have been and that the habanero sauce may have made it a bit too soggy. They did, however, think my filling combination was outstanding and they loved the texture of the mushrooms. But the win was all Andrea and Nessa's, wonderful competitors for a really fun Throwdown.

Bobby Flay's
Duck and Shiitake Mushroom Crêpes with Habanero Sauce
MAKES 8 CRÊPES

Duck

2 pounds (about 6) duck legs, skin removed

1¼ cups Mesa Grill Barbecue Sauce (see Sources, page 269) or your favorite barbecue sauce

3 cups homemade chicken stock (see page 220) or canned low-sodium chicken broth

Habanero Sauce (recipe follows)

3 tablespoons canola oil

4 large shiitake mushrooms, stemmed and thinly sliced

2 shallots, finely chopped

Kosher salt and freshly ground black pepper

3 tablespoons chopped fresh cilantro leaves, plus more for garnish

Crêpes

½ cup blue cornmeal

½ cup all-purpose flour

1 teaspoon baking powder

Pinch of kosher salt

2 large eggs, beaten

1 cup whole milk

2 tablespoons honey

2 tablespoons unsalted butter, melted

Cooking spray

1. *To cook the duck,* preheat the oven to 325°F.

2. Generously brush the duck legs with the barbecue sauce, and place them in a baking pan. Pour the stock and ½ cup of the Habanero Sauce around the legs. Cover the pan and braise in the oven until the meat begins to fall off the bone, about 2 hours.

3. Meanwhile, heat the oil in a large sauté pan over high heat until it begins to shimmer. Add the mushrooms and cook until they begin to release their juices, about 5 minutes. Add the shallots and continue cooking until the mushrooms are golden brown, about 5 minutes more. Season with salt and pepper, and set aside.

4. *To make the crêpes,* combine the cornmeal, flour, baking powder, and salt in a medium bowl. In a separate bowl, combine the eggs, milk, honey, and melted butter. Add this to the dry ingredients and mix until combined. Let rest for 1 hour at room temperature.

5. Place a 6-inch nonstick pan over high heat. Spray it with cooking spray and reduce the heat to medium. Ladle ¼ cup of the batter into the pan, swirling to evenly coat the pan with the mixture. Cook the crêpe until just set on the first side, about 1 minute. Flip it over and cook for an additional 20 to 30 seconds. Remove the crêpe to a plate and repeat with the remaining mixture, stacking the crêpes and covering them with foil to keep warm.

6. *To finish the duck filling,* remove the duck from the braising liquid and let it cool slightly. Strain and reserve the braising liquid. Shred the duck meat into bite-size pieces and discard the bones.

7. Combine the shredded duck meat, cooked mushrooms, and ½ cup of the braising liquid in a sauté pan, and warm over medium heat until heated through. Add the chopped cilantro, and season with salt and pepper.

8. Mound some of the duck mixture in the center of each crêpe. Fold the crêpes over the filling to make a semicircle, and drizzle with the remaining Habanero Sauce. Garnish with chopped cilantro.

Habanero Sauce

8 cups rich chicken stock (see page 220)

1 cup frozen apple juice concentrate, thawed

¼ cup firmly packed dark brown sugar

2 whole star anise

1 cinnamon stick

1 habanero chile, coarsely chopped

1 tablespoon fennel seeds, toasted

Kosher salt and freshly ground black pepper

Combine the stock, apple juice concentrate, brown sugar, star anise, cinnamon stick, chile, and fennel in a large saucepan. Bring to a boil over high heat and cook, stirring occasionally, until the sauce is thickened and reduced to about 1½ cups, about 30 minutes. Strain the sauce into a bowl, and season with salt and pepper to taste.

WINNER!

Nessa Higgins and Andrea Day-Boykin's Cuban Crêpes

MAKES 20 TO 24 (12-INCH) CRÊPES

Pulled Pork

4 pounds boneless pork butt

2 tablespoons kosher salt

1 tablespoon freshly ground black pepper

2 teaspoons onion powder

1 teaspoon red pepper flakes

Crêpes

6 large eggs

3 cups whole milk

3½ cups all-purpose flour

12 tablespoons (1½ sticks) unsalted butter, melted, plus more for cooking the crêpes

5 cups (1¼ pounds) shredded pepper jack cheese

1 cup yellow mustard

Tabasco sauce

2 cups finely diced dill pickles

1. *To cook the pork,* preheat the oven to 300°F.

2. Rub the pork with the salt, pepper, onion powder, and red pepper flakes and place it in a brown paper bag, fatty side up. Close the bag. Put the bag on a rimmed baking sheet and roast until an instant-read thermometer inserted into the center of the pork registers 185° to 190°F, about 4 hours.

3. Remove the pork from the bag, reserving any juices in the bag. When the pork is cool enough to handle, shred it into large pieces and toss it with the juices in a bowl.

4. *To make the crêpes,* whisk the eggs, milk, and 1 cup water together in a large bowl. Whisk in the flour until blended. Add the butter and mix again. Do not overmix.

5. Heat a 12-inch nonstick skillet over medium-high heat. Coat it with a little melted butter, and pour in ⅓ cup crêpe batter, swirling the skillet to spread it evenly over the bottom. Cook for about 2 minutes, until the underside has golden brown spots all over; then flip and cook until speckled on the other side, about 1 minute. Repeat to make the remaining crêpes. Stack the crêpes on a plate.

6. Turn the heat under the crêpe skillet to low, put a crêpe in the skillet, and fold it in half. Scatter ¼ cup of the cheese across the center of the crêpe, and top it with ⅓ cup pork. Then drizzle with some mustard and Tabasco, and scatter about 1 tablespoon or so diced pickles over the top. Fold one corner of the crêpe just over the filling; then roll the crêpe to make a closed package. Repeat with the remaining crêpes and filling.

PUFFY TACOS

ON THIS EPISODE OF THROWDOWN!...

I dared to mess with Texas, traveling to San Antonio to take on Diana Barrios Treviño and her amazing puffy tacos. Would this queen of Tex-Mex cuisine leave me in the dust? ○ San Antonio may be known first for the Alamo, but it's also home to the puffy taco: fresh tortillas, cooked in hot oil till they puff up, then shaped and stuffed with a really great filling . . . yum. And no one makes a puffy taco like chef, restaurateur, and cookbook author Diana, who is known as the Ambassador of Tex-Mex Cuisine—no small thing in Texas. It made a lot of sense for Food Network to ask her to star in an episode of their supposed new show, "North of the Border," about southwestern cuisine. ○ In fact, I'd met Diana about seven years earlier when I was taping *Food Nation* for Food Network. I had never eaten a puffy taco before that and remember being blown away by the process of making the shell, and by her recipe as a whole. Diana has had a lifetime of making and filling delicious puffy tacos. I needed to master the techniques and flavors pronto in order to ride off into the Texas sunset with a win.

Name: Diana Barrios Treviño
Establishment: La Hacienda de Los Barrios
Hometown: San Antonio, Texas
Website: www.lhdlb.com
Phone: (210) 497-8000

I made a pit stop on my way to the test kitchen and dropped in on my friend Aaron Sanchez, who showed me how to shape each tortilla by hand with a kitchen spider. Thanks to his help, I was ready to try these with my team. We used instant corn masa for our tortillas; Diana has freshly ground masa delivered to her restaurant daily (if you are lucky enough to find that, it makes all the difference). So I knew I had to bring big flavors to the table with my filling, a Yucatán-marinated chicken with a peanut–red chile barbecue sauce. For a crunchy touch of bright color and fresh taste, I topped the taco with a red cabbage slaw spiked with mint and cilantro.

The fiesta was just getting started at La Hacienda de Los Barrios when I came crashing in. Diana was shocked and a little disappointed not to be hosting "North of the Border," but she quickly stepped up to the challenge. I soon found out that when you go up against Diana, you go up against her whole family, including her mother, Viola, and her husband, Roland. Viola jumped that ship pretty quickly, taking pity on me and my taco shell—it seemed like everything that I'd learned from Aaron and did in the test kitchen was just a faint memory. Failure was sinking in and I was happy for Viola's support.

Diana's filling consisted of shredded poached chicken tossed in red salsa and topped with guacamole. We traded tacos and instantly I could tell the difference between the instant masa I used and hers made with fresh masa. Diana's taco was perfectly crisp on the outside and light, airy, and slightly chewy—and each bite was full of incredible corn flavor. Diana tasted mine and was proud of my effort, though she knew immediately that I hadn't used fresh masa.

I'd done the Texas two-step with Diana here in San Antonio, fed the lively crowd, and it was time to hear from judges Pat Mozersky, a food writer for the *San Antonio Express News,* and local chef Oscar Trejo Bertrand. As I knew they would, they said that the texture of Diana's puffy taco was perfect, and while the filling could have used a little more spice, they found it very fresh and loved the guacamole. My taco was way too crunchy, but they liked the kick of the spicy chicken and crisp cabbage. With the exception of the peanuts, they loved the overall flavor but didn't think it was authentic. Diana took the win.

I lost in San Antonio, and you know what? That's okay. I would never mind losing to Diana. I knew from the moment I met her all those years ago that her puffy taco was one of the best things I had ever eaten. I went home and practiced my technique and eventually put Yucatán Chicken Puffy Tacos on the menu at Mesa Grill. Every time I eat one, I think of Diana and her lovely mother, Viola, who died shortly after we taped this show. Viola was an amazing woman and I will never forget the kindness that she showed to me and my staff the day of the Throwdown.

Bobby Flay's
Yucatán Chicken Puffy Tacos with Peanut–Red Chile Barbecue Sauce and Red Cabbage Slaw
MAKES 8 TACOS

Yucatán Chicken

½ cup fresh orange juice

¼ cup fresh lime juice

2 tablespoons canola oil

2 tablespoons ancho chile powder

3 cloves garlic, coarsely chopped

6 boneless, skinless chicken thighs

Kosher salt and freshly ground black pepper

Peanut–Red Chile Barbecue Sauce (recipe follows)

1 cup homemade chicken stock (see page 220) or canned low-sodium chicken broth

Puffy Tacos

Canola oil, for deep-frying

1¾ cups instant corn masa mix

2 teaspoons kosher salt

Red Cabbage Slaw (recipe follows)

1. *To make the chicken,* whisk together the orange and lime juices, oil, chile powder, and garlic in a shallow baking dish. Add the chicken thighs, and turn to coat. Marinate for 1 to 4 hours in the refrigerator.

2. Heat a grill to high or a grill pan over high heat.

3. Remove the thighs from the marinade and season with salt and pepper on both sides. Grill until just cooked through, 4 to 5 minutes on each side, brushing with some of the peanut–red chile sauce during the last few minutes of grilling. Remove from the grill, let rest for 5 minutes, and then shred into bite-size pieces.

4. Heat the chicken stock and ½ cup of the peanut–red chile sauce in a sauté pan over medium heat. Add the chicken and toss to coat. Keep warm.

5. *To make the tacos,* heat 2 inches of oil in a large deep pot to 350°F.

6. Combine the masa mix, salt, and 1¼ cups warm water in a large bowl, and mix until a smooth dough forms; add more water, a tablespoon at a time, if needed. Pull off pieces of dough and roll them into balls about the size of a Ping-Pong ball. Keep them covered with a piece of plastic wrap or a clean dish towel so they don't dry out.

7. Cut a plastic food storage bag open down both sides, leaving the bottom attached, to form a rectangle. Lay one side of the plastic over the bottom of a tortilla press. Place a ball of dough in the center, and fold the other side of the plastic over the dough. Shut the top of the tortilla press and press firmly down on the dough to shape the tortilla.

8. Drop the tortilla into the hot oil. When the tortilla floats to the surface, use a metal spatula to repeatedly douse the top with hot oil until it begins to puff up. (If the tortilla does not begin to puff, gently pat it with the spatula.) Flip it over, and using another spatula to support the side, press the first spatula into the center of the tortilla to form a taco shape. This process takes approximately 60 seconds. Transfer the taco to paper towels to drain. Repeat with the remaining dough balls.

9. Fill each taco with some of the chicken, drizzle with a few tablespoons of the peanut–red chile sauce, and top with the slaw.

Peanut–Red Chile Barbecue Sauce

2 tablespoons canola oil

1 medium Spanish onion, coarsely chopped

1 (2-inch) piece fresh ginger, peeled and finely chopped

4 cloves garlic, coarsely chopped

2 cups canned plum tomatoes with juices, pureed

¼ cup ketchup

¼ cup red wine vinegar

¼ cup Worcestershire sauce

3 tablespoons Dijon mustard

3 tablespoons dark brown sugar

2 tablespoons honey

2 tablespoons molasses

2 tablespoons ancho chile powder

2 tablespoons pasilla chile powder

2 tablespoons pureed chipotle chiles in adobo

Kosher salt and freshly ground black pepper

1 cup homemade chicken stock (see page 220) or canned low-sodium chicken broth

2 tablespoons soy sauce

¼ cup creamy peanut butter

1. Heat the oil in a medium heavy-bottomed saucepan over medium-high heat. Add the onion and ginger, and cook until soft, about 5 minutes. Add the garlic and cook for 1 minute. Add the tomatoes and 1 cup water, bring to a boil, and simmer for 10 minutes. Add the ketchup, vinegar, Worcestershire, mustard, brown sugar, honey, molasses, chile powders, and chipotle. Simmer, stirring occasionally, until thickened to about 1½ cups, 30 to 40 minutes.

2. Puree the mixture in a food processor until smooth; season with salt and pepper to taste. Transfer to a clean saucepan and add the chicken stock and soy sauce. Boil over high heat until slightly thickened, about 5 minutes. Whisk in the peanut butter and cook for 1 minute. Pour into a bowl and cool to room temperature.

Red Cabbage Slaw

½ head red cabbage, finely shredded

1 small red onion, halved and thinly sliced

¼ cup rice vinegar

½ cup fresh orange juice

¼ cup canola oil

1 tablespoon honey

¼ cup chopped fresh cilantro leaves

2 tablespoons finely chopped fresh mint leaves

Kosher salt and freshly ground black pepper

Combine the cabbage and onion in a large bowl. Whisk the vinegar, orange juice, oil, and honey together in a small bowl, and pour over the cabbage. Add the cilantro and mint, and season with salt and pepper. Let sit at room temperature for 20 minutes before serving.

WINNER!

Diana Barrios Treviño's
Famous San Antonio Puffy Tacos

MAKES 13 TO 14 TACOS

Filling

1 (3- to 3½-pound) chicken, cut into 8 pieces
  (breasts halved)

1 small white onion, quartered, plus 1 medium
  white onion, halved and thinly sliced

3 celery stalks

3 cloves garlic

Kosher salt

1½ pounds (about 6) tomatoes, quartered

¼ cup vegetable oil

1 small green bell pepper, thinly sliced

¼ teaspoon garlic powder

¼ teaspoon ground cumin

Freshly ground black pepper

Tacos

Vegetable oil, for deep-frying

3 cups instant corn masa mix, such as Maseca

1½ teaspoons kosher salt

Guacamole, for topping (optional)

Shredded Monterey Jack or cheddar cheese, for
  topping (optional)

Shredded lettuce, for topping (optional)

Diced tomato, for topping (optional)

1. *To make the filling,* put the chicken in a large pot and add water to cover by 3 inches. Add the quartered onion, celery, and garlic. Season with salt, and bring to a simmer over medium heat. Simmer until the chicken is cooked through, about 30 minutes. Remove the chicken from the pot and let cool slightly. Discard the skin and bones and shred the meat.

2. Puree the tomatoes in a blender. Heat the oil in a medium skillet over medium heat. Add the sliced onion and bell pepper, and cook until soft, 3 to 5 minutes. Add the pureed tomatoes, garlic powder, and cumin. Season with salt and pepper, and bring to a simmer. Reduce the heat and simmer gently for about 45 minutes. Add the chicken and warm through.

3. *To make the tacos,* heat 2 inches of oil in a large deep pot to 350°F.

4. Whisk the masa mix and salt together in a large bowl. Stir in 2¼ cups warm water until a smooth dough forms. Pull off pieces of dough and roll them into 13 or 14 balls, each about the size of a Ping-Pong ball. Keep them covered with a piece of plastic wrap or a clean dish towel so they don't dry out.

5. Cut a plastic food storage bag open down both sides, leaving the bottom attached, to form a rectangle. Lay one side of the plastic over the bottom of a tortilla press. Place a ball of dough in the center, and fold the other side of the plastic over the dough. Shut the top of the tortilla press and press down firmly on the dough to shape the tortilla.

6. Drop the tortilla into the hot oil. When the tortilla floats to the surface, use a metal spatula to repeatedly douse the top with hot oil until it begins to puff up. (If the tortilla does not begin to puff, gently pat it with the spatula.) Flip it over, and using another spatula to support the side, press the first spatula into the center of the tortilla to form a taco shape. This process takes approximately 60 seconds. Transfer the taco to paper towels to drain. Repeat with the remaining dough balls.

7. Fill each taco with some of the shredded chicken, and add guacamole, cheese, shredded lettuce, and diced tomato as desired.

JERK STEAK

ON THIS EPISODE OF THROWDOWN!...

I heat things up with Jamaican jerk jockey Nigel Spence and his tantalizing jerk steak. **◯** Nigel's restaurant, Ripe, in Mount Vernon, New York, features all of the fantastic flavors of the Caribbean. This Culinary Institute of America graduate honed his skills as a Food Network intern—he even worked on one of my old shows, *Hot Off the Grill.* Nigel's mouthwatering jerk rib eye earned him a *Throwdown!* challenge and his turn in front of the camera. **◯** Ripe's menu boasts items inspired by the cuisines of Cuba and Trinidad, but Nigel's heart is definitely in his homeland of Jamaica. The marinade recipe for his jerk rib-eye steak has been handed down in his family for generations. Nigel marinates his steak for a minimum of 24 hours in a blend of Jamaican allspice, Jamaican thyme, nutmeg, garlic, Scotch bonnet peppers, brown sugar, and his "secret weapon," wild cinnamon.

"There was immense pressure once I realized that I would be competing against Bobby. I knew that in a sense I was representing Jamaica and jerk cuisine—a privilege but a daunting endeavor as well. After I fortified myself with a shot of Jamaican white rum, our cure-all, I was still nervous but ready for battle. Nothing could have prepared me for the onslaught of customers when the show first aired. My website crashed within a few hours, and my restaurant had a line down the street even before the doors opened. Everyone wanted to try the steak that beat Bobby Flay!"

—NIGEL SPENCE

Name: Nigel Spence
Establishment: Ripe Kitchen & Bar
Hometown: Mount Vernon, New York
Website: www.riperestaurant.com
Phone: (914) 665-7689

He serves his steak with a Caribbean sauce called *chadon beni.* Made with culantro (cilantro's cousin), parsley, lime juice, Scotch bonnet peppers, green onions, and garlic, it adds a fresh touch of incredible flavor to the jerk. The final result: one delicious, flavor-packed, and totally unforgettable dish! It's no wonder that Ripe has won rave reviews from the *New York Times* and its thousands of satisfied customers. I had to ask myself: Did I have what it took to out-grill this rib-eye royalty, or would the student become the master?

I have grilled a steak or two in my day, but I definitely needed to brush up on my jerk skills, so it was off to the test kitchen. Jerk rub is a full-flavored wet rub (as opposed to a typical dry rub), which, if done right, wakes up your senses at first bite. It requires a careful balance of sweet and heat. I got my rub under way. Fiery Scotch bonnet peppers definitely provide that heat, and fresh ginger is both sweet and spicy. Fresh thyme adds an herbaceous note, and red and green onions, garlic, cloves, cinnamon, and allspice complete the flavor profile of the oil and vinegar–blended rub. Rib eye, marbled with fat and ergo flavor, is one of my favorite cuts of beef. Since it is naturally so tender and the rub so flavorful, I decided against marinating my steak and would apply the jerk rub right before grilling.

It was a sweltering day when I headed off to Mount Vernon to issue my jerk steak Throwdown, and things were about to heat up even more. My steaks were thicker than Nigel's, and much to the dismay of the restless crowd, it took longer to grill them than expected. When watching Nigel plate his steaks, I noticed that the *chadon beni* sauce packed a powerful punch of flavor. I had to come up with a sauce of my own if I wanted a chance at winning this one, so I pulled together a green onion–habanero sauce with the ingredients I had on hand from the jerk rub. Would it do the trick?

After an afternoon spent grill-side going head to head, Nigel tasted my entry and even though he thought it was great, he stood firm in his conviction that his jerk steak was the best. We would have to see what judges Daniel Hinder, culinary arts director at Monroe College, and Allan Vernon, owner of Vernon's Catering and maker of Vernon's Jerk Sauce, had to say about that. They critiqued our steaks on tenderness, flavor, and authenticity. They gave me kudos for presentation and flavor—but the flavor, though tasty, wasn't that of an authentic jerk. Nigel's steak had excellent tenderness and that authentic flavor. Nigel was right to be so confident. These were two great jerk rib eyes—I actually thought I had a chance!—but Nigel got the well-deserved win.

Bobby Flay's
Jerk Rubbed Rib Eye with Green Onion–Habanero Sauce

SERVES 4

1 large red onion, coarsely chopped

4 green onions (white and green parts), coarsely chopped

2 to 3 Scotch bonnet or habanero chiles, to taste, coarsely chopped

1 (3-inch) piece fresh ginger, peeled and coarsely chopped

6 cloves garlic

3 tablespoons fresh thyme leaves

2 teaspoons ground cinnamon

2 teaspoons ground allspice

1 teaspoon ground cloves

2 tablespoons clover honey

Kosher salt and freshly ground black pepper

¼ cup fresh lime juice

¼ cup canola oil

2 (16-ounce) boneless rib-eye steaks, each 1½ inches thick

Green Onion–Habanero Sauce (recipe follows)

1. Combine the red and green onions, chiles, ginger, garlic, thyme, cinnamon, allspice, cloves, honey, 2 teaspoons salt, ½ teaspoon pepper, the lime juice, and the oil in a food processor and process until almost smooth (it should be just a little chunky).

2. Remove the steaks from the refrigerator 30 minutes before grilling.

3. Heat a grill to medium-high or a grill pan over medium-high heat.

4. Season the steaks on both sides with salt and pepper, and rub on both sides with the wet rub. Grill until they are golden brown and the rub has formed a crust, about 5 minutes. Flip the steaks over, reduce the heat to medium, close the cover (if using a grill), and continue cooking to medium-rare, about 7 minutes. Remove the steaks from the grill and let rest for 5 minutes before slicing.

5. Top each serving with some of the Green Onion–Habanero Sauce.

Green Onion–Habanero Sauce

½ cup olive oil

8 green onions (green and pale green parts), chopped

¼ habanero chile

2 cloves garlic

½ cup chopped fresh cilantro leaves

Juice of 1 lime

Kosher salt and freshly ground black pepper

Combine the oil, green onions, habanero, garlic, cilantro, and lime juice in a food processor and process until smooth. The mixture should have the texture of a slightly thin pesto. If it is too thick, add water, a tablespoon at a time, and process. Season with salt and pepper.

WINNER!

Nigel Spence's
Ripe's "Big Ass" Jerk Rib-Eye Steak
with *Chadon Beni* Sauce
SERVES 4 TO 6

5 cloves garlic

½ cup coarsely chopped green onions (white and green parts)

½ cup whole ajicito peppers (optional)

½ Scotch bonnet pepper

¼ cup fresh thyme leaves

1 teaspoon chopped fresh ginger

⅓ cup ground allspice

⅓ cup firmly packed dark brown sugar

¼ cup kosher salt

2 tablespoons freshly ground black pepper, plus more to taste

1 teaspoon ground white pepper

½ teaspoon ground nutmeg

¼ teaspoon ground cinnamon

¼ cup vegetable oil

4 (1-pound) boneless rib-eye steaks, each about 1¼ inches thick

Chadon Beni Sauce (recipe follows)

1. To make the rub, put the garlic cloves, green onions, ajicito (if desired), Scotch bonnet, and thyme in a food processor and pulse to make a paste. Add the ginger, allspice, brown sugar, ¼ cup salt, 2 tablespoons black pepper, the white pepper, and the nutmeg and cinnamon. Pulse to incorporate. With the processor running, slowly stream in the vegetable oil, processing until the mixture is almost smooth.

2. Season one side of the steaks generously with salt and pepper. Flip the steaks over and smear each one with about 2 tablespoons jerk rub. Cover and refrigerate for 1 or up to 24 hours.

3. Remove the steaks from the refrigerator 30 minutes before cooking.

4. Preheat a grill to high or a grill pan over high heat.

5. Place the steaks, rub side down, on the grill and cook for 7 minutes; the rub should form a nice crust. Flip and cook for about 6 more minutes for medium-rare. Let rest off the heat for 10 minutes.

6. Top with *Chadon Beni* Sauce, and serve.

Chadon Beni Sauce

1 cup densely packed fresh *chadon beni* (see Note) or cilantro leaves

¾ cup loosely packed fresh flat-leaf parsley leaves

1 cup fresh lime juice, or more if needed

½ Scotch bonnet pepper

¼ cup chopped green onions (white and green parts)

6 cloves garlic

1 tablespoon kosher salt

Combine all the ingredients in a blender and puree until smooth. Add a little extra lime juice if the puree is too thick to pour.

NOTE
Chadon beni—also called Shadow Benny in Trinidad and culantro or recao in Latin markets—has a broad, flat green leaf. Cilantro makes a fine substitute.

FRUIT PIE

ON THIS EPISODE OF THROWDOWN!...

I was off to picturesque Rockland, Maine (also known as Pie Town), where the fruit pie is a little slice of heaven and the local ambassadors, Janet LaPosta and Ally Taylor, are the "Pie Moms" of the Berry Manor Inn. Summer is peak pie time in Rockland, and it was Throwdown time as well. ○ Janet and Ally are the mothers of Rockland's Berry Manor Inn owners Cheryl and Michael. Brought together by their children's marriage, the two found something else to bond over: pie. The Pie Moms bake more than 500 pies each year for the inn's lucky guests and for Rockland's annual Pies on Parade event. Some of their favorites are apple, strawberry-rhubarb, and a mixed berry pie full of Maine's prized blueberries. They think they make the best pies in the world and aren't afraid to tell you so. After all, Janet and Ally have close to a hundred years of baking experience between them and the whole town behind them. ○ These local celebrities thought that they were going to be the stars of a Food Network series called "Pie à la Road," and planned on making a four-berry pie for their segment.

Names: Janet LaPosta and Ally (Alice) Taylor
Establishment: The Berry Manor Inn
Hometown: Rockland, Maine
Website: www.berrymanorinn.com
Phone: (800) 774-5692

Because my baking skills aren't quite up to par with my cooking skills, I had my work cut out for me and was off to the test kitchen to tackle what I decided would be a blackberry-peach pie, as those are my two favorite summer fruits. I macerated the sliced peaches in a mixture of white and brown sugars, ginger, cinnamon, nutmeg, and a touch of cornstarch, which helps thicken the filling. I added a splash of peach-flavored brandy to heighten the peach flavor and cold butter for a little richness. I then macerated the blackberries in a little blackberry liqueur and added it to the peach mixture. But I still had to deal with the crust.

The hardest part about baking a pie is getting a flaky, tender crust. I decided to make my dough with both butter, for flavor, and shortening to make the crust extra-flaky. There are several steps vital to making a good crust: start with cold ingredients, work quickly to get them all incorporated, and don't overwork the dough. Pastry rolled and fruit ready, I assembled the pie, brushing it with heavy cream and raw sugar before cutting slits for the steam to vent and baking it. Easy as pie . . .

We rolled up on the Pie Moms with our peach-blackberry pies all ready in the trunk of our car. Janet and Ally were shocked by my Throwdown challenge (not so shocked that they didn't make me try on a pie hat, though), but quickly regained their composure. The next thing you knew, those two sweet ladies turned into killer competition, stealing my flour and making fun of my pie-rolling technique. They told me that my pie was good, but they couldn't see waking up in the middle of the night to eat it.

Rockland's Mayor Brian Harden and Melanie Omlor, the owner of Helen's Restaurant, which is famous for its pies, judged our pies on presentation, overall taste, and crust. They thought our filling was thickened to just the right consistency and that both the top and bottom crusts were perfectly baked through. The mayor and Melanie loved the look of the Pie Moms' pie, and while they thought that the filling was sweetened perfectly, it wasn't thick enough and ran all over the plate. The winner of this Throwdown? Uh-oh, it was me.

The first thing I thought after winning was "My mother is going to kill me," and sure enough, I got an earful from her when the episode aired. I'm not sure how I did it, but I do know that I'd eat one of Janet and Ally's fine pies any day.

WINNER!

Bobby Flay's Peach-Blackberry Pie
MAKES 1 (9-INCH) PIE

Crust

2½ cups all-purpose flour, plus more for rolling

2 tablespoons granulated sugar

½ teaspoon fine salt

10 tablespoons (1¼ sticks) unsalted butter, cut into ½-inch cubes, cold

½ cup solid vegetable shortening, cut into pieces, cold

Filling

1 pint fresh blackberries

2 tablespoons blackberry liqueur

5 cups peeled, pitted, and (½-inch-thick) sliced ripe peaches (about 8)

⅓ cup firmly packed light brown sugar

⅓ cup granulated sugar

1 teaspoon ground cinnamon

1 teaspoon ground ginger

½ teaspoon freshly grated nutmeg

3 tablespoons peach brandy

¼ cup cornstarch or tapioca

2 tablespoons unsalted butter, cut into small pieces, cold

¼ cup heavy cream

3 tablespoons turbinado sugar, such as Sugar in the Raw

1. *To make the crust,* put the flour, sugar, and salt in the bowl of a food processor and pulse a few times to combine. Scatter the butter and shortening on top, and pulse until the mixture resembles coarse meal. Add ¼ cup ice-cold water and pulse until the dough just comes together. (You can add up to 3 tablespoons additional water, 1 tablespoon at a time, if needed.) Remove the dough from the machine and lightly knead it on a lightly floured flat surface until it just comes together. Form into a disk, wrap in plastic wrap, and refrigerate for at least 1 hour.

2. Preheat the oven to 375°F.

3. *To make the filling,* put the blackberries in a small bowl, add the blackberry liqueur, and toss gently to coat. Let sit for 5 minutes.

4. Combine the peaches, both sugars, cinnamon, ginger, nutmeg, peach brandy, and cornstarch in a large bowl and mix until well combined. Let sit for 10 minutes. Fold in the blackberries just before adding the filling to the pie.

5. Divide the dough in half and roll each half out on a lightly floured surface to a 13- to 14-inch round. Transfer one of the rounds to a 9-inch deep-dish pie plate. Using a slotted spoon, spoon the fruit mixture into the crust. Add some of the juices that have accumulated in the bowl. Scatter the butter over the filling. Roll up the remaining dough on your rolling pin, and unroll it atop the fruit mixture. Trim the edges of both crusts to a ¾-inch overhang. Fold the edges over, pressing to seal. Crimp the edges. Cut 6 slits in the top crust to allow steam to escape. Brush the top of the pie with the cream, and sprinkle with the turbinado sugar.

6. Put the pie plate on a rimmed baking sheet, and bake on the bottom rack of the oven until the crust is golden and the juices are bubbling thickly through the slits, about 1 hour and 10 minutes. (Cover the edges of the crust with foil if browning too quickly.)

7. Let the pie cool for at least 3 hours before serving.

Janet and Ally's
Berry Manor Inn Four-Berry Pie
MAKES 1 (9½-INCH) DEEP-DISH PIE

"Thick" Flaky Pie Crust

3 cups all-purpose flour

1½ teaspoons fine salt

1 heaping teaspoon sugar

1½ cups solid vegetable shortening, cold

4 tablespoons (½ stick) unsalted butter, cold

Filling

2 cups blueberries (fresh or fresh frozen)

2 cups sliced strawberries

1 cup raspberries

2 cups blackberries

2 tablespoons all-purpose flour, plus more for
   rolling the dough

2 cups sugar

¼ cup minute tapioca

Dash of fresh lemon juice

4 tablespoons (½ stick) unsalted butter,
   finely diced, cold

1. *To make the crust,* mix the flour, salt, and sugar together in a medium bowl. Cut the shortening into pieces and then cut into the dry ingredients until the mixture is sandy, with only a few larger pieces remaining. Using the large holes of a box grater, grate the butter into the mixture. Add ¼ cup ice-cold water, and mix with the dough. Continue to add water, a tablespoon at a time, until the dough sticks together and forms a ball. Divide the dough into 2 equal balls, wrap each in plastic wrap, and refrigerate while you make the filling.

2. Preheat the oven to 450°F.

3. *To make the filling,* gently toss the berries with the flour in a large mixing bowl. Mix in the sugar, tapioca, and lemon juice.

4. Put a large piece of plastic wrap (larger than the pie plate) on the counter and sprinkle it with flour. Set one of the dough balls in the center of the plastic wrap and cover with a second piece of plastic wrap. Roll the dough between the plastic wrap until it forms a round about 13 inches in diameter. Remove the top piece of plastic wrap and flip the dough into a 9½-inch deep-dish pie plate. Repeat the rolling process with the top crust, making it about 12 inches in diameter.

5. Put the filling in the bottom crust. Scatter the butter on top. Put the top crust over the filling. Roll the edge of the top crust under the bottom crust, pinch to seal the pie, and flute the edges. Make several small slits in the top crust for steam to escape.

6. Set the pie plate on a baking sheet and cover the edges of the pie with strips of foil. Bake for 15 minutes. Then lower the oven temperature to 425°F, and bake until the crust is golden brown and the filling is just bubbling through the slits, 45 to 50 minutes. (If the edge of the crust is not browning well, remove the foil for the last 10 minutes or so of the baking time.)

7. Let cool on a wire rack for at least 2 hours before serving.

MUFFULETTA

ON THIS EPISODE OF THROWDOWN!...

I'm making my way down to Louisiana to try my hand at muffuletta, a big-time sandwich in the Big Easy. ○ The Serios think that they are hosts of a new Food Network show called "Order Up," featuring regional deli sandwiches from across the country. Two big guys with even bigger appetites, Mike and Jack are the third generation to run their family's famed Serio's Deli in New Orleans. They pride themselves on what they do and feel their sandwich is the best one you'll find in the city. The lines out the door second their opinion. ○ The muffuletta is one of the many culinary contributions brought to New Orleans by Italian immigrants. They would buy one of these oversized and overstuffed sandwiches in the morning and eat it throughout the day—seriously, this is one sandwich that can take you through an eight-hour workday with ease! I had never made one before, so the Serio brothers definitely had the edge, not to mention the home court advantage! ○ Mike and Jack know that the sum of its parts is what makes this sandwich so great: a giant sesame-seeded loaf filled with layers of Italian cold cuts (Genoa salami, capicola, mortadella), big-eye Swiss and provolone cheeses, and their amazing olive salad. Dressed in extra-fruity olive oil and vinegar and composed of tangy green olives, capers, celery, and herbs, the olive salad is the muffuletta's defining ingredient; the flavorful juices soak into the bread and give the sandwich its distinct flavor and texture.

Names: Mike and Jack Serio
Establishment: Serio's Deli
Hometown: New Orleans, Louisiana
Website: www.seriosdeli.com
Phone: (504) 523-2668

I head to the test kitchen with some ideas of my own—and they are anything but traditional. I'm sticking with the bread and salami, but after that, I'm jumping the Italian ship. I look to Spain for inspiration and use Serrano ham, aged Spanish sausage, and Manchego cheese. Instead of the oil-and-vinegar-based olive salad, I decide to make my own special sauce with mayonnaise and mustard. Off camera, both Miriam and Stephanie are *not* happy with this decision and try to convince me to drop the mayonnaise—not a chance! (Of course this will come back to haunt me at the Throwdown . . .)

Once in New Orleans, I crash the Serios' party and issue them an invitation to a Throwdown. The brothers, who have made a few thousand muffulettas in their time, are totally unfazed and accept immediately. The New Orleans crowd knows how to enjoy a party and is not shy at all when it comes to telling me what they think about my changes to their classic sandwich. My use of mayonnaise and mustard in the dressing practically starts a riot! I hold my breath as I start to hand out wedges for folks to try, but I'm lucky—it's not as bad as it could be. They love my selection of meats and cheeses but I've lost them with the dressing. Miriam and Stephanie will never let me live this one down!

Local restaurateur Michael A. Bardelon and chef John Folse are the judges, critiquing our muffulettas on overall flavor, texture, and balance. They both love the flavor of the olive oil ("so good!") and praise the great olive and olive oil taste of the Serios' muffuletta while mine is . . . well . . . *different.* Ugh, did they say different? Neither is a fan of the mayonnaise and it's no big shock when Mike and Jack are named the winners. Oh yeah, I got my butt kicked. I think (okay, I know) it was the mayonnaise. I thought I was onto something, but sometimes you just don't mess with a classic.

Postscript: A few months after we taped this episode, Jack Serio passed away from a heart attack, never getting the chance to see the finished show. It is hard to believe that this man so full of life is no longer with us. I am thankful that I got the chance to know him and try his delicious, Throwdown-winning muffuletta sandwich. This episode was dedicated to him.

Bobby Flay's Muffuletta

SERVES 8

Special Dressing

1 cup mayonnaise

2 tablespoons Dijon mustard

3 tablespoons aged sherry vinegar

1½ cups mixed pitted green olives, such as picholine and cerignola

4 piquillo chiles, or 2 roasted red bell peppers (see Notes, page 22)

Cloves from 1 head garlic, roasted

4 anchovy fillets in oil, patted dry

½ small red onion, chopped

1 tablespoon chopped fresh oregano leaves

¼ cup chopped fresh flat-leaf parsley leaves

Kosher salt and freshly ground black pepper

Sandwich

1 (8- or 9-inch) round loaf Italian bread

⅓ pound thinly sliced Italian Genoa salami

⅓ pound thinly sliced Spanish salami

⅓ pound thinly sliced Serrano ham

⅓ pound thinly sliced capicola ham

⅓ pound thinly sliced Manchego cheese

1. *To make the dressing,* combine the mayonnaise, mustard, vinegar, olives, peppers, garlic, anchovies, onion, oregano, and parsley in a food processor and pulse until almost smooth (it should be a little chunky); season with salt and pepper.

2. Slice the bread in half horizontally. Remove a little of the inside of the top crust; then slather the bottom and top halves of the bread with the dressing. Layer the meats and cheese on the bottom half of the bread and cover with the top half.

3. Wrap the sandwich tightly in foil and place on a baking sheet. Put a heavy sauté pan on top, and put a few cans inside the pan to weight it down. Refrigerate for at least 4 and up to 24 hours. Serve at room temperature.

WINNER!

Mike and Jack Serio's Muffuletta

SERVES 4 TO 6

Olive Salad

¾ cup broken green olives stuffed with pimentos, drained

¼ cup pitted Kalamata olives

¼ cup giardiniera (jarred Italian pickled vegetables), drained

4 pepperoncini, halved

2 tablespoons pickled pearl onions (not sweet)

2 tablespoons diced carrot

2 tablespoons chopped celery

2 tablespoons brined capers, drained

½ clove garlic, minced

2 tablespoons extra virgin olive oil

1½ teaspoons finely chopped fresh oregano leaves

1½ teaspoons finely chopped fresh flat-leaf parsley leaves

1½ teaspoons finely chopped fresh basil leaves

Freshly ground black pepper

Sandwich

1 (9- to 10-inch) round loaf seeded Italian bread

4 ounces sliced boiled ham

4 ounces sliced Swiss cheese

4 ounces sliced mortadella

4 ounces sliced provolone cheese

4 ounces sliced Genoa salami

1. *To make the olive salad,* toss the olives, giardiniera, pepperoncini, pickled onions, carrot, celery, capers, and garlic with the olive oil in a bowl. Add the oregano, parsley, basil, and black pepper to taste, and toss again to combine. Cover and refrigerate for at least 4 hours and up to 2 days.

2. Cut the bread in half crosswise. Spread the top half with 1 cup of the olive salad. Layer the meats and cheeses on the bottom half. Put on the top with its salad. Serve cold. *Buon appetito and laissez les bons temps rouler!*

MEATBALLS

ON THIS EPISODE OF THROWDOWN!...

I head to Long Island's Northport to take on Italian superstar Mike Maroni and his award-winning meatballs. Mike's recipe was handed down to him from his grandmother. *My* grandmother's specialty was sauerbrauten. I may just need the luck of the Irish to win this Throwdown . . .

O Mike thinks that he is being filmed as a part of an upcoming Food Network special entitled "The Family Table." He's invited our crew to join his Italian dinner party where he'll be serving up his outstanding spaghetti and meatballs. Looks like he'll need to pull out an extra chair at the table, because look who's coming to dinner!

"I have to say between the time of the initial phone call when they said I was being considered for a new Food Network show called 'The Family Table' and the day they showed up for filming, there were some customers betting it was a Throwdown. But Rock Shrimp Productions, the company that filmed for the Food Network, did an amazing job at faking us out."
—MIKE MARONI

Name: Mike Maroni
Establishment: Maroni Cuisine
Hometown: Northport, New York
Website: www.maronicuisine.com
Phone: (631) 757-4500

Luckily, our host is well versed in hospitality. Maroni's, which opened in 2001, has its loyal customers to thank for this claim to fame: it regularly scores the highest Zagat ratings possible. Maroni's is obviously doing things right across the board, but it's their meatballs that get people talking. In fact, their meatballs are so popular, fanatic customers buy pots of them— 500 to 600 pots of meatballs a week of takeout alone!—to bring home to their own tables. Now that's a lot of meatball love. Mike's beloved meatballs are made with ground beef, lots of garlic, bread crumbs, onions, and eggs to bind the mixture together. He roasts them in the oven and serves them in a red sauce based on canned plum tomatoes and garlic.

It turns out we do have some Italian heritage of our own in the test kitchen; Stephanie's mother, Rose (also known as Rosa Pizzapella), and her family's recipe for meatballs may just be our best defense. I stop in Ottomanelli & Sons, where my friend butcher Frank Ottomanelli helps me out with what I hope is a winning combination of ground meat: beef for rich flavor, pork for fat and moisture, and light-flavored veal for balance. Like Mike, we flavor our meat with garlic and bread crumbs, but I prefer a lighter texture and use only one egg per pound of meat where Mike uses three. Stephanie's mom comes to the rescue with our sauce. She always adds a touch of red pepper flakes and a cubanelle pepper for a little heat and a lovely herbaceous flavor. Italian parsley and basil finish off Rosa Pizzapella's sauce. I brown the meatballs in a sauté pan with olive oil and serve them with the sauce atop al dente spaghetti. A sprinkling of freshly grated Parmesan, and Long Island, here we come!

I rolled up at Mike Maroni's party at his Long Island home and my challenge for a Throwdown was met with confidence. This is a man who believes in his meatball. Friends and family chose their favorites on the meatball marathon, but the final call goes to judges Richard Jay Scholem, a former *New York Times* food writer, and Julie Vegari, whose family owns Raphael Vineyard on Long Island. Scholem is looking for a rustic, peasant-like meatball with a rich sauce while Vegari prefers a softly textured, richly flavored meatball with a well-rounded sauce. Mike's meatball is judged to have great flavor and a more refined texture, while mine is deemed the more rustic, rich with garlic flavor. We could have a tie on our hands, but after much deliberation—and a bit of arguing—the winner is announced. Mike Maroni it is, and his reign as the meatball master of Long Island goes on.

Bobby Flay's
Spaghetti and Meatballs

SERVES 4 TO 6

Meatballs

1 cup plus 2 tablespoons olive oil

4 cloves garlic, finely chopped

2 large eggs

¼ cup finely chopped fresh flat-leaf parsley
  leaves

12 ounces ground beef chuck

4 ounces ground veal

4 ounces ground pork

½ cup freshly grated Parmesan cheese

Kosher salt and freshly ground black pepper

About 6 tablespoons plain dry bread crumbs

Sauce

2 tablespoons olive oil

1 medium Spanish onion, finely chopped

3 cloves garlic

¼ teaspoon red pepper flakes

2 tablespoons tomato paste

2 (28-ounce) cans plum tomatoes and juices,
  pureed in a blender

1 small cubanelle (or cubano or banana) chile

8 sprigs fresh flat-leaf parsley

Kosher salt and freshly ground black pepper

¼ cup chopped fresh basil leaves, plus more for
  garnish

1 pound spaghetti, cooked al dente

Freshly grated Parmesan cheese

1. *To make the meatballs,* heat the 2 tablespoons oil in a small sauté pan over medium heat. Add the garlic and cook until soft, about 1½ minutes. Remove from the heat and let cool slightly.

2. Whisk the eggs, 3 tablespoons cold water, and the parsley together in a large bowl. Add the garlic, beef, veal, pork, cheese, and salt and pepper and gently mix together until combined. Add the bread crumbs, a tablespoon at a time, until the mixture just holds together. Cover and refrigerate for at least 30 minutes and up to 1 day.

3. Form the meat mixture into 1½-inch balls. Heat the remaining 1 cup oil in a large sauté pan over high heat until it begins to shimmer. Add the meatballs and fry until golden brown on all sides. Drain on a baking sheet lined with paper towels.

4. *To make the sauce,* heat the oil in a medium saucepan over medium-high heat. Add the onion, garlic, and red pepper flakes, and cook until the onion is soft and the garlic is lightly golden brown on both sides, 5 minutes. Add the tomato paste and cook for 30 seconds. Stir in the pureed tomatoes. Make a slit in the side of the cubanelle chile with a paring knife, and add it and the parsley sprigs to the sauce. Bring to a boil and cook, stirring occasionally, until slightly thickened, 20 minutes. Season with salt and pepper.

5. Add the meatballs to the sauce, reduce the heat to medium, and simmer until the meatballs have cooked through and the sauce is thickened, about 20 minutes.

6. *To serve,* put the spaghetti on a platter and top with the meatballs (use a slotted spoon). Stir the chopped basil into the tomato sauce, and ladle some of the sauce over the spaghetti and meatballs. Top with lots of Parmesan and garnish with basil.

WINNER!

Mike Maroni's
Grandma Maroni's Meatballs
(100-Year-Old Recipe)

SERVES 4

Meatballs

Olive oil

1 pound ground beef chuck

1½ cups grated Pecorino Romano cheese

1¼ cups fresh bread crumbs

3 large eggs, lightly beaten

¼ cup whole milk

½ cup minced fresh flat-leaf parsley leaves

¼ cup chopped fresh basil leaves

½ small Spanish onion, grated

3 tablespoons minced garlic

Pinch of kosher salt, or to taste

Maroni Sauce

⅓ cup olive oil

12 cloves garlic, finely sliced

1 large Spanish onion, finely diced

2 (28-ounce) cans imported crushed tomatoes

1 teaspoon kosher salt

½ teaspoon freshly ground white or black pepper

1 large handful fresh basil leaves, thinly sliced

1 pound spaghetti, cooked al dente

1. *To make the meatballs,* preheat the oven to 350°F. Brush a rimmed baking sheet with olive oil.

2. Mix the beef, cheese, bread crumbs, eggs, milk, herbs, onion, garlic, and salt in a mixing bowl.

3. Roll the meatballs loosely about the size of a large golf ball, and place on the prepared baking sheet. Bake until cooked through and lightly browned, 35 to 40 minutes.

4. *To make the sauce,* heat the olive oil in a medium saucepan over medium heat until it begins to shimmer. Add the garlic and onion, and cook until soft and slightly browned, about 5 minutes. Add the tomatoes, salt, and pepper, and stir. Allow the sauce to come to a simmer and cook for 20 minutes. Remove from the heat and add the basil.

5. Add the meatballs to the sauce.

6. *To serve,* divide the spaghetti among 4 plates, and top with the meatballs and the sauce.

LASAGNA

ON THIS EPISODE OF THROWDOWN!...

I headed to Burlington, Vermont, to take on Mark Bove and his generations-old recipe for lasagna.

○ Mark Bove's grandparents came over from Italy and opened Bove's on Pearl Harbor Day in 1941 in the picturesque college town of Burlington. These days the family's landmark restaurant is run by Mark and his brother Rick—together the two are known as "The Sauceboys"—along with their father. Bove's booths are regularly filled with locals looking for a reminder of the comforting Neapolitan food they grew up with (or wish they had) and with the ever-hungry students from the nearby University of Vermont. Their menu's greatest draw is their eternally popular lasagna. What makes it so great? Mark believes it is the meatballs, which, along with their signature sauce, are made with the recipes first created by Mark's grandmother and grandfather when they opened Bove's way back when.

"Making lasagna in front of 200 people was great, but the realization then hit me . . . Bobby Flay challenged me in front of millions. Because of the success of the Throwdown we are selling our lasagna in grocery stores and now every night is lasagna night at Bove's Restaurant."
  —MARK BOVE

Name: Mark Bove
Establishment: Bove's of Vermont
Hometown: Burlington, Vermont
Website: www.boves.com
Phone: (802) 864-6651

Mark thought that he was selected to take part in an upcoming Food Network special called "Food for Thought," highlighting good food that students crave. The only way for me to win would be by bringing a lasagna that earned straight A's. It was time to study up in the test kitchen.

I made a lasagna that defies convention. Instead of the classic southern Italian version, I headed to northern Italy for my inspiration. I alternated my sheets of pasta with two different sauces: a Bolognese made with pork and beef shanks braised in red wine and chicken stock with onions, carrots, and garlic, and then shredded and mixed with diced tomatoes, crispy pancetta, and fresh rosemary; and a rich béchamel cheese sauce made with creamy, nutty fontina and sharp, salty Parmesan. I also included a layer of ricotta cheese, which had been mixed with eggs, more Parmesan, and herbs. The whole thing baked until golden brown and bubbly and then was topped with a simple marinara sauce made of onions, garlic, tomato, and basil.

On lasagna day, we made the trek north. Mark's lasagna was great. It reminded me of the food I ate as a child in the great Italian-American restaurants of New York City's Little Italy. It was cheesy and tomatoey with intense flavor from the dried herbs. The students' reactions were mixed. Most enjoyed the classic flavor and look of Mark's lasagna, but many also liked the unexpected flavor of mine. Ultimately it was Rod Rehwinkle, the ex-chef at UVM's Davis Center, and freelance food journalist Melissa Pasanen who were judging this competition based on our lasagna's texture, flavor, and layering.

Both judges commented that Mark's lasagna was full of good tomato flavor and was very savory. They loved the texture and the amount of cheese and liked the flavor of the herbs. Rod in particular loved the "comfort" flavor of the lasagna. My lasagna was up next. The judges found it very interesting—*not* like Mom used to make. Its flavors all remained separate yet still came together into one delicious dish. Rod loved the complexity of its flavors. Both Melissa and Rod felt my flavors were more distinct and awarded me the win.

This was a big surprise. Mark's lasagna is great classic Italian-American lasagna and there are lots of reasons why Bove's has been a Burlington favorite for more than sixty years. Their lasagna just might be the best one.

WINNER!

Bobby Flay's
Lasagna
SERVES 8

Bolognese Sauce

¼ cup olive oil

3 pounds bone-in pork shanks

3 pounds bone-in beef shanks

Kosher salt and freshly ground black pepper

12 ounces pancetta, finely diced

1½ cups finely diced Spanish onion

½ cup finely diced carrot

½ cup finely diced celery

4 cloves garlic

1 cup dry red wine

3 cups homemade chicken stock
   (see page 220)

1 (15-ounce) can diced tomatoes, with juices

4 sprigs fresh thyme

4 sprigs fresh rosemary

6 sprigs fresh flat-leaf parsley, plus
   2 tablespoons chopped fresh parsley leaves

Marinara Sauce (recipe follows)

2 cups chopped fresh basil leaves

Ricotta Mixture

3 cups ricotta, strained in a cheesecloth-lined
   strainer for at least 4 hours

2 large eggs, lightly beaten

½ cup freshly grated Parmesan cheese

¼ cup chopped fresh flat-leaf parsley leaves

3 tablespoons chopped fresh basil leaves

Kosher salt and freshly ground black pepper

Béchamel Sauce

3 tablespoons unsalted butter

3 tablespoons all-purpose flour

4 cups whole milk, or more if needed, warm

¼ teaspoon freshly grated nutmeg

Kosher salt and freshly ground black pepper

2 cups (8 ounces) grated fontina cheese

½ cup freshly grated Parmesan cheese

Unsalted butter, for the baking dish

4 sheets fresh pasta, or 1 pound dry lasagna
   noodles

1 cup freshly grated Parmesan cheese,
   plus extra for garnish

Whole fresh basil leaves, plus chopped leaves
   for garnish

Chopped fresh flat-leaf parsley leaves,
   for garnish

1. *To make the Bolognese,* preheat the oven to 350°F.

2. Heat the oil in a large Dutch oven over high heat. Season the pork and beef shanks on both sides with salt and pepper, place in the pan, and cook until golden brown all over, about 4 minutes per side. Remove the shanks to a plate.

3. Pour off all but 1 tablespoon of the fat from the pan. Add the pancetta to the pan and cook until golden brown, about 5 minutes. Remove the pancetta with a slotted spoon to a plate lined with paper towels.

4. Add the onion, carrot, celery, and garlic to the fat in the pan and cook until soft and light golden brown, about 5 minutes. Add the red

(recipe continues)

wine, scrape the bottom of the pan, and boil until completely reduced. Add the chicken stock, diced tomatoes, and the thyme, rosemary, and parsley sprigs, and bring to a simmer. Return the shanks and one-third of the pancetta to the pan, cover, and transfer it to the oven. Braise until the meat is tender and falling off the bone, about 2 hours.

5. Meanwhile, *make the ricotta mixture:* Stir together the ricotta, eggs, cheese, parsley, basil, and salt and pepper to taste in a bowl. Cover and refrigerate for at least 1 hour.

6. *Return to the Bolognese:* Remove the shanks to a cutting board, and when cool enough to handle, shred the meat into bite-size pieces and place in a bowl. Strain the cooking liquid into a second bowl; discard the solids. Pour 3 cups of the cooking liquid into a large deep sauté pan and bring to a boil over high heat. Cook until the liquid is reduced to about ¾ cup, about 2 minutes. Add the shredded meat and the remaining cooked pancetta to the pan, along with 1 cup of the marinara sauce, the chopped parsley, and the chopped basil. Stir to combine. Set the Bolognese aside.

7. *To make the béchamel sauce,* melt the butter in a medium saucepan over medium heat. Whisk in the flour and let cook for about 2 minutes. Slowly whisk in the warm milk and continue whisking until the sauce has thickened and lost its raw flavor, 5 to 7 minutes. Season the sauce with the nutmeg and salt and pepper to taste, and whisk in the cheeses. If the sauce is too thick, whisk in a little additional warm milk. Set the béchamel aside.

8. Preheat the oven to 375°F. Butter the bottom and sides of a 9 × 13-inch baking dish.

9. Cook the pasta in a large pot of boiling salted water until not quite al dente, 2 to 3 minutes for fresh and 5 for dry. Drain well.

10. Ladle a thin layer of béchamel evenly over the bottom of the prepared baking dish. Place a layer of pasta, cut to fit the inside of the pan, on top, and spread all the ricotta mixture evenly over the pasta. Ladle an even layer of béchamel over the ricotta, sprinkle with a few tablespoons of the Parmesan, and add some whole basil leaves. Top with another layer of pasta, and spread all the Bolognese evenly over the top. Ladle an even layer of béchamel over the Bolognese, again sprinkling with a few tablespoons of the Parmesan and some basil leaves. Place the final layer of pasta dough over the Bolognese, and ladle the remaining béchamel over the top to completely cover the pasta. Sprinkle with the remaining Parmesan cheese.

11. Place the pan on a rimmed baking sheet and cover loosely with aluminum foil. Bake for 20 minutes. Reduce the heat to 350°F, remove the foil, and continue baking until the top is golden brown and the filling is bubbling, 25 to 35 minutes. Remove from the oven and let rest for 15 minutes before cutting.

12. Cut into slices and top each serving with some marinara sauce, more grated cheese, and chopped parsley and basil.

Marinara Sauce

3 tablespoons olive oil

1 large Spanish onion, finely diced

3 cloves garlic, coarsely chopped

½ teaspoon red pepper flakes

1 (28-ounce) can crushed tomatoes

1 (15-ounce) can diced tomatoes, with juices

Kosher salt and freshly ground black pepper

¼ cup chopped fresh flat-leaf parsley leaves

¼ cup chopped fresh basil leaves

Heat the oil in a large sauté pan over medium-high heat. Add the onion and cook until soft, 3 to 4 minutes. Add the garlic and red pepper flakes and cook for 1 minute. Add both tomatoes, bring to a boil, season with salt and pepper, and cook until the sauce is reduced and thickened, 25 to 30 minutes. Stir in the parsley and basil.

Mark Bove's
Bove's Lasagna

SERVES 6 TO 8

Meatballs

1 cup grated Pecorino Romano cheese

¾ cup plain dry bread crumbs

2 to 4 tablespoons minced garlic, to taste

1 teaspoon red pepper flakes

½ teaspoon freshly ground black pepper

3 large eggs, lightly beaten

1 pound ground beef (80% lean)

¼ cup olive oil

Lasagna

2 (26-ounce) jars Bove's Marinara Sauce or
   your favorite tomato sauce

2 tablespoons olive oil, plus more for the
   baking dish

16 dry lasagna noodles

4 cups (2 pounds) ricotta cheese

6 cups (1½ pounds) shredded mozzarella
   cheese

4 tablespoons grated Pecorino Romano cheese

4 tablespoons chopped fresh flat-leaf parsley
   leaves

1. *To make the meatballs,* preheat the oven
to 375°F.

2. Mix the cheese, bread crumbs, garlic, red pepper flakes, and black pepper with your hands in a large bowl. Work in the eggs, and then mix in the beef.

3. Pour the olive oil onto a rimmed baking sheet. Roll the meat mixture into 24 balls, transfer them to the baking sheet, and roll to coat in the olive oil. Bake for 20 minutes. Flip the meatballs over, and bake until just cooked through and golden brown, about 10 minutes. Remove from the oven.

4. *To make the lasagna,* put the meatballs and marinara sauce in a large saucepan and bring to a simmer. Simmer, stirring occasionally, for 1 hour. Cool for 1 hour or overnight in the refrigerator.

5. Bring a large pot of salted water to a boil over high heat. Add the olive oil and the lasagna noodles and cook according to the package instructions until al dente. Drain, rinse under cold water to stop the cooking process, and drain on a cotton dish towel.

6. Preheat the oven to 350°F.

7. Lightly grease a 9 × 13-inch baking dish with oil. Spoon about 1 cup of the marinara sauce over the bottom. Arrange 4 lasagna noodles over the sauce, three lengthwise and one at the short end, so that the bottom of the baking dish is covered. Crumble one-third of the meatballs over the noodles. Dot with one-third of the ricotta. Scatter 1½ cups of the mozzarella, 1 tablespoon of the Pecorino Romano, and 1 tablespoon of the chopped parsley on top. Repeat to make two more layers, alternating the side on which you place the single lasagna noodle. Top with the remaining noodles and 1½ cups marinara sauce, making sure you cover all the noodles. Scatter 1½ cups mozzarella and 1 tablespoon each Pecorino Romano and parsley on top. Cover with foil and bake for 20 minutes. Remove the foil, and bake until the cheese is browned, another 20 minutes. Let rest for 10 minutes before serving.

ICE POPS

ON THIS EPISODE OF THROWDOWN!...

I headed to Nashville, Tennessee, to learn about the world of *paletas* (that's "ice pops" in Spanish) and to see them made by the masters, Norma and Irma Paz. ○ Sisters Norma and Irma grew up in the Mexican city of Guadalajara, where ice pops are a part of the daily diet. Not your standard popsicle, these ice pops aren't fruit flavored, they *are* fruit! The outstanding local produce is blended and frozen into flavor-packed, refreshingly cool icy treats, perfect for the hot climate. Watching the Nashville marathon a few years back, Norma and Irma thought back to their childhood days and realized how perfect those healthy ice pops would be to cool down the exhausted runners. Why not introduce their favorite childhood treat to the residents of Nashville?

Before Norma and Irma could bring their ice pops stateside, they'd have to learn how to make them. Finding a *paleta* mentor wasn't easy, as women making ice pops was practically unheard of in their native Guadalajara. But they persevered and finally found the right person who was willing to pass on the technique to them. And now Las Paletas has more than a hundred fantastic ice pop flavors. The one I'll have to face? A super-fresh pineapple, lime, salt, and chile pop.

Names: Norma and Irma Paz
Establishment: Las Paletas Gourmet Popsicles
Hometown: Nashville, Tennessee
Website: www.wheresthesign.com
Phone: (615) 386-2101

My mission was to come up with a unique ice pop flavor, so I paid a visit to pastry chef Sam Mason. A mad scientist of the kitchen, Sam gave me a quick chemistry lesson on how to achieve the proper consistency and flavor in my ice pops. Armed with my new information, I went to the test kitchen and got to work. I decided on a red wine–pomegranate pop, something akin to frozen sangria, made from reduced red wine, fruit, and pomegranate, orange, and grape juices. Concentrated simple syrup and corn syrup add sweetness and do wonders for the consistency, keeping it smooth and creamy. Before freezing, everything gets refrigerated for the flavors to meld.

It was ice pop weather when we arrived in Nashville, just minutes away from Las Paletas. Norma and Irma were completely surprised, but their southern hospitality immediately kicked in; they even shed a few tears—happy ones, I hope. The crowd's anticipation was almost "paleta-able." I was flat-out shocked when some of the crowd preferred my ice pops; I know when I have been outdone and have no problem admitting it.

Robin Riddell, of Slow Food Nashville, and Carrington Fox, food critic for *Nashville Scene,* set out to judge our ice pops on their overall taste, texture, and appearance. The liked the tart start and sweet finish to mine and its nice wine flavor, but Norma and Irma's ice pop got an immediate *"Wow!"* Its salty, spicy notes were totally unexpected. They both loved the pulpy texture of the pineapple and its great fresh pineapple taste. Las Paletas took the win.

The right ice pop won this Throwdown. Norma and Irma's pops are proof positive that some-times the simplest things are the best. Their smooth, creamy texture and incredible fruit flavor is unlike any popsicle I have ever eaten.

Bobby Flay's
Sangria Ice Pops

MAKES 10 TO 12 POPSICLES

1 (750-ml) bottle fruity red wine

1 large Granny Smith apple, cored and chopped

1 large ripe pear, cored and chopped

2 plums, pitted and chopped

1 orange, chopped (with skin on)

1 cup unsweetened pomegranate juice

¼ cup fresh orange juice

¼ cup red grape juice

¼ cup Simple Syrup (see page 177)

2 tablespoons light corn syrup

1. Combine the wine, apple, pear, plums, and orange in a large saucepan and boil over high heat until the wine is reduced by half, about 12 minutes. Transfer to a large bowl or pitcher. Stir in the pomegranate, orange, and grape juices, the simple syrup, and the corn syrup. Cool to room temperature. Then cover and refrigerate for at least 4 hours and up to 2 days. (The longer it sits, the more flavor it will have.)

2. Place the pop molds in the freezer 1 hour before filling.

3. Strain the mixture into a bowl or pitcher and fill the ice pop molds, leaving a little room at the top. Freeze until solid, at least 4 hours.

4. Dip the molds in lukewarm water to loosen the ice pops, and then pull them out.

WINNER!

Norma and Irma Paz's
Pineapple-Chile Ice Pops
MAKES 10 POPSICLES

1 medium ripe pineapple, peeled and cored

½ cup fresh lime juice

4 pinches fine salt

2 cups sugar

10 pinches chile de árbol powder or cayenne
   pepper, or to taste

1. Puree the pineapple with an immersion blender or in a food processor, but keep some texture to it. Stir in the lime juice, salt, and sugar by hand until dissolved. Add the chile powder. Fill 3-ounce molds and freeze the popsicles for at least 24 hours and up to 2 days.

2. Dip the molds in lukewarm water to loosen the ice pops, and then pull them out.

EGGPLANT PARMESAN

ON THIS EPISODE OF THROWDOWN!...

I was on Arthur Avenue in the Bronx, ready to take on the Italian-American classic, eggplant Parmesan. I went up against David Greco, a man whose version of the dish is the pride of that borough's Little Italy. It was a Throwdown full of music, trash talk, and celebrities, all with a photo finish. ○ Mike's Deli was opened by David Greco's father back in 1951 on a stretch of Arthur Avenue already littered with Italian delis. In a neighborhood full of the real deals, Mike's Deli is a standout, beloved for its legendary eggplant Parmesan, made with homemade mozzarella from his grandmother's recipe. The dish is so popular that David and his dad even serve it up at Yankee Stadium. So why not show it off as the star of Arthur Avenue for a Food Network show called "Culinary Streets"?

"Before the celebration, some of my guests asked if it was going to be a Showdown, so I called Food Network to ask and they said no, and that's the truth. During the party, when Bobby Flay walked out of the crowd, I immediately thought it had to be a joke. He just looked at me and said, 'I told you it wasn't going to be a showdown . . . this is a Throwdown.'"
—DAVID GRECO

Name: David Greco
Establishment: Mike's Deli
Hometown: Bronx, New York
Website: www.arthuravenue.com
Phone: (718) 295-5033

There are three major components to think about when making great eggplant Parmesan: the cheese; the tomato sauce, which has to have good flavor yet not be overpowering; and of course the eggplant, which can be bland, bitter, and chewy if not cooked right. I decided to cut the eggplant into thick rounds for a meaty texture and to leave its skin on because I love the flavor.

I gave my tomato sauce an extra flavor kick with roasted red peppers and layered everything with a blend of four cheeses: fontina, two mozzarellas, and Romano. Our test kitchen trial was the first time either Stephanie, Miriam, or I had made eggplant Parmesan and we were thrilled with the results.

The *Throwdown!* team crossed the river to Mike's Deli, and after a few jabs at my Irish heritage, I received a warm Bronx welcome and David and I both got down to business. I was thinking I might have had the edge with my roasted red pepper tomato sauce . . . until David and I exchanged plates. I adored his thin layers of eggplant, his savory sauce, and especially his creamy homemade mozzarella. It was obvious that this man had been making this dish for years. David wasn't a fan of the fact that I had left the skin on my eggplant, saying that it is a big no-no in Italian cooking. He did say my dish was good, but was he just being polite?

Maria Garcia, freelance food writer with *Ambassador* magazine, and Robert Cacciola, culinary adviser to the Westchester Italian Cultural Center, stepped up to judge our dishes on their taste, texture, and adherence to tradition. They tasted David's first and thought the sauce was sweet and nice. Maria thought there was a lot of cheese but Robert did not. The judges were on opposite sides with mine, too. Maria liked the skin on my eggplant while Robert didn't. The judges were locked for what seemed like forever. They begged for a tie, but in the end they decided that tradition would win out, and David was announced the winner.

It was pretty scary taking my eggplant Parmesan up to Arthur Avenue because not only was I going up against David, I was going up against years and years of Italian tradition. That is where good food comes from: tradition, love, and family—and that is what David's dish is all about.

Bobby Flay's
Eggplant Parmesan
SERVES 6 TO 8

Roasted Red Pepper Tomato Sauce

3 tablespoons olive oil

1 large onion, coarsely chopped

4 cloves garlic, coarsely chopped

¼ teaspoon red pepper flakes

4 red bell peppers, roasted (see Notes, page 22) and chopped

2 (28-ounce) cans plum tomatoes with juices, crushed with your hands

¼ cup chopped fresh flat-leaf parsley leaves

3 tablespoons finely chopped fresh basil leaves

1 tablespoon finely chopped fresh oregano leaves

Kosher salt and freshly ground black pepper

Honey, if needed

Eggplant

5 cups fresh bread crumbs (made from day-old bread)

2 tablespoons unsalted butter, softened

2 cups all-purpose flour

Kosher salt and freshly ground black pepper

6 large eggs

3 tablespoons finely chopped fresh flat-leaf parsley leaves

1 tablespoon finely chopped fresh oregano leaves

1 tablespoon finely chopped fresh thyme leaves

2 to 3 medium eggplants (about 2¼ pounds) total, cut into ½-inch-thick rounds (about 18 slices)

Olive oil

3 cups (12 ounces) grated mozzarella cheese (not fresh)

3 cups (12 ounces) grated fontina cheese

¾ cup grated Pecorino Romano cheese

½ cup fresh basil leaves, torn

8 ounces fresh mozzarella cheese, thinly sliced

1. *To make the sauce,* heat the oil in a large Dutch oven over medium heat. Add the onion and cook until soft, 5 minutes. Add the garlic and red pepper flakes, and cook for 1 minute. Add the roasted red peppers and cook for 1 minute. Add the tomatoes, bring to a boil, and cook, stirring occasionally, until thickened, 25 to 30 minutes.

2. Transfer the mixture to a food processor and process until smooth. Return the mixture to the pot, add the parsley, basil, and oregano, and season with salt and pepper. Cook for 10 minutes. Season with honey, if needed, and set aside.

3. *To cook the eggplant,* preheat the oven to 350°F.

4. Spread the bread crumbs evenly on a large baking sheet and bake, stirring once, until dry, about 10 minutes. Remove from the oven.

5. Raise the oven temperature to 400°F. Grease the bottom and sides of a 10 × 15-inch baking dish with the butter.

6. Combine the flour with 1 teaspoon salt and ¼ teaspoon pepper in a medium shallow bowl or on a large plate. In another medium shallow bowl, whisk the eggs with 2 tablespoons water. In a large shallow bowl, mix the bread crumbs with the parsley, oregano, thyme, 1½ teaspoons salt, and ½ teaspoon pepper.

7. Season each eggplant slice on both sides with salt and pepper. Dredge each slice in the flour, tapping off any excess; then dip it in the egg; and finally dredge it in the bread crumb mixture. Shake off any excess breading and transfer the eggplant to a baking sheet.

8. Heat ½ inch of oil in 2 large straight-sided sauté pans over medium heat until the oil begins to shimmer. Working in batches, fry the eggplant slices, turning once, until golden brown on both sides, about 3 minutes. Using tongs, transfer the eggplant to a paper-towel-lined baking sheet.

9. Cover the bottom of the prepared baking dish with some of the tomato sauce, and arrange a third of the eggplant slices over the sauce. Cover the eggplant with some of the sauce, grated mozzarella, fontina, Pecorino, and basil. Repeat to make two more layers, ending with the sauce. Top with the fresh mozzarella and remaining Pecorino, and bake until hot and just beginning to brown, about 30 minutes. Let rest for 10 minutes before serving.

WINNER!

David Greco's
Mike's Deli Famous Eggplant Parmigiana
SERVES 6 TO 8

6 large eggs

1 heaping cup grated Pecorino Romano cheese

2 tablespoons minced fresh flat-leaf parsley
    leaves

Kosher salt and freshly ground black pepper

2 cups all-purpose flour

3 cups Italian-seasoned dry bread crumbs

2 eggplants (about 2 pounds total), peeled and
    sliced ¼ inch thick lengthwise

⅔ cup vegetable oil

⅓ cup olive oil

4 cups Arthur Avenue Italian Deli Marinara or
    your favorite tomato sauce

1 pound mozzarella, thinly sliced (see Note)

1. Preheat the oven to 350°F.
2. Beat the eggs with 1 tablespoon of the
Pecorino and the parsley in a large bowl or
baking dish. Season with salt and pepper. Put
the flour in another baking dish, and the bread
crumbs in a third dish. Coat both sides of the
eggplant slices with the flour, then the egg
mixture, then the bread crumbs.
3. Heat the vegetable and olive oils in 1 or
2 large straight-sided skillets over medium
heat until the oil begins to shimmer. Fry the
eggplant, in batches, until golden brown on
both sides, about 3 minutes per side. Transfer
the eggplant to a paper-towel-lined plate or a
wire rack to drain.

4. Spread a little of the marinara sauce in the
bottom of a 10 × 15-inch baking dish. Add a
layer of eggplant, one-third of the remaining
sauce, one-third of the mozzarella, and one-
third of the remaining Pecorino. Continue to
layer until you have reached the top of the
dish. Top off with sauce, mozzarella, and
Pecorino—a little heavier than the preceding
layers. Bake on a rimmed baking sheet until
the top is lightly crisp, 25 to 30 minutes. Let
rest for 10 minutes before serving.

NOTE
If using fresh mozzarella, let the slices dry
out, uncovered, in the refrigerator overnight to
remove excess moisture.

CHICKEN AND WAFFLES

ON THIS EPISODE OF THROWDOWN!...

Harlem was calling with a sweet and savory classic—chicken and waffles—and Melba Wilson is the queen bee of this specialty. ○ Harlem has been one of New York City's most vibrant neighborhoods since the city's early days. It's home to lots of culture, amazing cuisine, and a thriving jazz scene harkening back to Harlem's golden age. After performing into the early hours of the morning, musicians would come into Wells Restaurant, some hungry for dinner while others wanted breakfast. Joseph Wells satisfied both by serving his chicken and waffles. ○ Melba Wilson keeps this jazzy tradition alive at her Harlem restaurant, Melba's, with her twist on the generations-old recipe. Descended from soul-food royalty, Melba received her culinary education in the kitchen of her aunt Sylvia's legendary restaurant, Sylvia's. Melba credits mustard, her ninety-six-year-old grandmother's secret ingredient, for her chicken's deep golden color and tangy flavor. The secret addition to Melba's waffles came about out of necessity. While making a batch at home one day, and out of heavy cream, she used eggnog instead and was so pleased with the waffles that she has used eggnog ever since.

Name: Melba Wilson
Establishment: Melba's Restaurant
Hometown: New York, New York
Website: www.melbasrestaurant.com
Phone: (212) 864-7777

In the test kitchen, Stephanie and Miriam quickly reminded me that the last time I had showed up at a Throwdown with my chicken recipe (Fried Chicken in Saratoga, New York), I had lost. I wasn't about to let that deter me. I've been serving my chicken and waffles at Bar Americain for years and I knew that I had a winning recipe. I first marinate my chicken overnight in buttermilk and chile de árbol powder before giving it a double dipping in seasoned flour for an extra-crunchy crust. The secret to my waffle batter is buttermilk and the addition of cooked wild rice, which gives the waffles a great texture and a nutty flavor. I was set with my honey-pink peppercorn butter, but I decided that my maple syrup could use a savory touch as well, so I added a little Dijon mustard and horseradish to it.

I was off to Harlem's legendary jazz club the Lenox Lounge to issue Melba her chicken and waffles *Throwdown!* challenge. We immediately started cooking, and I had to hand it to her: Melba put on a good show. It was hard to keep up, especially after I snuck a taste of her waffles; compared to hers, mine weren't crispy enough. I thought that adding melted butter to the batter might solve the problem, and thankfully, I was right. We plated our dishes and fed the crowd, who raved over my waffles but couldn't get their heads—or mouths—around my mustard and horseradish maple syrup. It seemed they far preferred Melba's sweet strawberry butter and plain maple syrup. We turned it over to judges Joyce White, a food writer, and Grammy Award–winning jazz musician Loren Schoenberg to see what they had to say.

They judged us on our chicken's crispiness, the texture of the waffle, and the overall flavor of the dish. Joyce and Loren both loved the sweetness of the strawberry butter and maple syrup in Melba's dish and gave a big thumbs-up to her chicken's flavor and crispiness. They also loved the traditional look of Melba's entry. Then my dish came up, which definitely didn't look traditional; its appearance and taste got a lot of "interestings." My savory-flavored syrup also threw them for a loop. Joyce and Loren did love the crispiness of my chicken and felt it had more flavor than Melba's, but my waffle could have been a bit crisper. While they liked both, the judges were won over by the total package of Melba's chicken and waffles.

It served me right for going to Harlem and trying to beat the hometown girl. But I learned a lot about the history of a classic American dish, met wonderful people, and had a great time doing it.

Bobby Flay's
Fried Chicken and Wild Rice Waffles with Pink Peppercorn Butter

SERVES 4 TO 6

Wild Rice Waffles

1½ cups all-purpose flour

1½ cups whole wheat flour

1½ tablespoons sugar

1 tablespoon plus 1 teaspoon baking powder

2 teaspoons baking soda

1 teaspoon kosher salt

1 quart buttermilk

4 large eggs

⅓ cup vegetable oil

½ cup cooked wild rice (the rice should be overcooked), well drained

4 tablespoons (½ stick) unsalted butter, melted and cooled slightly, plus more for the waffle maker

Chicken

Fried Chicken (page 50)

Pink Peppercorn Butter (recipe follows), for serving

Maple-Horseradish Syrup (recipe follows), for serving

1. *To make the waffles,* whisk together the flours, sugar, baking powder, baking soda, and salt in a large bowl. Whisk the buttermilk, eggs, and oil together in a separate large bowl. Add the wet ingredients to the dry ingredients, and whisk until the mixture just comes together. Add the wild rice and melted butter, and fold until just combined. Let sit for 15 minutes.

2. Heat the waffle maker. Brush the waffle grates with some melted butter, and cook the waffles according to the manufacturer's directions.

3. Spread the waffles with some of the Pink Peppercorn Butter, top with a piece or two of fried chicken, and drizzle the waffles and chicken with some of the Maple-Horseradish Syrup.

Pink Peppercorn Butter

12 tablespoons (1½ sticks) unsalted butter, slightly softened

1 teaspoon pink peppercorns, coarsely crushed

3 tablespoons clover honey

Kosher salt

Combine the butter, peppercorns, honey, and salt to taste in a small bowl. Cover and refrigerate for at least 30 minutes and up to 1 day to allow the flavors to meld. Remove from the refrigerator 15 minutes before serving.

Maple-Horseradish Syrup

1 cup pure maple syrup

1 tablespoon prepared horseradish, drained

1 tablespoon Dijon mustard

Stir the syrup, horseradish, and mustard together in a small bowl.

WINNER!

Melba Wilson's
Southern Fried Chicken and Eggnog Waffles
SERVES 4

Chicken

1 (3-pound) chicken, cut into 8 pieces

2 teaspoons kosher salt

1 teaspoon freshly ground black pepper

1 teaspoon sweet Spanish paprika

1 teaspoon poultry seasoning

½ teaspoon garlic powder

1 tablespoon brown mustard

2 cups buttermilk

Peanut or vegetable oil, for frying

2 cups all-purpose flour

2 teaspoons Sazonador seasoning

Eggnog Waffles

2 cups all-purpose flour, sifted

2 teaspoons baking powder

Pinch of ground cinnamon

Pinch of ground nutmeg

2 cups eggnog

2 large eggs, separated

4 tablespoons (½ stick) unsalted butter, melted

Cooking spray, for the waffle iron

Strawberry Butter (recipe follows), for serving

Maple syrup, for serving

1. *To cook the chicken,* put the chicken pieces in a bowl and sprinkle with the salt, pepper, paprika, poultry seasoning, and garlic powder. Add the mustard and use your hands to work everything into the chicken. Pour in the buttermilk, cover with plastic wrap, and refrigerate for 2 hours.

2. Heat 3 inches of oil to 325°F in a deep cast-iron skillet over medium heat. Combine the flour and Sazonador seasoning in a brown paper bag. Add a few pieces of chicken at a time and shake it like you mean it! Working in batches, fry the chicken until it is beautifully brown and crispy on one side, about 15 minutes. Turn and cook until a meat thermometer inserted into the meat registers 160°F, about 15 minutes. Drain on paper towels.

3. *To make the waffles,* combine the flour, baking powder, cinnamon, and nutmeg in a medium bowl. Whisk the eggnog, egg yolks, and butter in another bowl. Stir the wet ingredients into the dry until combined; you don't want the batter to be lumpy or too smooth—just right.

4. Whisk the egg whites until almost stiff; fold them into the batter.

5. Heat a waffle iron. Spray the waffle iron with cooking spray. Pour some of the batter into the middle of the iron, following the manufacturer's instructions. Close and cook until golden brown and cooked through, 3 to 4 minutes. Repeat with the remaining batter.

6. Top the waffles with fried chicken, Strawberry Butter, and maple syrup. Are you ready to *Paaarrrtyyy!?*

Strawberry Butter

1 cup (2 sticks) unsalted butter, slightly
   softened

4 ounces strawberries, hulled and sliced
   (about ¾ cup)

A few drops of grenadine syrup

Put the butter in a food processor fitted with
the metal blade, and blend until smooth. Add
the berries and grenadine and pulse until
combined, but with small pieces of berry still
visible.

ARROZ CON POLLO

ON THIS EPISODE OF THROWDOWN!...

I headed up to Spanish Harlem to whip up a mellow Latin classic as Puerto Rican as salsa music—arroz con pollo. But could Jorge Ayala handle it when I salsa'd through the door? It was tradition versus nuevo, complete with dancing and a guest appearance by my archenemy: rice. (If you've seen the mess I made of the rice in the Jambalaya episode, no further explanation is necessary.) ● For the last decade, La Fonda Boricua has delivered the best Puerto Rican food in New York City, thanks to its founder and head chef, Jorge Ayala. This former psychology professor attributes his success to fresh ingredients, loyal customers, and a popular dish that keeps them coming back—his arroz con pollo is the real thing, just like (if not better than) your mom used to make.

Name: Jorge Ayala
Establishment: La Fonda Boricua
Hometown: New York, New York
Website: www.fondaboricua.com
Phone: (212) 410-7292

Chicken and rice—it sounds simple enough, right? But simple doesn't mean easy. Jorge knows that to get this dish right, the flavors of the chicken and rice need to meld together, and the chicken can't be overcooked and the rice undercooked or vice versa. Jorge marinates his chicken in adobo spices overnight and sautés it in annatto oil for its great color and distinct flavor. You can't have Puerto Rican food without sofrito, a fragrant blend of onions, peppers, garlic, and herbs (cilantro and its pungent cousin recao). Jorge sautés his sofrito with bay leaves, tomato paste, and olives—it's this arroz con pollo magic that Jorge thought had earned him a spot in a Food Network show called "Latin Spice."

In the test kitchen, I started with the chicken, creating my own adobo spice rub to give it a great yellow color and incredible flavor. My sofrito started off traditionally enough until I added a few serrano chiles. Puerto Rican food is known for being full of spice, not heat, but no matter what I'm cooking, it seems a chile pepper always makes its way into the dish. Rice, stock, and the chicken are added, and peas, red peppers, and citrus zest finish the dish. If all had gone according to plan, the chicken would have been perfectly cooked and the rice tender and fluffy. Well, at least the chicken was good. Again I struggled with the rice. (Dissatisfied with my soggy rice, I decided to go back to my apartment and make the dish again for my wife. I changed my method, cooking the rice and chicken separately and combining the two at the end. Classic? No. Good? Definitely.)

This fun and lively Spanish Harlem Throwdown was full of flavor, but the time came to kill the music, clear the dance floor, and give our attention to the judges. Debbie Quinones and Jordy Lavanderos are experts in the field of Latin cuisine and they judged us on the rice's texture, the seasoning of the chicken, and the overall flavor of the dish. They said that mine was very peppery and had lots of flavor, though it was more of an American taste. Jorge's chicken could have used more flavor, but the rice was cooked much better than mine. This win went to Jorge.

He did a great job, and it's good to know that I can come to La Fonda Boricua for Jorge's fabulous arroz con pollo any time the craving strikes. I can even get in a little salsa dancing, too.

Bobby Flay's
Adobo-Seasoned Chicken and Rice
SERVES 4

Adobo Seasoning

2 tablespoons kosher salt

2 teaspoons granulated garlic

2 teaspoons granulated onion

1 teaspoon ground cumin

1 teaspoon sweet Spanish paprika

2 teaspoons freshly ground black pepper

2 teaspoons ground turmeric

1 tablespoon finely chopped fresh oregano
  leaves

Chicken and Rice

4 bone-in, skin-on chicken thighs, cut in half

4 bone-in, skin-on chicken breasts, cut in half
  lengthwise

Kosher salt and freshly ground black pepper

2 tablespoons olive oil

1 large Spanish onion, finely diced

2 medium red bell peppers, finely diced

1 serrano chile, finely diced

2 plum tomatoes, seeded and finely diced

4 cloves garlic, finely chopped

3 cups long-grain rice

5½ cups homemade chicken stock (see
  page 220)

1 bay leaf

1 cup frozen peas (not thawed)

1 cup pitted picholine olives

3 tablespoons finely chopped fresh cilantro or
  flat-leaf parsley leaves

2 teaspoons finely chopped fresh oregano
  leaves

Grated zest and juice of 1 fresh lime

1. *To make the adobo seasoning,* mix together the salt, granulated garlic, granulated onion, cumin, paprika, black pepper, turmeric, and oregano in a small bowl.

2. *To cook the chicken,* preheat the oven to 375°F.

3. Season both sides of the chicken pieces with salt and pepper, and then with the adobo seasoning mixture.

4. Heat the oil in a large Dutch oven over medium heat. Place the chicken in the oil, skin side down, in batches if necessary, and sauté until golden brown, about 4 minutes. Turn the chicken over and cook until the second side is golden brown, about 4 minutes. Transfer the chicken to a baking sheet, place it in the oven, and roast until tender and just cooked through, about 12 minutes.

5. Meanwhile, pour off all but 2 tablespoons fat from the Dutch oven, and place it back over high heat. Add the onion, bell peppers, and serrano chile, and cook until soft, 5 minutes. Add the tomatoes and garlic and cook for 1 minute.

6. Add the rice to the pan, stir to coat it in the mixture, and cook for 1 minute. Add the chicken stock and bay leaf, season with salt and pepper, and bring to a boil. Cook for 5 minutes, uncovered. Then stir well, cover, reduce the heat to medium, and cook until all the stock has been absorbed and the rice is tender, 10 to 12 minutes. During the last few minutes of cooking, quickly stir in the peas, cover, and continue cooking.

7. Remove the pan from the heat and let sit for 5 minutes, covered. Then remove the lid, fluff the rice, and gently fold in the olives, cilantro, oregano, lime zest, and juice. Add the chicken and stir to combine.

WINNER!

Jorge Ayala's Arroz con Pollo

SERVES 4

4 cups long-grain white rice

2 tablespoons granulated garlic

1 tablespoon granulated onion

1½ teaspoons ground cumin

1½ teaspoons dried oregano

Kosher salt and freshly ground black pepper

Juice of 2 limes

4 bone-in, skinless chicken drumsticks
    (about 1 pound)

4 bone-in, skinless chicken thighs
    (about 1 pound)

¼ cup olive oil

1½ teaspoons annatto seeds

1 small white onion, chopped

4 cloves garlic, chopped

1 small green bell pepper, chopped

1 small red bell pepper, chopped

2 tablespoons chopped fresh cilantro leaves

2 tablespoons chopped fresh recao leaves

¼ cup diced dried Spanish chorizo
    (about 2 ounces)

¼ cup tomato paste

¼ cup pimento-stuffed Spanish olives

3 bay leaves

5 cups homemade chicken stock
    (see page 220)

1 (12-ounce) bottle light beer

1. Swish the rice in a bowl of cold water and drain; repeat until the water is clear. Set aside.
2. Combine the granulated garlic, granulated onion, cumin, oregano, 1½ tablespoons salt, and 1½ teaspoons black pepper in a small bowl. Rub about 3 tablespoons of this adobo mixture and the lime juice into the chicken pieces. Reserve the remaining adobo mixture.
3. Heat the olive oil in a large, wide Dutch oven over low heat, and add the annatto seeds. Cook, stirring frequently, until the oil has turned orange, about 5 minutes. Be careful not to burn the seeds or the oil will be bitter. Strain, discarding the seeds.
4. Return the oil to the pot. Raise the heat to medium and cook the chicken, in batches if necessary, until golden brown on both sides, about 8 minutes total. Remove to a platter.
5. Add the onion, garlic, green and red bell peppers, cilantro, and recao to the pot and cook for another 5 minutes; season generously with salt to taste. Stir in the chorizo, tomato paste, olives, bay leaves, ¼ teaspoon black pepper, and 3 tablespoons adobo mixture. Cook, stirring, for 1 to 2 minutes. Then return the chicken and any juices on the platter to the pot. Continue cooking, turning to coat the chicken in the sofrito-chorizo mixture, for 2 to 3 minutes.
6. Stir in the rice. Then stir in the chicken stock and beer, raise the heat to medium-high, and bring to a boil. Boil, uncovered, until most of the liquid has evaporated, about 10 minutes. Reduce the heat to low, give the ingredients a stir, cover, and cook until the rice is tender and the chicken is cooked through, about 10 minutes. Remove the bay leaves.

GRILLED CHEESE

ON THIS EPISODE OF THROWDOWN!...

If it's griddled and gooey, it must be . . . grilled cheese. It seems my spatula has some other ideas. Can I keep my team from melting down long enough to take the crown or will a guy named "Stink" be the big cheese of this Throwdown? ○ Connie and Bill "Stink" Fisher are on a mission to spread their love of great grilled cheese around the world. Their restaurant, The Pop Shop in Collingswood, New Jersey, offers thirty-one varieties of grilled cheese composed from a pantry stocked with eight styles of artisan bread, nine types of cheese, and countless fillings. Toasted bread and luscious melted cheese are the constants, but as the award-winning grilled cheese sandwiches at The Pop Shop prove, it doesn't have to be ordinary to be delicious!

CASE FILE: 4.8

"Suddenly the crowd goes nuts and gets really loud. I look at Connie and give her a look like 'What's going on?' And then I see him: Bobby Flay, standing inside our restaurant with a giant grin plastered on his face. At that point I think both Connie and I touched Heaven."
　　　—BILL FISHER

Names: Connie and Bill Fisher
Establishment: The Pop Shop
Hometown: Collingswood, New Jersey
Website: www.thepopshopusa.com
Phone: (856) 869-0111

The Fishers were trying to polish their act for a Food Network special called "All Grown Up." The concept of the special was one that the Fishers were definitely familiar with: highlighting favorite kids' menus that have received a grown-up twist. Always happy to share the love, Connie and Stink had invited friends and family to The Pop Shop for a gourmet grilled cheese party featuring "The Calvert," a grilled cheese of focaccia bread filled with turkey, Monterey Jack, bacon, and balsamic vinegar. Excellent choice—excellent sandwich.

We all grew up eating the classic grilled cheese made with American cheese—which I love to this day—but for this competition, I needed to do something a little more refined. So I was off to the test kitchen to come up with the perfect combination for my grown-up grilled cheese. My first thought was to use an aged cheddar, but while it has great flavor, cheddar doesn't melt especially well; it tends to get a little grainy. I decided to use a combo of Brie and goat cheese—creamy Brie for its "gooey" factor and aged goat cheese for its great pungent flavor. My cheese choices weren't winning approval from Stephanie and Miriam, but I worked hard to convince them. We'd have to leave this one up to the judges. In addition to the cheese, I added crispy bacon and tart green tomatoes.

In Collingswood and headed for The Pop Shop . . . Will Stink be able to smell me coming? He didn't, but both he and Connie gladly accepted my challenge to a grilled cheese Throwdown. Sensing the crowd was firmly on the Fishers' side, I had to work extra-hard to win them over. Both sides were flipping grilled cheeses like short-order cooks to get this hungry crew fed. They looked pleased with both offerings, but The Pop Shop's loyal fan base seemed to lean toward theirs.

Luckily for me, food blogger Arthur Etchells and *Philadelphia City Paper* food editor Drew Lazor—not the crowd—were the ones calling this race. Their judging criteria were taste, texture, and originality. They praised the Fishers' atypical bread choice with the focaccia, as well as their avocado and bacon. The bacon was a hit in both sandwiches; mine also got high marks for its simple bread, and they loved the Brie and goat cheese combo, calling it a "taste explosion" (take that, Stephanie and Miriam). After quite a bit of back-and-forth discussion, the judges had their winner and . . . these two came down on my side.

The Fishers and I both had excellent versions of the grilled cheese sandwich, and in my mind, it was a tie; I just got lucky this time. Connie and Stink couldn't have been more gracious to me and my staff, and the audience of their friends and fans made us feel welcome from the moment we stepped into The Pop Shop.

WINNER!

Bobby Flay's
Grilled Brie and Goat Cheese with Bacon and Green Tomato
SERVES 4

8 (¼-inch-thick) slices center-cut bacon

10 tablespoons (1¼ sticks) unsalted butter, at room temperature

8 (1-inch-thick) slices Pullman bread

12 ounces really good Brie, thinly sliced with a serrated knife

2 green tomatoes, sliced ¼ inch thick

8 ounces soft goat cheese, such as Bûcheron, cut into 8 slices

Kosher salt and freshly ground black pepper

1. Put the bacon in a large skillet or on a griddle and cook, flipping it once, over medium heat until golden brown and crisp, about 10 minutes. Remove to a paper-towel-lined plate. Break each piece in half and set aside.

2. Heat a cast-iron griddle or cast-iron pan over medium heat.

3. Spread butter on one side of each slice of bread. Flip over 4 of the bread slices and layer each with 3 to 4 slices of Brie, 2 green tomato slices, 2 slices of goat cheese, and 4 slices of the bacon. Season with salt and pepper. Place the remaining bread slices on top, butter side up, and cook on the griddle until the bottom is golden brown, 3 to 4 minutes. Flip the sandwich over, cover with a heatproof bowl (to melt the cheese), and continue cooking until the bottom is golden brown and the Brie has melted, 3 to 4 minutes.

Connie and Bill "Stink" Fisher's
The Calvert

SERVES 2

½ cup mayonnaise

1 tablespoon balsamic vinegar

2 (5-inch) round or square pieces rosemary
   focaccia, split

Vegetable oil or butter, for the griddle

10 slices Monterey Jack cheese

8 ounces sliced oven-roasted turkey

4 slices applewood-smoked bacon, cooked
   until crisp

1 avocado, halved and thinly sliced

1. Preheat a griddle to 350°F.

2. Combine the mayonnaise and vinegar in a
small bowl. Spread 1 tablespoon on each cut
side of the focaccia.

3. Add a little oil to the griddle. Place the
focaccia, mayonnaise side up, on the griddle.
Put 2 slices of cheese on top of each piece of
bread, and cover with a heatproof bowl to melt
the cheese.

4. Meanwhile, divide the turkey into 2 portions
and put on the griddle to warm. Place the
bacon slices in an "X" over each portion, and
cover with the avocado and remaining cheese.
Once the cheese is melted all around, put a
mound of turkey on 2 bottom halves, and top
with the remaining bread.

5. Add a bit more oil to the griddle and press
the sandwiches with a cast-iron pan or other
heavy thing, turning once, until the bread is
crisp on both sides.

DUMPLINGS

ON THIS EPISODE OF THROWDOWN!...

It's everyone's favorite appetizer—Asian dumplings. Sohui Kim of Brooklyn makes a mean dumpling and she can't wait to tell the world about it. ○ Though it's been open for only a few years, Sohui's restaurant, The Good Fork in Brooklyn's Red Hook neighborhood, has received its fair share of attention, popular with patrons and praised by the critics for its fine-tuned and delicious dumplings. Sohui started her culinary career by working in some of New York's top kitchens, but she wanted to break out on her own and serve what made *her* happy, and that's just what she does with her signature dish: pork and chive dumplings. Her generations-old recipe makes dumplings that are at once delicate, aromatic, well balanced, and packed with flavor. Tofu gives a silky texture to her meat filling, and though simple, her dipping sauce of dark soy sauce, brown sugar, and rice vinegar is incredibly flavorful.

Name: Sohui Kim
Establishment: The Good Fork
Hometown: Brooklyn, New York
Website: www.goodfork.com
Phone: (718) 643-6636

I had my work cut out for me. My mission was to learn the delicate technique of making dumplings, come up with a dynamite recipe, and be prepared to fill, fold, steam, and fry them by the hundreds. One small problem: I'd never made dumplings before! I made a quick call to my friend and fellow chef Anita Lo, who just happens to own Rickshaw Dumplings, to see if she could give me a few pointers, including, and most important, how to fold the dumplings.

In the test kitchen, I decided on a filling of finely ground duck and shredded savoy cabbage flavored with chives, green onion, cilantro, Chinese five-spice powder, ginger, allspice, chili paste, and hoisin. I added a little cornstarch (a tip I picked up from Anita) to the filling to help absorb any additional liquid. My filling and dough were just where I wanted them to be, but my shaping technique . . . not so much. Thankfully, Miriam mastered that art, so she was put on shaping duty for the Throwdown.

Red Hook was echoing with the click of chopsticks as we got down to business. My dumplings' filling and dipping sauce may have rattled Sohui, but she quickly regained her confidence when she saw my filling technique. The first thing I noticed when trying her dumplings was their incredibly smooth, moist, and perfectly seasoned filling. She was gracious enough to compliment the chewy texture of my dough, the flavor combinations in my filling, and the heat from my dipping sauce. Ultimately it was up to judges Lucas Lin, chef and creator of The Dumpling Man, and food blogger Yung Jung to make their choice based on our dumplings' taste, texture, and presentation.

The judging seemed endless. They loved my unexpected choice of duck, calling the dumplings spicy and meaty. And while we tied on presentation, Sohui got high marks for her silky, juicy dumplings and was praised for their simple, clean flavors. When it came down to it, the dumpling they wanted a second plate of was Sohui's.

I have to say that I loved this Throwdown. I have eaten Asian dumplings since I was a kid but, before this, had never even attempted to make them. I learned a lot and had the opportunity to compete against an extremely talented, extremely nice cook. And that is what *Throwdown!* is all about.

Bobby Flay's
Duck and Hoisin Dumplings
MAKES 48 DUMPLINGS

Dough

4 cups all-purpose flour, plus extra for dusting

¼ teaspoon kosher salt

Filling

2 skin-on, boneless duck breasts and legs
   (about 1½ pounds total), ground

1 cup finely chopped savoy cabbage

2 green onions (green parts only), thinly sliced

2 tablespoons chopped fresh cilantro leaves

2 tablespoons chopped fresh chives

1 large egg, lightly beaten

2 tablespoons Asian chili paste

2 tablespoons hoisin sauce

1 teaspoon ground ginger

1 teaspoon Chinese five-spice powder

1 teaspoon ground allspice

2 tablespoons cornstarch

Kosher salt and freshly ground black pepper

Canola oil

Spicy Dipping Sauce (recipe follows)

Lime slices, for garnish

1. *To make the dough,* mix the flour, salt, and 2 cups hot water in a large bowl until the dough just comes together. Turn it out onto a lightly floured surface and knead until smooth. The dough should be soft and pliable, not sticky. Form into a ball, cover with a clean cloth, and let rest at room temperature for 15 minutes.

2. *To make the filling,* gently mix the duck, cabbage, green onions, cilantro, chives, egg, chili paste, hoisin, ginger, five-spice powder, allspice, and cornstarch in a large bowl; season with salt and pepper. To check for seasoning, fry a bit of the mixture in some hot oil until just cooked through; taste, and adjust the seasoning as necessary.

3. Lightly flour a work surface and roll the dough, or pieces of it, about ⅛ inch thick (too thin and the dough will tear as you fill the dumplings). Cut out rounds with a 3-inch round cutter. Cover the dough with a towel or piece of plastic wrap as you work. Have a small bowl of water next to you.

4. Spoon a scant tablespoon of the filling onto the middle of a dough round, and press it so that it spreads slightly toward the side edges of the dough. Using your fingertip or a small pastry brush, wet the edge of the dough. Fold the dough up around the filling so that the filling sits on the work surface—that's the bottom of your dumpling—and the seam is between your fingers. Pleat the dough that is facing you about six times, pressing it against the back to seal—only the front of the dumpling should be pleated. The corners of the dumpling should curl slightly away from you, toward the unpleated side.

5. Heat 2 tablespoons canola oil in a 10-inch skillet over high heat until it begins to shimmer. Add the dumplings (in batches of about 8) in concentric circles. They should be touching. Cook until the bottoms are golden brown, 2 to 3 minutes (reduce the heat if they are browning too quickly). Add enough water to reach about a quarter of the way up the sides of the dumplings. Be careful; it will spatter. Cover the skillet, adjust the heat so that the water is simmering, and cook for about 5 minutes. Uncover the skillet, and if there is water left, let it cook off. Check the dumpling bottoms—if they need to brown a bit more, let them, adding a bit more oil if necessary.

6. Serve the dumplings immediately, with the dipping sauce and lime slices.

Spicy Dipping Sauce

1 cup Asian black vinegar

¼ cup rice vinegar

2 tablespoons hoisin sauce

2 tablespoons fresh lime juice

1 tablespoon Asian chili paste

2 tablespoons chopped fresh cilantro leaves

2 tablespoons chopped fresh mint leaves

1 tablespoon chopped fresh Thai basil leaves

½ habanero pepper, minced

Whisk all the ingredients together in a bowl.

WINNER!

Sohui Kim's
Pork and Chive Dumplings
MAKES 70 DUMPLINGS

2 tablespoons canola oil, plus more for frying

1 large onion, finely diced

3 tablespoons minced garlic

2 tablespoons minced fresh ginger

1 cup chopped garlic chives or Chinese chives

Kosher salt and freshly ground black pepper

1½ pounds ground pork

1 (8-ounce) package firm tofu, cut into 1-inch squares

3 tablespoons hoisin sauce

70 dumpling wrappers (from one 16-ounce package), such as Twin Marquis Hong Kong style (available in Asian food stores)

1 egg, beaten

Dipping Sauce (recipe follows)

1. Heat the oil in a large sauté pan over medium heat. Add the onion, garlic, ginger, and garlic chives and cook for 8 minutes. Season with salt and pepper and let cool.

2. In a large bowl, combine the pork, tofu, and hoisin sauce with the chive mixture. Test-fry a small portion of the pork mixture and adjust the seasoning if needed.

3. Holding a dumpling wrapper flour side down, place a tablespoon of the pork mixture onto the middle of the wrapper. Dip your index finger into the beaten egg and rub it over half of the outer edge of the dumpling. Fold the dumpling in half, crimping it in the middle and sealing along the egg-moistened edge, taking care not to leave any air pockets.

4. Heat a thin film of canola oil in a medium skillet over medium heat. Working in batches, fry the dumplings until crisp and brown on both sides, 3 to 4 minutes per side. Serve with the Dipping Sauce.

Dipping Sauce

¼ cup soy sauce, preferably dark

¼ cup rice vinegar

1 tablespoon light brown sugar

1 whole star anise

1 teaspoon sesame seeds

Combine the soy sauce, rice vinegar, brown sugar, and star anise in a small bowl. Scatter the sesame seeds over the top.

PULLED PORK

ON THIS EPISODE OF THROWDOWN!...

I was down in the woods of Virginia to take on decorated pitmaster Lee Ann Whippen and her pulled pork sandwich.  Lee Ann Whippen worked in hotel catering for fifteen years while perfecting her killer dry rub on the state barbecue championship circuit, including earning an almost unheard-of perfect 180 score in competition. She won the Georgia State Championship in 1996, and her pork took first place in the prestigious American Royal National Championship. Lee Ann had enough wins under her belt by 2002 to leave hotels behind and start up her own catering and competition team called Wood Chick's BBQ, which was soon followed by a restaurant. ○ Lee Ann has a few rules for her fantastic pulled pork. First, she treats her bone-in pork butt (FYI, the "butt" actually comes from the shoulder of the pig) to a dry rub before smoking it over a combination of fruit and hickory woods that have been aged for a minimum of 3 months. Her flavorful, slightly spicy sauce keeps the pork moist. This award-winning combination has won Lee Ann a spot stoking the fires under her own Food Network special called "Grillin' Gals." Or so she thinks.

"I was just glad I cooked the butts all night long not knowing Bobby was coming, because when he showed up they were done. I had no time to be nervous because at that point they were going to be what they were going to be . . . thank goodness smoky, flavorful, and oh soooo tender!"
—LEE ANN WHIPPEN

Name: Lee Ann Whippen
Establishment: Wood Chick's BBQ
Hometown: Chesapeake, Virginia
Website: www.woodchicksbbq.com
Phone: (757) 549-9290

Back at the test kitchen, we seasoned our bone-in butt with my Mesa Grill spice rub, which contains, among other things, chile powders, cumin, and coriander, and then gave it a quick sear on the stovetop to ensure a great crusty exterior. Since we couldn't use a smoker indoors, we braised our bone-in butt in chicken stock in a low oven for 4 hours. While it braised, I made up a fresh red cabbage slaw tossed in a spicy green onion mayonnaise–based dressing and got to work on a mustard-based sauce with rice vinegar, black pepper, and honey. The cooked pork was shredded into bite-size pieces and dressed with the mustard sauce. We piled that on a soft bun with the slaw and took a taste—perfect. All we needed was some actual smoke, which we would get at the Throwdown.

We went to Virginia the night before the Throwdown to start our pork so that by the time I busted in on Lee Ann, it had already been smoking for about 10 hours. My arrival and challenge left Lee Ann overwhelmed with emotion, but this seasoned pitmaster pulled herself together and before you knew it, her game face was back on and she was ready to go. I tried Lee Ann's sandwich and *wow*—her pork was perfectly smoked and moist, and every component, from the well-seasoned coleslaw to the sauce with its just-right amount of spice, was incredibly flavorful.

The crowd was pretty much on Lee Ann's side; her talent and expertise just can't be denied. I still wanted to win this battle, but it was all up to the judges. They ranked our entries on taste, texture, and smokiness of the meat. Lee Ann's sandwich was up first and they had nothing but praise: good taste, plenty of moisture, great texture, and lots of fantastic smoke flavor. They moved on to mine and noted its unusual spice and lots of pepper flavor. It was definitely good, but different. The judges said my sandwich was really tasty but just not spiced the way that they were used to on the barbecue circuit. They announced their winner and Lee Ann had another "blue ribbon" to add to her collection.

I would qualify myself as a barbecue enthusiast, and Lee Ann—well, she's a barbecue champion. I honestly think her pulled pork sandwich might be the best I have ever had the pleasure to eat.

Lee Ann Whippen's Wood Chick's BBQ Award-Winning Smoked Pork

Bobby Flay's
Pulled Pork with Black Pepper Vinegar Sauce
SERVES 8 TO 10

1 (5- to 6-pound) pork shoulder, excess fat trimmed

Kosher salt and freshly ground black pepper

1 cup ancho chile powder

⅓ cup sweet Spanish paprika

3 tablespoons ground dried oregano

3 tablespoons ground coriander

3 tablespoons dry mustard

1 tablespoon ground cumin

2 teaspoons chile de árbol powder

Black Pepper Vinegar Sauce (recipe follows)

1. Place the pork, fat side up, on a large rimmed baking sheet. Season on both sides with salt and pepper. Mix all the remaining ingredients together in a small bowl, and add 1 tablespoon kosher salt and 1 tablespoon black pepper. Rub this all over the pork. Cover with plastic wrap and refrigerate for at least 1 hour and up to 8 hours.
2. Following the manufacturer's instructions and using lump charcoal and ½ cup drained soaked wood chips for a smoker or 1 cup for a grill, start a fire and bring the temperature of the smoker to 225° to 250°F.
3. Set the pork on a rack in the smoker. Cover and cook, turning the pork every 45 minutes, until a meat thermometer inserted into the center of the pork registers 165°F, about 6 hours. Add more charcoal as needed to maintain the temperature and more drained wood chips to maintain the smoke level.
4. Transfer the pork to a clean rimmed baking sheet, and let stand until cool enough to handle. Then shred the meat into bite-size pieces. Mound them on a platter and drizzle with some of the Black Pepper Vinegar Sauce. Pour any accumulated juices from the baking sheet over the pork.

NOTE
Serve the pork topped with coleslaw on a hamburger bun.

Black Pepper Vinegar Sauce

½ cup rice vinegar

¼ cup Dijon mustard

1 tablespoon honey

1½ teaspoons kosher salt

1 teaspoon coarsely ground black pepper

¾ cup plus 2 tablespoons canola oil

Combine the vinegar, mustard, honey, salt, and pepper in a blender and blend until smooth. With the motor running, slowly add the oil until emulsified.

WINNER!

Lee Ann Whippen's
Wood Chick's BBQ
Award-Winning Smoked Pork
SERVES 12

1 (6- to 7-pound) bone-in Boston butt pork
 shoulder, with ¼-inch fat cap
Wood Chick's BBQ Championship BBQ Rub
 (recipe follows)
6 to 8 cups apple juice, for the roasting pan and
 for spraying
3 to 4 cups Wood Chick's Mild BBQ Sauce or
 your favorite barbecue sauce

1. The night before you roast the pork, coat it
heavily with the dry rub. Wrap in plastic wrap
or place in a plastic bag, and refrigerate
overnight.
2. Remove the pork from the refrigerator
2 hours prior to cooking.
3. Preheat the oven to 250°F.
4. Put the pork butt, fat side up, in a roasting
pan with enough apple juice to cover the
bottom of the pan. Cook in the oven until the
exterior of the pork is mahogany colored,
about 4 hours, adding more apple juice as
needed. If the exterior is drying out, spray the
pork with apple juice.
5. Carefully transfer the pork to long pieces of
double-layered heavy-duty foil. Pull up the
sides of the foil, add ½ cup apple juice to the
foil, and wrap so it's as airtight as possible.
Return to the oven and cook until the internal
temperature of the pork is 190° to 195°F, 4 to
5 hours.
6. Unwrap, let cool slightly, and pull the
pork to the desired consistency. Top with the
barbecue sauce.

Wood Chick's BBQ
Championship BBQ Rub

 1 tablespoon kosher salt
 2 tablespoons dark brown sugar
 ¼ cup chili powder
 1½ tablespoons sweet Spanish paprika
 1½ teaspoons freshly ground black pepper
 1¼ teaspoons cayenne pepper
 1 teaspoon garlic powder
 1 teaspoon taco spice
 1 teaspoon onion powder
 1 teaspoon dry mustard
 ¼ teaspoon ground cinnamon
 ¼ teaspoon freshly grated nutmeg
 ⅛ teaspoon curry powder
 ⅛ teaspoon ground coriander
 ⅛ teaspoon ground cumin
 ½ cup granulated sugar

Combine the salt and brown sugar in a food
processor or blender, and process until well
blended. Add all the remaining ingredients
except the granulated sugar, and process until
blended. Then add the granulated sugar and
process until the ingredients are evenly
distributed.

NOTE
Serve the pork topped with coleslaw on
a hamburger bun.

AREPAS

ON THIS EPISODE OF THROWDOWN!...

They were fried, they were stuffed . . . we were throwing down arepas with Venezuela natives Maribel Araujo and Aristides Barrios, the owners of New York City's shrine to arepas, the Caracas Arepa Bar. ○ Indigenous to the Andes and particularly loved in Venezuela, arepas are fluffy corn-flour cakes split open in the middle and stuffed with a variety of flavorful fillings. Like a sandwich, they should be eaten with your hands, not a fork and knife. The arepa cake is made from a mixture of corn flour, salt, and oil—simple enough, but the consistency is paramount to their success and can take years to perfect. The dough is shaped into a hand-size disk before first being griddled to create a crispy exterior and then finished in the oven for a steamy-soft middle. Venezuelans enjoy these tasty treats everywhere from the fanciest restaurants to neighborhood street stands.

"Being able to bring arepas to the big picture by the hand of Bobby has been the most amazing experience ever, not only because we won over an amazing chef, but because his humbleness only made people believe what an amazing product we have to offer. People fly in to NYC to taste the arepa that we bit Bobby with. No joke! Thanks, Bobby!"
— MARIBEL AND ARISTIDES

Names: Maribel Araujo and Aristides Barrios
Establishment: Caracas Arepa Bar
Hometown: New York, New York
Website: www.caracasarepabar.com
Phone: (212) 529-2314

Friends Maribel and Aristides came to New York from Venezuela dreaming of careers in architecture and the film industry. Dissatisfied with their prospects and nostalgic for their favorite food from home, they struck out upon a new dream, realized in 2003 with their restaurant, the Caracas Arepa Bar. Fueled by fond, delicious memories of watching their mothers and grandmothers make arepas, the women, along with their chef, Ilse Parra, poured their hearts and souls into their restaurant. You can taste it with every bite. Maribel and Aristides thought they had been selected to share their homeland's national dish with Food Network for a special called "Stuffed," for which they planned to showcase their restaurant's most popular arepa, filled with beef, beans, and plantains.

These little corn cakes may look easy to make, but we found out very quickly in the test kitchen that they are anything but. And while most arepa cake batters call for mixing the arepa flour (an instant white cornmeal) with water, we found that using milk made a more tender finished product. Knowing that Maribel and Aristides would be serving up a meat-filled version, I decided to go with seafood. I tested two different filling possibilities, the first a grilled salmon tossed in a slightly spicy mayonnaise with black olives and drizzled with an avocado crema. Stephanie, Miriam, and I decided that this combination just didn't work. The creaminess of the mayonnaise and avocado left our filling with no contrast of texture. We also tested a lobster and octopus filling tossed in a citrus–yellow pepper vinaigrette—much better!

Maribel and Aristides accepted our challenge with good humor. We had arepa makers flown in directly from Venezuela when, according to the duo, all we needed was a nonstick griddle. And my arepa-shaping technique was all wrong. They both quickly offered to give me lessons. Apparently I needed them.

Our arepas would be judged by food writer Nicole Cotroneo and chef Jorge Fortune on three criteria: texture, filling flavor, and authenticity. Even though I felt that my filling was good, I doubted my arepa could compare to their light, pillowy version. The judges loved the crispy exterior and fabulous balance of flavors of Aristides and Maribel's arepa; it was at once sweet, savory, spicy, and salty. Jorge, who was born and raised in Venezuela, said it reminded him of his childhood. Moving on, the judges noticed immediately that the shape of my arepa was smaller than usual, but both loved the flavor of my filling. They had a hard time deciding between the two—Maribel and Aristides's delicious arepa was classic and mine was a flavor explosion in the mouth. After some flip-flopping, Nicole and Jorge made the right call: the women of the Caracas Arepa Bar won. The best part: now I know how to make arepas!

Bobby Flay's Arepas with Lobster-Octopus Salad and Avocado Crema

Bobby Flay's
Arepas with Lobster-Octopus Salad and Avocado Crema

MAKES 12 AREPAS

Lobster-Octopus Salad

2 yellow bell peppers, roasted (see Notes, page 22)

2 tablespoons Dijon mustard

2 tablespoons sweet Spanish paprika

¼ teaspoon cayenne pepper

Juice of 1 lemon

⅓ cup extra virgin olive oil

Kosher salt and freshly ground black pepper

8 ounces cooked octopus, coarsely chopped

8 ounces cooked lobster meat, coarsely chopped

¼ cup chopped fresh cilantro leaves

Arepas

2½ cups whole milk

4 tablespoons (½ stick) unsalted butter, cut into pieces

1½ cups white arepa flour (precooked cornmeal)

1½ teaspoons kosher salt

½ teaspoon freshly ground black pepper

½ cup grated Cotija cheese

1 tablespoon honey

Canola oil

Avocado Crema (page 252)

1. *To make the lobster-octopus salad,* combine the bell peppers, mustard, paprika, cayenne, and lemon juice in a blender and blend until smooth. With the motor running, add the oil and blend until emulsified; season with salt and pepper.

2. Put the octopus and lobster in a bowl, add the yellow pepper vinaigrette and the cilantro, and toss to combine; season with salt and pepper. Cover and refrigerate for at least 30 minutes and up to 2 hours to allow the flavors to meld.

3. *To make the arepas,* preheat the oven to 350°F.

4. Bring the milk to a simmer in a small saucepan; then remove from the heat and stir in the butter. Combine the arepa flour, salt, pepper, and cheese in a large bowl. Add the hot milk and the honey, and stir until combined. Let the mixture stand until the milk is absorbed enough for a soft dough to form, 1 to 2 minutes; the dough will continue to stiffen.

5. Form the dough into 12 balls, each about 2 inches in diameter, and flatten them between your palms into 3-inch patties, each about ⅓ inch thick.

6. Heat 2 tablespoons oil in a large nonstick skillet over medium heat until the oil begins to shimmer. Fry 4 arepas at a time until light golden brown and just cooked through, 2 to 3 minutes per side, adding more oil as needed; transfer to a plate lined with paper towels. Transfer the arepas to a baking sheet, and bake in the oven until just heated through, about 5 minutes.

7. Slice the arepas in half crosswise, spread the Avocado Crema on the bottom layer, and top with the lobster-octopus salad. Cover with the top layer.

WINNER!

Maribel Araujo and Aristides Barrios's Pabellon Arepa
MAKES 12 LARGE AREPAS

Shredded Beef

1½ pounds eye of round

¼ cup vegetable oil

1 medium Spanish onion, finely diced

2 small red bell peppers, finely diced

6 jalapeño peppers, finely diced

6 cloves garlic, finely chopped

2 ounces Panela, or ¼ cup firmly packed light brown sugar

2 tablespoons Worcestershire sauce

1 (8-ounce) can tomato paste

4 tablespoons (½ stick) unsalted butter

Kosher salt and freshly ground black pepper

Black Beans

8 ounces dried black beans

1 medium Spanish onion, chopped

1 small red bell pepper, chopped

4 cloves garlic, chopped

1 teaspoon ground cumin

2 ounces Panela, or ¼ cup firmly packed light brown sugar

Kosher salt and freshly ground black pepper

Fried Plantains

Vegetable oil, for deep-frying

3 ripe sweet plantains

Arepas

2 tablespoons kosher salt

6 cups precooked corn flour (found in the Latin markets)

6 tablespoons canola oil, plus more for cooking the arepas

2 cups crumbled white salty cheese, such as Venezuelan Queso de Año or Mexican Cotija

1. *To cook the beef,* put it in a medium pot and add enough water to cover by 2 inches. Bring to a boil over high heat, reduce the heat to medium-low, and simmer, uncovered, until just tender, about 3 hours, adding more water if needed to cover.

(recipe continues)

2. Meanwhile, *cook the black beans:* Combine the beans with the onion, bell pepper, garlic, cumin, and Panela in a large pot and add cold water to cover by 2 inches. Bring to a boil over high heat, reduce the heat to medium, and simmer, uncovered, until tender, about 3 hours.

3. Remove the beef to a plate and let it cool slightly; reserve the cooking broth. Once it is cool enough to handle, shred the beef into bite-size pieces.

4. Heat the oil in a large sauté pan over medium-high heat until it begins to shimmer. Add the onion, red bell peppers, and jalapeños, and cook until soft, about 5 minutes. Add the garlic and cook for 1 minute. Add the Panela and cook until the vegetables become slightly caramelized, about 5 minutes. Add the Worcestershire and simmer for 5 minutes. Add the tomato paste and 2 cups of the reserved cooking broth. Bring to a simmer and cook until slightly reduced, about 7 minutes. Add the butter and cook until melted. Add the beef and cook until just warmed through. Season with salt and pepper to taste. If the mixture is a little too dry, add more of the reserved broth.

5. *To cook the plantains,* heat a scant ¼ inch of oil in a deep skillet to 375°F. Slice the plantains on the diagonal into ¼-inch-thick slices, and fry them, turning occasionally, until they are caramelized and dark brown, about 1½ minutes. Remove from the skillet and drain on a paper-towel-lined plate.

6. *To make the arepas,* preheat the oven to 375°F.

7. Combine 7½ cups lukewarm water and the salt in a large bowl and stir until the salt dissolves. Add the flour slowly, and mix with your hands until the dough comes together. Transfer the dough to a lightly floured flat surface and knead until smooth. Shape into a ball and let rest for 3 minutes.

8. Remove a small piece of dough and roll it into a ball; if the dough cracks slightly, add a little more water, continue kneading, and let rest again. Once you reach the perfect texture, add the oil and knead it into the dough for a couple of minutes until blended. Using wet hands, divide the dough into 12 equal pieces and form each piece into a ball. Form the balls into flat round cakes about 1-inch thick and 5 inches in diameter.

9. Heat about 2 tablespoons oil on a griddle or in a large frying pan over medium heat until it begins to shimmer. Fry 4 arepas at a time until golden brown on each side, about 7 minutes per side. Transfer to a baking sheet. When all of the arepas have been cooked, bake in the oven for 10 minutes.

10. Season the beans with salt and pepper. Slice the arepas in half, and stuff them with the beans, beef, plantains, and cheese.

COCONUT CAKE

ON THIS EPISODE OF THROWDOWN!...

I headed down to Charleston, South Carolina, for a twelve-layer slice of heaven. Would I be able to take down the man who makes one of my all-time favorite desserts? It was a battle of the Bobs! ○ Robert Carter thinks that he is part of a Food Network special called "Crème de la Crème," celebrating the "best of the best" of this country's food. He may be in for a surprise when I reveal the real reason for the film crews, but if Food Network *were* making that special, there is no doubt that Robert would deserve his featured role—the man has some serious talent. ○ Executive chef Robert Carter opened picturesque Charleston's Peninsula Grill in 1997, and while his robust menu has consistently wowed satisfied diners, it's his Ultimate Coconut Cake that cemented his place among the "crème de la crème." Charleston, in the heart of the Low Country, has lofty culinary traditions, and coconut, which first came to the city's port in the 1880s, has long been a staple in Charleston's kitchens; coconut cake is a dessert near and dear to the city's heart. If you're going to call yours the "ultimate," it better be! And Robert Carter does not disappoint. Combine his years of experience with his grandmother's treasured recipe—not to mention almost 3 pounds of butter, 6 cups of heavy cream, and layer upon layer of cream-cheese-enriched frosting and nutty coconut—and what you get is one decadent showstopper of a cake.

"The Throwdown was an incredible experience! Fun, exciting, rewarding, and memorable. The production staff was incredible. They were around the house for about eight hours with our two kids and our golden retriever, Halsey—that in itself was patience at its best!"
—ROBERT CARTER

Name: Robert Carter
Establishment: Peninsula Grill
Hometown: Charleston, South Carolina
Website: www.peninsulagrill.com
Phone: (843) 723-0700

Hard to imagine how I could top this man's masterpiece, but I headed off to the test kitchen to try. In my mind, the key to the perfect coconut cake is all about moisture and lots of coconut flavor. I started with a buttery white cake and brushed each layer with a coconut milk and coconut rum–enriched simple syrup. I filled those layers with a rich coconut cream, frosted the stack with—you guessed it—coconut butter-cream, and crowned it all with a blizzard of crunchy toasted coconut, and I had my cake.

Once in Charleston, I made my appearance at the "Crème de la Crème" Coconut Cake party and challenged Robert to a Throwdown. We submitted our desserts to a blind tasting by our two expert judges, renowned southern cookbook author Nathalie Dupree and Kevin Jordan, owner of Charleston's Kennedy's Market & Bakery. We would see who took the cake when they reached their verdict.

Nathalie loved the coconut flavor of my cake, praising the toasted coconut and its moist consistency. She found it to have a clean taste, which allowed you to keep going back for another bite. Kevin gave kudos to Robert for his cake's impressive height, saying its tall layers were perfect for a southern layer cake. He also noted the cake's intense sweetness. Both Kevin and Nathalie said that both cakes were great and they would happily take either one—or both!—home, but as for a winner . . . it was mine.

As much as I loved our version, Robert's cake is still my favorite layer cake of all time. I strongly urge anyone planning a trip to Charleston to stop in at the Peninsula Grill to try it. If that's not an option, order one online and have it shipped to your home for your next special occasion. You won't be disappointed.

WINNER!

Bobby Flay's
Toasted Coconut Cake with Coconut Filling and Coconut Buttercream

SERVES 8

Cake

2 tablespoons butter, at room temperature, for the pans

1 cup whole milk, at room temperature

6 large egg whites, at room temperature

1 vanilla bean, split lengthwise, seeds scraped out and reserved

½ teaspoon pure vanilla extract

2¼ cups cake flour, plus more for the pans

1¾ cups granulated sugar

1 tablespoon plus 1 teaspoon baking powder

1 teaspoon fine salt

12 tablespoons (1½ sticks) unsalted butter, cut into 12 pieces, slightly cold

Coconut Filling

¾ cup Coconut Custard (recipe follows), cold

¾ cup heavy cream, cold

Coconut Buttercream

1½ cups (3 sticks) unsalted butter, at room temperature

⅓ cup confectioners' sugar

¾ cup Coconut Custard (recipe follows), cold

Pinch of fine salt

Coconut Simple Syrup (recipe follows)

2 cups sweetened flaked coconut, lightly toasted

1. *To make the cake,* preheat the oven to 350°F. Butter and flour two 9 × 2-inch round cake pans and line the bottoms with parchment paper.

2. Whisk together the milk, egg whites, vanilla seeds, and vanilla extract in a medium bowl.

3. In the bowl of a mixer fitted with the paddle attachment, mix together the flour, sugar, baking powder, and salt. With the mixer running at low speed, add the butter, one piece at a time, and continue beating until the mixture resembles moist crumbs. Add all but ½ cup of the milk mixture and beat on medium speed until pale and fluffy, about 1½ minutes. With the mixer on low speed, add the remaining ½ cup milk mixture. Increase the speed to medium and beat for 30 seconds more. Scrape the sides of the bowl and mix for 20 seconds longer. Divide the batter evenly between the cake pans and smooth the tops with a rubber spatula.

4. Bake until a toothpick inserted into the center comes out with a few crumbs attached, 22 to 24 minutes. Cool in the pans on a baking rack for 10 minutes. Then run a small knife around the sides of the pans and invert the cakes onto the baking rack. Remove the parchment paper and let cool completely, about 45 minutes.

5. *To make the coconut filling,* combine the custard and cream in a bowl and whip until soft peaks form.

6. *To make the coconut buttercream,* beat the butter and confectioners' sugar in a stand mixer fitted with the paddle attachment until light and fluffy, about 4 minutes. Add the coconut custard and salt, and beat until smooth.

(recipe continues)

7. *To assemble the cake,* use a long serrated knife to slice each cake horizontally into 2 layers. Reserve one of the flat bottom layers for the top of the cake. Place another one of the layers on a cardboard round, cut side up, and brush with some of the coconut simple syrup. Spoon one-third of the coconut filling onto the cake, and using a small offset metal spatula, spread it into an even layer, leaving a ½-inch border around the edge of the cake. Repeat with 2 more layers. Brush the cut side of the reserved cake layer with the remaining syrup. Place the layer, cut side down, on top of the cake. Frost the sides and top of the cake with the buttercream. Pat the toasted coconut onto the sides of the cake and sprinkle some on the top.

Coconut Custard

¾ cup whole milk

¾ cup unsweetened coconut milk

½ vanilla bean, seeds scraped out, bean and
     seeds reserved

4 large egg yolks

⅓ cup sugar

3 tablespoons cornstarch

2 teaspoons Malibu coconut rum

½ teaspoon pure vanilla extract

1. Combine the milk, coconut milk, and vanilla bean and seeds in a medium nonreactive saucepan and bring to a simmer over low heat.
2. Whisk the egg yolks, sugar, and cornstarch together in a large bowl. Slowly whisk the warm milk into the egg mixture. Then return the mixture to the pan, set it over medium heat, and bring to a boil. Cook, whisking constantly, until thickened. Scrape the mixture into a bowl, remove the vanilla bean, and whisk in the rum and vanilla extract. Let cool to room temperature; then cover with plastic wrap and refrigerate until cold, at least 2 hours.

Coconut Simple Syrup

1 tablespoon sugar

¾ cup sweetened flaked coconut

1. Combine 1½ cups water and the sugar in a saucepan, and bring to a boil. Stir in the coconut, remove from the heat, and let sit for at least 30 minutes and up to 4 hours.
2. Strain the liquid into a clean saucepan. Bring to a boil and cook until the mixture is slightly reduced, about 5 minutes. Let cool.

Robert Carter's
Peninsula Grill Coconut Cake
SERVES 12 TO 16

Filling

5 cups heavy cream

3 cups granulated sugar

2 cups (4 sticks) unsalted butter

¼ cup cornstarch

1 teaspoon pure vanilla extract

9 cups sweetened flaked coconut

Cake

Cooking spray

2 cups (4 sticks) unsalted butter, at room
    temperature

3 cups granulated sugar

6 large eggs

4½ cups all-purpose flour

1½ tablespoons baking powder

½ teaspoon fine salt

1½ cups heavy cream

1½ tablespoons pure vanilla extract

1 teaspoon coconut extract

To Assemble

Simple Syrup (recipe follows)

Frosting

1 cup (2 sticks) unsalted butter, at room
    temperature

1 (8-ounce) package cream cheese, at room
    temperature

1 vanilla bean, split lengthwise, seeds scraped
    out and reserved, or 2 tablespoons pure
    vanilla extract

5 cups confectioners' sugar

2 cups sweetened flaked coconut, toasted

1. *To make the filling,* combine the cream, sugar, and butter in a medium saucepan and bring to a boil over high heat. Mix the cornstarch, vanilla, and 1 tablespoon water together in a small bowl, and slowly add this to the boiling cream mixture, stirring constantly. Bring to a boil and cook, stirring constantly, for 1 minute. Remove from the heat and add the coconut. Cover and refrigerate for at least 6 and up to 12 hours.

2. *To make the cake,* preheat the oven to 325°F. Spray three 10-inch cake pans with cooking spray and line the bottoms with parchment paper.

3. Beat the butter and sugar together in the bowl of an electric mixer fitted with the paddle attachment. Add the eggs, one at a time, scraping down the sides of the bowl, and mix until creamy.

4. Sift the flour, baking powder, and salt together into a separate bowl.

5. Mix the cream, vanilla, and coconut extract together in a third bowl. Alternate adding the dry ingredients and wet ingredients to the batter in three additions, starting and ending with the dry.

6. Divide the batter evenly among the 3 pans and bake until a toothpick inserted into the centers comes out clean, 40 to 45 minutes. Remove to a baking rack and let cool for 10 minutes in the pans. Then remove from the pans, remove the parchment, and let cool completely, about 2 hours.

7. In an electric mixer fitted with the paddle attachment, whip the filling just until soft and creamy.

8. *To assemble,* trim off the domed top of each cake. Brush the top of one layer with simple syrup. Spread 1½ cups of the filling evenly on top. Continue with the remaining 2 cake layers, stacking them on top of each other and brushing each layer with simple syrup before spreading with filling. Refrigerate the cake until firm to the touch, about 4 hours.

9. *To make the frosting,* combine the butter and cream cheese in the bowl of a mixer fitted with the paddle attachment and beat on high speed until light and fluffy, scraping the sides and bottom of the bowl occasionally, about 5 minutes. Add the vanilla seeds and beat for 30 seconds. Slowly add the confectioners' sugar on low speed. Then raise the speed to high and beat until smooth and fluffy, about 2 minutes.

10. Ice the top and sides of the cake with the frosting, and pat the toasted coconut around the outside. Chill for at least 2 hours before slicing.

Simple Syrup

¾ cup sugar

Combine ¾ cup water and the sugar in a small saucepan over high heat, and bring to a boil. Cook until the sugar has dissolved, about 2 minutes. Transfer to a bowl and let cool.

SEAFOOD GUMBO

ON THIS EPISODE OF THROWDOWN!...

The pot is talking and it's saying "seafood gumbo." Poppy Tooker is the Food Diva of New Orleans cuisine, complete with a deep knowledge of Creole cooking and the kitchen chops to back it up.

○ Poppy is passionate about three things: cooking, teaching, and New Orleans. She has found a way to satisfy all three, leading critically acclaimed cooking classes starring authentic New Orleans cuisine. The city's vast culinary tradition was in jeopardy after Hurricane Katrina, and Poppy, along with her fellow food friends, worked tirelessly to get it up on its feet again. In New Orleans, known for any number of specialties from beignets to jambalaya, étouffé to muffulettas, there is one dish that reigns supreme: gumbo. As Poppy thought that she had been tapped to host a culinary tour of New Orleans for Food Network, she was going to show just how things are done at her Good Friday Gumbo Party.

"I was extremely grateful to Bobby and Food Network for the positive light the show shed on my beloved New Orleans and our recovery efforts following Hurricane Katrina. It aired originally at a time when I think people still thought we were not a good vacation destination due to the damages from the storm and resulting flood. It worked as a virtual travelogue, encouraging and inviting visitors to come to our city."

—POPPY TOOKER

Name: Poppy Tooker
Hometown: New Orleans, Louisiana
Website: www.poppytooker.com

The most important element to a successful gumbo is the roux; the flour and butter are cooked to a rich, dark chocolate color. This is the foundation of the gumbo's flavor, and it works as a thickening agent while adding great color. Seafood, of course, is a must; shrimp, scallops, and oysters are most often used. After that, there's the andouille sausage and okra. In my research, I learned that Creole gumbo contains seafood and Cajun gumbo is made with andouille sausage and chicken.

It was off to the test kitchen to try to perfect my own gumbo recipe. I began my roux with flour and unsalted butter (I learned at the competition that Poppy makes hers with oil). I opted for shrimp, scallops, and lump crabmeat, an atypical choice. Now for that okra . . . I decided to cut the okra into small rounds, which I dredged in cornmeal and fried in canola oil. This reduces the slime factor that is often associated with okra, and the crispy wheels were a nice contrast to the silky-smooth broth. Gumbo is typically served over plain white rice, but I went with crispy okra in its place. (You know my record with rice on *Throwdown!* . . . 0-3.)

We arrived in Louisiana with an 0-2 record, having lost both the muffuletta and jambalaya battles, but we would not be deterred. Honestly, I felt pretty good about this dish. I challenged Poppy and she laughed—literally—in my face before accepting. That's okay; I'd been laughed at before.

I had made a few changes to my gumbo since the test kitchen. Since this was a Good Friday party, after all, I decided to omit the sausage so that everyone in the crowd would be able to partake. My lump crabmeat (from Maryland, no less) got some groans from Poppy and her crew, but I was able to get my hands on some fresh Gulf shrimp and beautiful local oysters, which I added to the pot instead of the scallops, which Stephanie and Miriam had not liked. The legendary New Orleans chef Leah Chase lent me a few words of wisdom and I was starting to feel good about my chances.

Local food writers Dale Curry and Jay Forman stepped up to the judges' table, grading our dishes on their taste, texture, and presentation. They noticed the coloring of the roux in Poppy's gumbo right off the bat. They loved her gumbo's thick texture but felt it needed a touch more seasoning. Moving on to my dish, they loved the contemporary touches of oysters and fried okra. Dale and Jay agreed that both were delicious, well-executed dishes, but they went for Poppy's more traditional New Orleans–style gumbo.

I'll hand it to her; Poppy's gumbo was lovely, the color was incredible, and even though her roux was extremely dark and concentrated, you could still taste the shrimp stock and seafood. It was perfect.

Bobby Flay's Shellfish Gumbo

SERVES 6 TO 8

8 tablespoons (1 stick) unsalted butter

½ cup all-purpose flour

2 celery stalks, finely diced

2 carrots, finely diced

1 large Spanish onion, finely diced

1 red bell pepper, finely diced

3 cloves garlic, finely chopped

4 cups Shrimp Stock (recipe follows), or more
if needed, hot

2 tablespoons honey

Kosher salt and freshly ground black pepper

4 tablespoons canola oil, plus more for deep-
frying the okra

1½ cups yellow cornmeal

8 ounces okra, cut into ¼-inch-thick rounds

1 pound large (21- to 24-count) shrimp, peeled
and deveined, tails left on

18 shucked oysters

6 ounces jumbo lump crabmeat

¼ cup coarsely chopped fresh flat-leaf parsley
leaves

3 green onions (green and pale green parts),
thinly sliced

1. Melt the butter in a large Dutch oven over medium heat. Gradually whisk in the flour until smooth. Cook the roux, stirring occasionally with a wooden spoon, until it's a light caramel color, 5 to 7 minutes. Then stir in all the vegetables and the garlic, and cook until the mixture begins to turn a deep chocolate color, about 5 minutes.

2. Whisk the 4 cups hot stock into the roux mixture, and bring to a boil. Then reduce the heat to low and simmer for about 20 minutes. Add more stock if the mixture is too thick. Season with the honey and salt and pepper to taste.

3. Meanwhile, heat 2 inches of canola oil in a deep sauté pan over medium-high heat until it begins to shimmer. Put the cornmeal in a shallow baking dish and season with salt and

pepper. Season the okra with salt and pepper, and toss it in the cornmeal. Fry the okra, in batches, in the hot oil until golden brown, 2 minutes. Remove with a slotted spoon to a paper-towel-lined baking sheet and season with salt.

4. Heat 2 tablespoons of the oil in a large sauté pan over high heat until almost smoking. Season the shrimp with salt and pepper. Add half of the shrimp to the pan and cook until just pink on both sides, about 2 minutes. Set aside on a plate. Repeat with the remaining 2 tablespoons oil and shrimp.

5. Add the shrimp, oysters, and crabmeat to the sauce and simmer until the oysters are plump and cooked through, about 1 minute. Divide the seafood among 6 to 8 shallow bowls, ladle in some of the sauce, and garnish with the fried okra, chopped parsley, and green onions.

Shrimp Stock

2 tablespoons canola oil

4 cups raw shrimp shells and tails

1 medium onion, coarsely chopped

1 small carrot, coarsely chopped

½ medium celery stalk, coarsely chopped

1 cup dry white wine

1 medium tomato, chopped, or ½ cup chopped
canned plum tomatoes

1 bay leaf

8 black peppercorns

Heat the oil in a large saucepan over high heat until almost smoking. Add the shrimp shells and tails, onion, carrot, and celery, and sauté, stirring, for 5 minutes. Add the wine and boil until reduced by half. Add 8 cups cold water, the tomato, bay leaf, and peppercorns. Reduce the heat to medium, cover partially, and simmer for 40 minutes. Strain the stock through cheesecloth or a fine-mesh strainer into a bowl.

WINNER!

Poppy Tooker's Seafood Gumbo

SERVES 10 TO 12

4 pounds medium shrimp, peeled, shells and
   tails reserved

1 onion, chopped, skin and trimmings reserved

1 cup plus 3 tablespoons vegetable oil

2 pounds okra, sliced ¼ inch thick

1½ cups all-purpose flour

1 green bell pepper, cut into medium dice

3 celery stalks, cut into medium dice

4 gumbo crabs (see Sources, page 269),
   cleaned, halved if small, quartered if large

1 (14½-ounce) can crushed tomatoes

2 teaspoons dried thyme

1 bay leaf

1 clove garlic, minced

Kosher salt and freshly ground black pepper

1 bunch green onions (white and green parts),
   sliced about ¼ inch thick

Cooked white rice, hot, for serving

1. Put the shrimp shells and tails in a saucepan. Add the onion skin and trimmings and 12 cups cold water. Boil over high heat for 10 minutes. Strain and reserve. You will need about 8 cups stock.

2. Heat the 3 tablespoons oil in a large skillet over medium-high heat. Add the okra and fry until very lightly browned, about 2 minutes. Drain on a plate lined with paper towels.

3. Heat a large saucepan over medium heat and add the remaining 1 cup oil. Add the flour and cook, stirring constantly, until the color of milk chocolate, 6 to 8 minutes. Add the chopped onion and cook, stirring, until the roux darkens to a bittersweet-chocolate brown, 6 to 8 minutes. Add the bell pepper and celery and cook, stirring, for 5 minutes.

4. Stir in the 8 cups shrimp stock. Then add the fried okra, gumbo crabs, tomatoes, thyme, bay leaf, garlic, and salt and pepper to taste. Simmer for 45 minutes.

5. Add the shrimp and green onions, and simmer until the shrimp are just cooked through, 8 to 10 minutes. Serve on top of cooked rice.

PAELLA

ON THIS EPISODE OF THROWDOWN!...

I went cruising down California's Highway 1 in search of paella and the pied piper of this saffron-scented dish, Gerard Nebesky. ○ The "Paella Man" of California's Sonoma County, Gerard first began making paella after eating it on a backcountry ski trip in Spain. He brought his newfound passion for the dish home with him to California and started his catering company, Gerard's Paella, with it as the starring dish. His paellas range from those with meat and/or seafood to a vegetarian version, but he has one firm rule for all paella: no stirring! Gerard is so dedicated to his paella that he dives into the Pacific Ocean to collect the freshest possible seafood. I assure you, I wouldn't be doing that! ○ I have been making paella for many years, and it was the bestselling dish at my restaurant Bolo, so I had a few tricks up my sleeve.

Saffron is paella's most important ingredient; it's expensive, but you only need a little bit. A paella pan is also key; it has a nice thick bottom with lots of surface area (and it also happens to look cool).

○ You can't have paella without rice. Short or medium grains are best for absorbing a lot of the broth and making the dish creamy and moist.

Name: Gerard Nebesky
Hometown: Occidental, California
Website: www.gerardspaella.com
Phone: (707) 874-2711

Bone-in, skin-on chicken adds lots of flavor and texture, and then there's the fun part: deciding which seafood to throw in. For this Throwdown, I planned on using shrimp, lobster, squid, clams, and mussels. I had a couple of other secret ingredients in mind, including chorizo for its smoky flavor and a lemon aioli to add sheen and give the dish a burst of citrus intensity. In the test kitchen, I made enough to feed about six people, but when we hit the Throwdown, I'd be serving sixty! That would require some skill.

The Paella Man was engrossed in teaching his hungry class at The Cannery in San Francisco and had no idea that I was headed his way with a question to ask. Gerard was totally taken off guard when I arrived with my challenge, but he agreed with gusto. As we set up, he kept motoring on, adding a few surprising ingredients to his paella: chickpeas and Meyer lemons. I love both and only wished I had thought of using them first!

We both spent the afternoon assembling our paellas, and now it was time to taste. Gerard's rice and seafood were perfectly cooked, and I loved the spices—saffron and smoked paprika—that perfumed his dish. He in turn loved the smoky, slightly spicy flavor of mine. We fed the crowd and their opinions seemed knotted up, so we let our well-qualified judges untangle a winner.

David Olivella, Barcelona-born chef and owner of San Francisco's Spanish bistro B44, and Andy Booth, owner of The Spanish Table, a retail store that specializes in all things Spanish, assessed the overall flavor, the texture of the rice, and the balance of flavors in our paellas. Tasting mine, they commented on its spicy heat right away. They thought its flavors were well balanced, but a bit on the spicy side. Gerard's rice was perfectly cooked, and while Daniel found the all-important crust on the bottom to be a little burnt, Andy thought it was fine. And so the judges declared Gerard the paella Throwdown winner.

I think we both had really beautiful paellas, and I know Gerard was right-on with his flavorings and textures. It was a great day to be in beautiful San Francisco, eating paella and working side by side with a true master of the art of paella-making.

Bobby Flay's
Shellfish and Chicken Paella with Chorizo and Green Peas
SERVES 8

9¾ cups homemade chicken stock (see page 220) or canned low-sodium chicken broth

9 tablespoons olive oil

2 tablespoons unsalted butter

1 large Spanish onion, diced

2 cups short-grain rice

Large pinch of saffron threads

4 plum tomatoes, halved lengthwise

1 tablespoon honey

Kosher salt and freshly ground black pepper

2 (2½-pound) chickens, each cut into 8 pieces

2 (1½-pound) live lobsters

8 ounces dried chorizo, cut into ½-inch-thick slices

24 mussels, debearded and scrubbed

24 littleneck clams, scrubbed

8 large shrimp, peeled and deveined

4 baby squid, cleaned and sliced into rings

1 cup shelled fresh peas

½ cup Lemon Aioli (recipe follows)

½ cup chopped fresh flat-leaf parsley leaves

1. Preheat the oven to 375°F. Bring 7¾ cups of the stock to a simmer in a saucepan.
2. Meanwhile, heat 2 tablespoons of the olive oil and the butter in a large saucepan over medium-high heat. Add the onion and cook until soft, 5 minutes. Add the rice and stir to coat.
3. Add the saffron to the simmering stock and cook for 1 minute. Then add the stock to the rice and bring to a boil. Reduce the heat to low, cover the pan, and simmer until the liquid has been absorbed and the rice is tender, 15 to 18 minutes. Uncover and fluff with a fork.

4. Put the tomatoes in a small baking dish, and drizzle with the honey and 2 tablespoons of the olive oil. Season with salt and pepper, and roast in the oven until soft, about 30 minutes. Set aside.

5. Raise the oven temperature to 450°F.

6. Heat 3 tablespoons of the olive oil in a large ovenproof skillet until almost smoking. Season the chicken pieces with salt and pepper, place in the skillet (in batches if necessary), and brown all sides. Pour off the fat, and transfer the skillet to the oven. Roast until cooked through, 25 to 30 minutes. Let rest for 15 minutes.

7. Bring a large pot of salted water to a boil. Add the lobsters and cover the pot. Return to a boil, reduce the heat, and simmer until cooked through, 12 to 15 minutes. Let cool slightly, then shell the lobsters. Keep the claws whole; coarsely chop the tail meat.

8. Cook the chorizo in a medium sauté pan over medium-high heat until browned on both sides, 6 minutes. Remove the chorizo to a plate lined with paper towels.

9. Combine the mussels and clams in a pot, add 1 cup water, cover the pot, and cook over high heat until they open, 3 to 4 minutes. Discard any that do not open.

10. Heat the remaining 2 tablespoons olive oil in a large sauté pan or paella pan until almost smoking. Season the shrimp with salt and pepper and sauté for 1 minute. Season the squid with salt and pepper and add to the pan. Cook until just cooked through, 2 to 3 minutes. Add the rice, remaining 2 cups stock, the peas, tomatoes, chicken, lobster meat, and chorizo, and stir to combine. Add the mussels and clams.

11. Fold in the Lemon Aioli and parsley, and mix until combined; season with salt and pepper to taste. Serve immediately.

Lemon Aioli

4 cloves garlic

½ teaspoon kosher salt, or more if needed

2 large egg yolks

¼ cup fresh lemon juice

1 tablespoon chopped lemon zest

¾ cup olive oil

Freshly ground white pepper

Combine the garlic, salt, egg yolks, lemon juice, and zest in a food processor or blender, and process until smooth. Slowly add the oil, drop by drop at first, processing until thickened. Season with salt and white pepper to taste. Refrigerate until ready to use.

WINNER!

Gerard Nebesky's
Paella
SERVES 6 TO 9

⅓ cup olive oil, plus more for serving

1 red bell pepper, cut into ½-inch-wide strips

1 nora or cascabel chile

Kosher salt

6 bone-in, skin-on chicken thighs

8 cloves garlic

1 large onion, diced

1 (15-ounce) can diced tomatoes, with juices

4 cups homemade chicken stock (see page 220) or canned low-sodium chicken broth

1 tablespoon smoked sweet Spanish paprika

Pinch of saffron threads

6 littleneck clams

2 cups medium-grain rice

6 jumbo shrimp, preferably with heads on

6 mussels

8 ounces green beans, cut into 2-inch pieces (about 2 cups)

½ cup canned chickpeas, drained, liquid reserved

8 ounces rockfish fillets, or other firm-fleshed white fish, cut into 2-inch chunks

2 Meyer lemons, cut into wedges

¼ cup chopped fresh flat-leaf parsley leaves

1. Heat a 12-inch heavy-bottomed skillet over medium-high heat, or heat a paella pan on a grill over medium-high heat. Add the olive oil, red bell pepper, and nora chile and sauté until lightly browned, about 3 minutes. Season with salt and scrape out onto a plate.

2. Season the chicken thighs all over with salt. Put them in the skillet, skin side down, and brown thoroughly on both sides, about 8 minutes. Transfer to a plate.

3. Reduce the heat under the skillet to medium and add the garlic cloves and onion; season with salt. Cook until the onion is translucent, about 12 minutes. Add the diced tomatoes and cook until syrupy, 10 minutes. Add the chicken stock, raise the heat to medium-high, and bring to a boil. Crush the paprika, saffron, and 1 teaspoon salt with a mortar and pestle, and stir into the sauce.

4. Add the clams, cover, and remove them as they open, 5 to 10 minutes; set the clams aside. (Discard any that do not open.)

5. Return the chicken to the pan and simmer for 10 minutes. Scatter the rice evenly in the pan, turning the chicken to let the rice fall to the bottom of the pan, but do not stir! Nestle the shrimp, mussels, green beans, and chickpeas into the liquid. Adjust the heat to maintain a brisk simmer.

6. Turn the shrimp over to cook them through. Add the bell pepper mixture. Cook until all of the liquid has been absorbed and the rice is caramelized on the bottom of the pan, 20 to 25 minutes. About 5 minutes before the rice is fully cooked, add the fish to the pan along with the cooked clams, lemon wedges, and parsley. If you need more liquid, add the reserved chickpea liquid.

7. Let stand for 5 minutes. Then drizzle with olive oil, and serve.

CHILES RELLENOS

ON THIS EPISODE OF THROWDOWN!...

I was stuffed with excitement for chiles rellenos, which I absolutely love. Ramiro Arvizu and Jaime Martin Del Campo are the kings of Los Angeles's authentic Mexican food, and the jewel in their crown is their roasted and stuffed chiles. ○ Co-chefs and co-owners Ramiro and Jaime opened their L.A.-area restaurant La Casita Mexicana with a mission to preserve and share the culinary traditions of their ancestors. Ramiro and Jaime left their jobs in the airline industry in 1999 because both keenly missed the food their mothers and grandmothers made back in Jalisco, Mexico. Though there are plenty of Mexican restaurants in southern California, none had the authentic taste of home—the carne asada, enchiladas, flautas, and most important, the mole. They opened La Casita, ten miles south of Los Angeles, to curb that craving, and their passion for real Mexican food has satisfied their strong roster of customers ever since. One of the menu's perennial standouts is chiles rellenos, made from Ramiro's grandmother's recipe.

Names: Ramiro Arvizu and Jaime Martin Del Campo
Establishment: La Casita Mexicana
Hometown: Bell, California
Website: www.casitamex.com
Phone: (323) 773-1898

Versions of chiles rellenos differ from house-hold to household in Mexico. One of Ramiro and Jaime's favorite ingredients to use in their poblano filling is *nopales* (Spanish for "cactus"), a staple in Mexican cuisine, which they pair with mushrooms, onions, garlic, and the "skunk plant," the herb epazote. Ramiro and Jaime have gifted their version to L.A. and were ready to share it with Food Network's viewers in the special "Home Cooking."

Not wanting to show up empty-handed, I made my way to the test kitchen to work on my version. The chile is the most important ingredient, and like Jaime and Ramiro, I use poblanos. I love their flavor, with its fresh pepper background and good amount of heat; its presence is undeniable without burning your mouth out. (My competitors have a tip for judging a chile's level of heat: If its stem is straight, it won't be spicy. If its stem is curved . . . watch out!) My filling has a Spanish flair and comprises roasted eggplant and Man-chego cheese—sort of like eggplant Parmesan in a chile relleno. (Don't laugh—it works!) Once roasted in the oven, the chiles are stuffed, dredged in seasoned flour, dipped in beer batter, coated in cornmeal, and fried. A balsamic glaze and a crema–roasted red pepper sauce finish the dish.

It was time to head west and challenge Jaime and Ramiro to a chiles rellenos Throwdown. While getting our dishes in order, I decided that my red pepper sauce could use a touch of heat; Jaime and Ramiro came to my aid and let me borrow some chipotle. Over in my "kitchen," they immediately saw the difference between our chiles rellenos as I mixed up my batter. Theirs aren't battered or fried. I have to say that I loved that they use cactus; it's an underutilized ingredient in America and absolutely delicious!

We fed the hungry crowd, and as usual, the audience's allegiance was split. They loved the traditional flavor of Jaime and Ramiro's dish, yet appreciated the creativity and crispy texture of mine. The judges were called to the table. They were making their decision based on our dishes' taste, texture, and presentation. They loved the creamy filling and the careful balance of sweet and spicy in my chiles rellenos. Its crisp coating and beautiful presentation were also given high marks. They noticed the lack of batter on Ramiro and Jaime's chiles, considering it the lighter and healthier of the two, with a fresh, authentic taste. While the lack of cheese was a strike against Jaime and Ramiro, the judges felt that the flavors of their chiles rellenos tasted truly Mexican and so the win was theirs. These were two different takes on one outstanding dish—I may not have been the winner of this battle, but there was no losing to be had.

Bobby Flay's
Eggplant and Manchego Chiles Rellenos with Red Pepper–Balsamic Sauce
SERVES 6

3 Japanese eggplants, cut into ½-inch dice

4 cloves garlic, coarsely chopped

2 teaspoons finely chopped fresh oregano leaves, plus more for garnish

3 tablespoons olive oil

Kosher salt and freshly ground black pepper

1½ cups (6 ounces) grated Manchego cheese

¼ cup finely chopped fresh flat-leaf parsley leaves, plus whole leaves for garnish

1 (12-ounce) bottle dark beer

3 large eggs

½ cup plus 2 tablespoons all-purpose flour, plus more for dredging

6 poblano peppers, roasted and carefully peeled (see Notes, page 22)

6 (6-inch) wooden skewers, soaked in water

1½ cups white or yellow cornmeal

4 cups canola oil

Red Pepper Sauce (recipe follows)

Balsamic Reduction (recipe follows)

1. Preheat the oven to 425°F.

2. Toss the eggplant, garlic, and oregano with the olive oil on a rimmed baking sheet, and season with salt and pepper. Roast, stirring once, until light golden brown and soft, about 20 minutes. Transfer to a bowl and let cool slightly. Then fold in the cheese and chopped parsley.

3. Whisk the beer, eggs, and flour together in a medium bowl until smooth, and season with salt and pepper.

4. Make a 3-inch slit lengthwise down the center of each chile, and carefully remove the seeds using a small spoon. Divide the eggplant filling among the chiles, compressing it into the shape of the pepper (the roasted chiles are very delicate and may begin to tear but will be fine). Thread a skewer through each slit to close.

5. Scoop about a cup of flour onto a plate, and season it with salt and pepper. Scoop the cornmeal onto a plate, and season it with salt and pepper. Dredge the chiles completely in the flour and tap off any excess. Dip the chiles into the beer batter and allow the excess to drain off. Then dredge the chiles in the cornmeal and tap off any excess.

6. Heat the canola oil to 370°F in a large frying pan or shallow pot. Fry the peppers in batches, turning them, until lightly browned, about 4 minutes. Drain on paper towels.

7. Ladle the Red Pepper Sauce onto the center of 6 plates, drizzle with some of the balsamic glaze and oregano leaves, and place the chiles rellenos on top. Garnish with parsley.

Red Pepper Sauce

3 large red bell peppers, roasted and chopped
(see Notes, page 22)

6 cloves roasted garlic

3 cloves fresh garlic, chopped

1 to 2 chipotle chiles in adobo, to taste

3 tablespoons red wine vinegar

¼ cup canola oil

3 tablespoons crema, crème fraîche,
or sour cream

Kosher salt and freshly ground black pepper

Combine the red peppers, roasted and fresh
garlic, chipotle, vinegar, and oil in a blender
and blend until smooth. Transfer to a bowl,
whisk in the crema, and season with salt and
pepper.

Balsamic Reduction

3 cups balsamic vinegar

1 tablespoon honey

Kosher salt and freshly ground black pepper

Bring the vinegar to a boil in a small nonreactive saucepan and cook, stirring occasionally,
until thickened and reduced to about ¾ cup,
about 30 minutes. Stir in the honey and
season with salt and pepper.

WINNER!

Ramiro Arvizu and Jaime Martin Del Campo's
Chiles Rellenos with Cactus and Mushrooms
SERVES 4

Sauce

1 pound ripe tomatoes, coarsely chopped

2 guajillo chiles, stemmed and seeded

¼ small white onion, coarsely chopped

1 clove garlic

Leaves from 2 sprigs fresh oregano

1¼ cups homemade chicken stock (see page 220) or canned low-sodium chicken broth

Kosher salt

Chiles

4 poblano chiles

12 ounces cactus paddle, spines removed, cut into ½-inch slices

1 medium white onion, halved

2 cloves garlic

2 tablespoons corn oil

1 ripe tomato, diced

8 ounces white button mushrooms, thickly sliced

4 epazote leaves, chopped

Kosher salt

1. *To make the sauce,* combine the tomatoes, guajillo chiles, onion, garlic, oregano, and chicken stock in a saucepan, and bring to a simmer over medium-high heat. Cook until the onion and tomato are tender, about 15 minutes. Transfer to a blender and puree until smooth. Season with salt to taste. Keep warm while you make the rellenos.

2. Roast the poblano chiles over an open flame until blackened—the flesh will still be firm. Put them in a plastic bag to steam for 5 minutes; then peel. To seed the chiles, make a T-shaped cut on one side: cut across the chile at the stem end, then slit the flesh down the length of the chile to about 1 inch from the tip. Pull out the seeds and discard. Set the chiles aside.

3. Bring a large pot of salted water to a boil. Add the cactus, 1 onion half, and 1 of the garlic cloves. Cook until soft, 10 minutes. Drain, rinse the cactus under cold water, and drain well.

4. Finely dice the remaining onion half and garlic clove. Heat the oil in a medium skillet over medium-high heat. Add the onion and garlic and cook, stirring, until softened, about 4 minutes. Add the tomato and cook, stirring, for about 1 minute. Add the cactus and cook for a minute or two. Add the mushrooms and cook for about 4 minutes. Stir in the epazote and cook for another minute. Season with salt to taste.

5. Stuff the chiles with the hot cactus mixture—the mixture should be spilling out. Serve with some sauce spooned over.

FALAFEL

ON THIS EPISODE OF THROWDOWN!...

It's all about falafel. Einat Admony is New York City's queen of this crunchy fried chickpea delight. Can she keep it together when her old boss (that's me) barges in? ○ Tel Aviv native Einat and her husband, Stefan Nafzinger, opened Taïm Falafel and Smoothie Bar in picturesque Greenwich Village in 2005 with the aim of bringing the food, spices, and seasonings of the Middle East to New York. Einat spent twelve years working in some of New York's finest restaurants (one of which just happened to be my Spanish-influenced restaurant Bolo), but when it came time to open her own place, she decided to focus on a dish she'd been eating and making her whole life—falafel. Taïm, which means "delicious" in Hebrew, puts a gourmet spin on this popular street food. Einat's falafel, either served as part of a Middle Eastern salad

platter or tucked in a pita, won *New York* magazine's title of "Best Falafel"—no small feat in this falafel-loving city. ○ My mission: to find out as much as I can about falafel and give it my own gourmet kick. I enlisted chef Muhammed Rahman of Kwik Meal, one of NYC's most famous street carts, to help me out. He gave me some much needed tips: Soak the chickpeas overnight and don't cook them— check. Grind the hydrated chickpeas with spices—check. Form and deep-fry—check. It sounded easy enough, right? Wrong!

Name: Einat Admony
Establishment: Taïm Falafel and Smoothie Bar
Hometown: New York, New York
Website: www.taimfalafel.com
Phone: (212) 691-1287

I needed some serious practice if I was going to be able to pull off this Throwdown upset, so it was off to the test kitchen. We tried grinding the soaked chickpeas in a food processor, but found that a meat grinder gave them a fluffier texture. For seasonings, we went with garlic, serrano chiles, mint, cilantro, coriander, and cumin. It may be cheating, but a touch of baking powder adds to the fluffy factor. I used the same technique I use with my French fries and double-fried the falafel for extra crispiness. (Einat says this step isn't necessary and makes the falafel greasy, but I didn't find that to be the case.) Still not satisfied with the texture of my falafel, I moved on to the dips and sauces, a piquillo pepper–smoked paprika yogurt sauce in the test kitchen, and later rounded out my selections with a creamy white bean hummus, tomato-mint relish, and a feta and roasted red pepper dip.

As Einat kicked off her falafel party, I headed her way with a special hello from her former boss. She accepted my challenge with two words: "Good luck!" The bar was set high, and while confident in every other component in my platter, I asked Einat for her honest opinion about my falafel. She liked the flavor, but not the texture. The problem, she told me, was that I formed my falafel by hand, which automatically made them on the dense side. She has a special instrument to mold her falafel, making them as light as a feather. Einat's sides were equally excellent, too.

Marking us on texture, presentation, and authenticity were executive chef of the United Nations New York headquarters Darryl Schembeck, former player for the New York Knicks basketball team John Starks, and former WNBA player Kym Hampton. Einat scored with her beautiful presentation, and they loved the seasonings, allover flavor, and texture of her dish.

Mine got points for its side dishes, and while my falafel didn't have as much herb flavor as did Einat's, they did think the chickpea flavor came through more. John set his vote for Einat, but Kym and Darryl ultimately preferred mine.

I was in shock, as were Stephanie and Miriam. It's not that we didn't think our falafel was good, but we knew it wasn't great—and Einat's was. In the test kitchen, I could not figure out how to get the light and fluffy texture that Einat did.

Winning or losing is honestly not important to me on *Throwdown!*; the show is more about showcasing the great food of my competitors and sometimes stepping outside of my comfort zone to learn new dishes. But, with all due respect to our judges on this particular episode, my falafel didn't even come close to Einat's and I decided to do something that I have never done in the history of *Throwdown!*: I reversed the decision of our judges and I awarded Einat the win. Of course, *Throwdown!* rules don't permit that . . . so let's consider this one a draw.

Bobby Flay's
Falafel
MAKES ABOUT 20 BALLS

2 cups dried chickpeas

Canola oil, for deep-frying

1 tablespoon olive oil

3 cloves garlic, chopped

1 to 2 serrano chiles, to taste, chopped

2 green onions (green and pale green parts),
   thinly sliced

¼ cup finely chopped fresh parsley leaves

3 tablespoons finely chopped fresh mint leaves

3 tablespoons finely chopped fresh cilantro
   leaves

1 tablespoon fresh lemon juice

1½ teaspoons ground cumin

1½ teaspoons ground coriander

Scant 2 teaspoons baking powder

Kosher salt and freshly ground black pepper

Piquillo Pepper Yogurt Sauce (recipe follows)

1. Soak the chickpeas in cold water to cover for at least 18 hours and up to 24 hours.

2. Drain the chickpeas, transfer them to a baking sheet lined with paper towels, and set aside for 30 minutes to drain completely.

3. Heat 4 inches of canola oil in a medium saucepan over medium heat until it reaches 330°F on a deep-frying thermometer.

4. Meanwhile, heat the olive oil in a small sauté pan over medium heat. Add the garlic and serrano chiles and cook until soft, about 3 minutes.

5. Transfer the chickpeas to a meat grinder or food processor, and add the garlic mixture, green onions, parsley, mint, cilantro, lemon juice, cumin, coriander, and baking powder. Season with salt and pepper. Grind until the mixture is finely ground. Transfer to a bowl.

6. Line a baking sheet with paper towels. Using a small ice cream scoop, form the mixture into Ping-Pong-size balls and place them on a plate. Fry, in batches, in the hot oil until a pale blond color, about 45 seconds, spooning oil over the falafel constantly. Remove with a slotted spoon to the lined baking sheet.

7. Raise the heat of the oil to 350°F. In batches, return the falafel to the oil, cover the pan with a lid for 30 seconds, and then uncover and fry, spooning the oil over the falafel constantly, until a deep brown color, about 1 minute. Remove with a slotted spoon to the lined baking sheet, and immediately season with salt. Serve with the sauce.

Piquillo Pepper Yogurt Sauce

2 cups Greek yogurt

3 piquillo peppers or 2 roasted red bell peppers
   (see Notes, page 22)

2 teaspoons smoked sweet Spanish paprika

4 cloves garlic, coarsely chopped

1 teaspoon grated lemon zest

Kosher salt and freshly ground black pepper

Put the yogurt, peppers, paprika, garlic, and lemon zest in a blender and blend until smooth. Season with salt and pepper, and transfer to a small bowl. Refrigerate for at least 30 minutes, covered, to allow the flavors to meld.

NOTE
Serve the falafel balls and sauce in a pita with sliced cucumber, sliced red onion, chopped tomato, and fresh parsley leaves.

Einat Admony's Falafel

MAKES 38 BALLS

2 cups dried chickpeas

1 small onion, coarsely chopped

1 clove garlic, coarsely chopped

1 cup coarsely chopped fresh flat-leaf parsley
   leaves

¼ cup coarsely chopped fresh cilantro leaves

2 fresh mint leaves, chopped

1½ tablespoons kosher salt

1½ teaspoons freshly ground black pepper

1 teaspoon ground cumin

1 teaspoon ground coriander

Vegetable oil, for deep-frying

1. Put the chickpeas in a large bowl, add water to cover by about 2 inches, and refrigerate overnight.

2. The next morning, drain the chickpeas and toss them in a bowl with the onion and garlic. Run the mixture through the medium blade of a meat grinder. Toss the chickpea mixture with the parsley, cilantro, mint, salt, pepper, cumin, and coriander, and run through the grinder again.

3. Heat 4 inches of oil to 350°F in a large pot over medium heat. Using a tablespoon, shape the falafel mixture into balls and fry, adjusting the heat as necessary, until browned, about 3 minutes. Drain on paper towels.

NOTE

Serve the falafel in pitas with chopped cucumber and tomato, fresh parsley, and yogurt, if desired.

CHOCOLATE BREAD PUDDING

ON THIS EPISODE OF THROWDOWN!...

I was on a collision course with New York City's Dessert Truck and their creamy concoction of chocolate and bread known as chocolate bread pudding. But hold on—this wasn't supposed to be a Throwdown! The Dessert Truck was doing their own dessert special until they started gabbing on the Internet and challenged me to a Throwdown. Well, they wanted it and they got it. **O** Co-owners Jerome Chang and Chris Chen's Dessert Truck, a postal truck remade into a sweets haven on wheels, could be found every day parked on various corners throughout the borough of Manhattan. Dessert Truck is now Dessert Truck Works, a pastry shop and café on the Lower East Side of Manhattan. Jerome, who trained as a pastry chef and worked in some of the city's best restaurants, makes the truck's bestselling chocolate bread pudding with an unusual addition: he infuses the pudding's base with bacon, and the resulting dish is touched with a caramelized flavor, a hint of salt, and a pleasing smokiness.

Names: Jerome Chang and Chris Chen
Establishment: Dessert Truck Works
Hometown: New York, New York
Website: www.dt-works.net

Jerome and the Dessert Truck were supposed to be on a Food Network special called "Food Roadies," but for some reason, some NYC food bloggers thought that I would be showing up for a Throwdown and began spreading the word. As we already know, *Throwdown!* doesn't work like that. You can't challenge me—I have to find you. But I was willing to make an exception because I liked these guys and had heard that they made an amazing bread pudding. I found them taping their special in Washington Square Park and put up my challenge. It seemed my offer had them a little bit speechless. I hoped they would have more to say when we went head to head the next day . . .

You can use pretty much any kind of bread for this dessert: French, challah, brioche, croissants, even a good-quality white bread will work. The key is that the bread is stale so it holds up in the custard and doesn't turn to mush when mixed with the liquid ingredients. Even though the word "pudding" appears in its title, in my mind the dish should have a slightly chewy texture to balance the custard's smooth consistency.

I decided to do a rich chocolate-coconut bread pudding served with a creamy coconut crème anglaise as well as a sweet and tart passion fruit sauce. I went with brioche soaked in a custard of eggs, coconut milk, heavy cream, and bittersweet chocolate. I reinforced the chocolate flavor by drizzling the layers of bread with a bittersweet chocolate ganache.

Just because they knew I was coming didn't mean that I wasn't going to make an entrance. So, to make sure we were on an equal playing ground, I rented my own dessert truck and showed up in style! We immediately got to work. We had a difference of opinion when it came to whether or not to bake the bread pudding in a water bath; I'm all for it, but Chris and Jerome think it's overrated. We were, however, in total agreement when it came to the addition of crème anglaise, and they had come up with a bacon-flavored sauce to serve with their bread pudding.

For a typical Throwdown my producers search for judges who can be considered experts in the food field, but because this was far from a typical event, I asked Chris and Jerome to search the streets of Manhattan and find two people with no formal training in the food world to judge our bread puddings. It should have been easy—who wouldn't want to eat and share their thoughts on some great desserts?—but we were in Manhattan and everyone had somewhere else to be and something else to do. Finally they found special-ed teachers and best friends Kate and Amy. Neither had eaten bread pudding before but they were game to judge our desserts on their chocolate intensity and overall flavor. The teachers loved Jerome's combination of chocolate and bacon and the dish's smooth, molten texture. While neither Kate nor Amy grooved on my passion fruit sauce, they did love my dessert's intense chocolate flavor and felt that the coconut sauce added a nice subtle flavor to the dish as a whole.

Jerome and Chris were good sports, good competitors, and most important, they made an incredible bread pudding that was worthy of this Throwdown victory.

Bobby Flay's
Chocolate-Coconut Bread Pudding with Passion Fruit Sauce

SERVES 8

Ganache

6 ounces bittersweet chocolate, finely chopped

¾ cup heavy cream

Bread Pudding

1 (12-inch) loaf brioche, crust removed, cut into
   1½-inch dice (about 10 cups)

3 tablespoons unsalted butter, melted

3 cups heavy cream

2 cups unsweetened coconut milk

1¼ cups sugar

½ vanilla bean, split lengthwise, seeds scraped
   out, bean and seeds reserved

8 ounces bittersweet chocolate, such as
   Valrhona Manjari 64%, finely chopped

4 large eggs

2 large egg yolks

1 cup unsweetened shredded coconut

Coconut Anglaise (recipe follows)

Passion Fruit Sauce (recipe follows)

1. *To make the ganache,* put the chocolate in a small heatproof bowl. Bring the cream to a simmer in a small saucepan, and pour it over the chocolate. Let sit for 30 seconds; then whisk until smooth. Keep warm.

2. *To make the bread pudding,* preheat the oven to 325°F.

3. Line a large baking sheet with parchment paper, add the diced bread, drizzle with the butter, and toss to coat. Bake, tossing the cubes several times, until light golden brown, about 12 minutes. Let cool slightly.

4. Combine the cream, coconut milk, sugar, and vanilla bean and seeds in a medium saucepan, and bring to a simmer over high heat. Whisk until the sugar has dissolved. Remove from the heat, add the chopped chocolate, and whisk until melted. Strain into a clean bowl.

5. Whisk the eggs and yolks together in a medium bowl, and slowly whisk in the warm chocolate mixture.

6. Scatter half of the bread cubes over the bottom of a 9 × 13-inch baking dish. Pour half of the chocolate custard on top, then half of the ganache. Sprinkle with ½ cup of the coconut. Press down on the bread to allow the liquid to soak in. Scatter the remaining bread cubes over the top, add the remaining custard and ganache, and again press down to submerge the bread. Top with the remaining ½ cup coconut, cover, and let sit for at least 30 minutes to allow the bread to soak up the custard mixture.

7. Place the baking dish in a larger roasting pan and fill the roasting pan with warm water until it comes halfway up the sides of the baking dish. Place the roasting pan in the oven and bake until the sides of the pudding are slightly puffy and the center is slightly set but still jiggles a bit, about 40 minutes. Remove the baking dish from the water bath, place it on a wire rack, and let it sit for at least 20 minutes before serving.

8. To serve, spoon some of the Coconut Anglaise into a bowl, drizzle with some of the Passion Fruit Sauce, and top with a large scoop of the bread pudding.

Coconut Anglaise

1 cup whole milk

1 cup unsweetened coconut milk

½ vanilla bean, split lengthwise, seeds scraped
   out, bean and seeds reserved

4 large egg yolks

3 tablespoons sugar

1. Combine the milk, coconut milk, and vanilla
bean and seeds in a small saucepan, and bring
to a simmer.

2. Meanwhile, prepare an ice bath in a large
bowl.

3. Whisk the egg yolks and sugar together in a
medium bowl until pale. Slowly whisk in the
warm milk mixture until combined. Remove
the vanilla bean, return the mixture to the pan
over medium heat, and cook, stirring with a
wooden spoon until the mixture coats the back
of the spoon, about 4 minutes. Immediately
strain the mixture into a bowl and then set the
bowl in the ice bath to chill.

4. Once the anglaise is cool, cover and refrigerate for at least 1 hour before serving.

Passion Fruit Sauce

¾ cup passion fruit juice

¼ cup sugar

¼ cup fresh orange juice

2 tablespoons white rum

Pour the passion fruit juice into a small saucepan. Add the sugar, orange juice, and rum, and
cook over high heat until the sugar has melted
and the sauce has thickened, 5 to 7 minutes.
Transfer to a bowl and chill in the refrigerator.

WINNER!

Jerome Chang's
Warm Chocolate Bread Pudding
SERVES 10

1 (1½-pound) loaf Pullman bread, crusts
   removed, cut into ½-inch cubes
   (about 10 cups)

4 cups heavy cream

¾ cup sugar

9 ounces good-quality bittersweet chocolate,
   finely chopped

7 large egg yolks

Pinch of fine salt

Bacon Crème Anglaise (recipe follows)

Whipped Cream (recipe follows)

1. Preheat the oven to 300°F. Put the bread
cubes in a large bowl.

2. Bring the cream and sugar to a boil in a
medium saucepan, stirring until the sugar has
dissolved. Remove from the heat and whisk in
the chocolate until it has melted and the
mixture is smooth and uniform in color. Whisk
in the egg yolks and salt.

3. Pour the chocolate custard over the bread
cubes and toss to combine. Ladle into ten
6-ounce ramekins, until it is about ½ inch
from the top. Bake until almost set but still
jiggly, 30 to 35 minutes. Let cool at least
slightly.

4. To serve, spoon some Bacon Crème
Anglaise over the top of each pudding and
top with a dollop of whipped cream.

Bacon Crème Anglaise

4 strips applewood-smoked bacon

2 cups half-and-half

5 large egg yolks

⅓ cup sugar

1. Cook the bacon in a skillet over medium
heat until well caramelized, about 5 minutes.
Transfer to a paper-towel-lined plate.

2. Bring the half-and-half to a boil in a small
saucepan, and remove from the heat. Add
the bacon strips, cover, and let steep for
15 minutes. Remove and discard the bacon
strips.

3. Put a medium bowl or a 4-cup measuring
cup into a larger bowl filled with ice water.

4. Put the egg yolks in a medium bowl, and
whisk.

5. Add the sugar to the half-and-half and bring
just to a boil over medium heat. Whisk about
half of the hot mixture into the egg yolks in a
steady stream; then whisk that mixture back
into the saucepan. Return the pan to medium
heat and cook, stirring with a wooden spoon,
until the custard no longer looks watery when
you draw your finger across the back of the
spoon, about 7 minutes.

6. Strain the custard into the bowl in the ice
bath, and let it cool to room temperature.
Refrigerate until ready to serve.

Whipped Cream

½ vanilla bean, split lengthwise

1 cup heavy cream

2 tablespoons sugar

Scrape the vanilla seeds into the cream in a
mixing bowl. Add the sugar and whip until soft
peaks form.

CIOPPINO

ON THIS EPISODE OF THROWDOWN!...

We made our way to northern California in search of a regional classic: cioppino. Making this seafood chowder is second nature to Phil DiGirolamo, and his cioppino was the one to beat.

○ Cioppino originated in the San Francisco Bay Area. Legend has it that this great American dish was first made with the scraps that local fishermen who worked the docks were able to pull for their own use. The dockworkers would "chip in" those seafood odds and ends (thus the name "cioppino") to a stew pot of tomatoes and fish stock. ○ Phil's Fish Market, down the coast in Moss Landing, near Monterey, began as just that when it opened in 1982. A Sicilian American who grew up by the sea, surrounded with a family who loved to fish and to cook, Phil started his business by selling what interested him most: fresh, locally caught fish.

But Phil soon realized that there was a growing clientele interested in buying prepared dishes made with his first-rate seafood. So he raided his family's treasure trove of recipes and expanded his business.

"Before the show originally aired I was asked repeatedly, 'Who won?' My answer was and still is 'Win, lose, or draw . . . no matter what, I won!' My staff and I had a great time. Bobby is a heck of a chef and an extremely gracious person! The Throwdown challenge also has been an incredible boon for the business. Across the board we have seen an amazing customer response since the show aired—and in this economy we feel lucky to say, 'It was a great year for Phil's!'"

—PHIL DIGIROLAMO

Name: Phil DiGirolamo
Establishment: Phil's Fish Market & Eatery
Hometown: Moss Landing, California
Website: www.philsfishmarket.com
Phone: (831) 633-2152

The critical acclaim that Phil has received helped to put the once-sleepy town and the waters of Moss Landing, full of halibut, striped bass, sardines, and calamari, on the map.

Phil's famous cioppino, his top-selling dish, is based on the delicious seafood soup that his grandmother Nina made. It contains seven different types of seafood, including crab, calamari, scallops, snapper, cod, and prawns, which he cooks with a pinch of saffron and a splash of sweet wine. His sauce contains sautéed onions and garlic, fresh herbs, and tomatoes. His secret for balanced flavors is to cut the acidity of the tomatoes by sneaking in a little brown sugar and cinnamon.

I have a lot of experience with cioppino and have served versions of the dish at both Bar Americain and Mesa Grill. My seafood of choice usually includes sea bass, shrimp, clams, and oysters, but varies according to what is freshest on any given day. I bathe the seafood in a garlicky tomato broth. And I also have a secret ingredient that puts this stew over the top: anchovies. I don't add them to the broth; instead, I blend them with butter to spread on grilled sourdough bread.

Now, I knew that Phil wouldn't want an Irish boy beating him, but we headed toward Monterey anyway. Would Phil stay as happy as a clam when faced with my Throwdown challenge? After a glass or two of wine, of course he was! The audience loved both of our cioppinos, and it was beginning to look as though it could go either way as the judges made their way in to critique our choice of seafood, broth, and authenticity.

They found Phil's to be a classic Monterey cioppino. Packed with seafood, it was fit for a king. They loved his broth, too, but would have liked a touch more heat. Ours was praised for its perfumed broth and savory anchovy-buttered bread. We may have had the winning broth, but Phil garnered the top prize for authenticity and seafood. I loved what Phil made and know we made a valiant effort. Maybe we could have used a little more tomato in our broth. Hey, Phil, you ready for a rematch?

Bobby Flay's Cioppino

SERVES 4 TO 6

6 tablespoons olive oil

1 large onion, finely chopped

6 cloves garlic, finely chopped

¼ teaspoon red pepper flakes

1 cup dry white wine

5 cups fish stock (see Sources, page 269)

1 (16-ounce) can diced tomatoes, drained

1 bay leaf

6 sprigs fresh thyme

Kosher salt and freshly ground black pepper

1½ pounds sea bass fillets, cut into 2-inch squares

12 large shrimp, shelled and deveined

32 littleneck clams

24 mussels, scrubbed and debearded

¼ cup coarsely chopped fresh flat-leaf parsley leaves, plus whole leaves for garnish (optional)

2 tablespoons chopped fresh tarragon leaves

2 tablespoons honey

Few dashes of hot sauce

Sourdough Croutons (recipe follows)

1. Heat 2 tablespoons of the oil in a large Dutch oven over medium-high heat. Add the onion and cook until soft, about 3 minutes. Add the garlic and red pepper flakes, and cook until fragrant, 1 minute. Add the wine and cook until reduced by half. Add the fish stock, drained tomatoes, bay leaf, and thyme sprigs. Season with salt and pepper. Bring to a boil and cook, stirring occasionally, until slightly thickened, about 15 minutes.

2. While the broth is cooking, heat 2 tablespoons of the oil in large sauté pan over high heat. Season the bass on both sides with salt and pepper, and cook until golden brown, about 2 minutes per side. Remove to a plate.

3. Add the remaining 2 tablespoons oil to the same pan. Season the shrimp and sauté until light golden brown, about 1 minute per side. Remove to the plate with the bass.

4. Add the clams and mussels to the thickened broth and cook until they open (discarding any that do not), about 3 minutes. Add the bass and shrimp, and cook just to heat through, about 1 minute. Stir in the parsley and tarragon, and season with the honey, hot sauce, and salt and pepper to taste. Remove the bay leaf.

5. To serve, place a crouton in each of 4 to 6 bowls, ladle some of the cioppino on top, and top with the remaining croutons. Garnish with parsley leaves, if desired.

Sourdough Croutons

12 tablespoons (1½ sticks) unsalted butter, at room temperature

6 anchovies packed in oil, patted dry

Kosher salt and freshly ground black pepper

8 (½-inch-thick) slices sourdough bread

Olive oil

1. Preheat a grill pan over medium-high heat, or preheat your broiler.

2. Combine the butter and anchovies in a food processor, and process until smooth. Season with salt and pepper, and scrape into a bowl.

3. Brush one side of the bread with olive oil, and season with salt and pepper. Grill, oil side down (or broil, oil side up), until light golden brown. Turn over and continue grilling until light golden brown on both sides.

4. Remove the bread to a platter, and spread some of the butter mixture on the seasoned side. Cut each slice in half crosswise, to make 16 croutons.

WINNER!

Phil DiGirolamo's
Famous Cioppino
SERVES 4 TO 6

1 tablespoon olive oil

1 tablespoon unsalted butter

1 clove garlic, chopped

1 pound littleneck clams

¼ cup dry white wine

8 ounces mussels, scrubbed

2 quarts Cioppino Sauce (recipe follows)

2 dashes Worcestershire sauce

Pinch of saffron threads

8 ounces medium shrimp in the shell

8 ounces cleaned squid tubes, cut into rings

8 ounces firm-fleshed white fish fillets, cut into
   2-inch cubes

4 ounces bay scallops

1 pound lump crabmeat, preferably Dungeness

1. Combine the olive oil, butter, and garlic in a wide, deep pot over medium heat. Cook, stirring, until the garlic is fragrant but not browned, 2 minutes. Add the clams and wine, cover, increase the heat to medium-high, and steam until the clams start to open, about 5 minutes. Add the mussels, cover, and steam until the mussels just start to open, about 2 minutes. (Discard any clams or mussels that do not open.)

2. Stir in the Cioppino Sauce, Worcestershire, and saffron, and bring to a simmer. Add the shrimp and simmer for about 5 minutes. Then gently stir in the squid, fish, and scallops, and simmer until they are all just cooked through, about 5 minutes. Gently stir in the crabmeat during the last minute or so of cooking time.

Cioppino Sauce

½ cup olive oil

2 medium onions, halved and thinly sliced

6 cloves garlic, chopped

3 bay leaves

½ cup chopped fresh flat-leaf parsley leaves

¼ cup chopped fresh basil leaves

1 (28-ounce) can peeled tomatoes with juice,
   crushed by hand

1 (28-ounce) can tomato puree

1 tablespoon clam base without MSG (optional)

1 tablespoon brown sugar

1 tablespoon celery salt

Dash of Worcestershire sauce

Dash of ground cinnamon

Kosher salt and freshly ground black pepper

Red pepper flakes

1. Heat the olive oil in a large saucepan over medium heat. Add the onions and sauté until soft, about 5 minutes. Add the garlic, bay leaves, parsley, and basil, and cook for 1 minute; do not brown.

2. Stir in the crushed tomatoes, tomato puree, 3½ cups water, the clam base (if using), brown sugar, celery salt, Worcestershire, and cinnamon. Season with salt, black pepper, and red pepper flakes to taste. Bring to a boil. Reduce the heat to medium-low, and simmer, stirring occasionally, until thickened, 1¼ hours. Remove the bay leaves before serving.

NOTE
Serve over pasta, if desired.

RAVIOLI

ON THIS EPISODE OF THROWDOWN!...

I've got one word for you: *ravioli.* I faced a father-and-son team carrying on generations of tradition by stuffing cherished family secrets into their famous pasta purses. Would they welcome me into the family? It was the battle of the Bobbys . . . ○ Durso's Pasta and Ravioli Company, in Flushing, Queens, is a family-owned business started by Robert's grandfather. Since 1967, it has been *the* neighborhood Italian food shop—that's four decades and counting! Today Durso's is run by Robert, his brother Jerry, and his son Bobby Jr. With aging cheeses and meats hanging from the ceiling, this shop regularly boasts lines out the door with customers who come from all over New York City for its selection of more than fifty prepared foods. And with all it has to offer, nothing is more popular than Durso's always fresh, daily made ravioli.

○ The Bobbys Durso learned that they were getting a shot to show their stuff to Food Network's Italian-loving viewers, and for their big shot they went with a big dish: double-cheese ravioli and osso buco with white wine jus. Wanting to learn a new trick or two myself, I went to Raffetto's on West Houston Street, where Nonna Raffetto taught me how to make the perfect spinach and ricotta ravioli.

Names: Robert Durso Sr. and
Robert "Bobby" Durso Jr.
Establishment: Durso's Pasta and Ravioli Company
Hometown: Flushing, New York
Website: www.dursos.com
Phone: (718) 358-1311

Lesson completed, I was off to the test kitchen to try two versions of my own: one stuffed with a black olive tapenade and the other with a brandade and shrimp filling. Miriam, our resident dough expert, made a rich pasta dough from flour, eggs, salt, and water. For the first ravioli, I marbled briny tapenade into a mixture of ricotta, goat cheese, egg, and woodsy thyme and served the finished ravioli with a chunky tomato–red pepper sauce. The brandade stuffing began in the traditional manner by combining salt cod and potatoes flavored with lots of shallots and garlic and mixed with heavy cream until smooth and rich. Sautéed shrimp joined the brandade to stuff the pasta.

Over in Queens the Bobbys had set their table and were ready to feed their guests. The Dursos accepted our invitation for the "Bobby, Bobby, and Bobby Ravioli Throwdown." The crowd's opinions were mixed, but we had two judges who definitely knew a thing or two about Italian cuisine on hand to make the final call.

Cooking school owner Daniel Rosati and *Sopranos* star Lorraine Bracco did the honors. My offering was lauded for being different, popping with unexpected flavors. They loved the traditional cheese ravioli and the thin, light texture of my pasta. They didn't feel the Dursos' pasta was delicate enough, finding it thicker than mine, but they loved the rich flavor of the veal and the surplus of cheese in the ravioli. In the end, Daniel and Lorraine, citing the creativity of my brandade and shrimp ravioli, gave me the win. I don't know how we did it. The Durso family has been steeped in culinary tradition for years, and it was an honor to cook alongside them. If you're in need of a taste of Italy, it's worth the trip to Flushing. Your hunger will surely be curbed at Durso's Pasta and Ravioli Company.

Robert Durso and Robert "Bobby" Durso Jr.'s Osso Buco Ravioli

WINNER!

Bobby Flay's
Ricotta and Black Olive Ravioli
with Roasted Red Pepper Tomato Sauce
SERVES 4 TO 6

Pasta Dough

5 cups all-purpose flour, plus more for dusting

1½ teaspoons kosher salt

5 large eggs

2 large egg yolks

1 tablespoon extra virgin olive oil, plus more
   for brushing

Black Olive Tapenade

1 cup black Niçoise olives, pitted

2 tablespoons pine nuts

3 cloves garlic, chopped

1 tablespoon brined capers, drained

2 anchovy fillets in oil, patted dry

1 teaspoon grated lemon zest

¼ cup extra virgin olive oil

Kosher salt and freshly ground black pepper

Cheese Filling

1½ cups fresh ricotta cheese

¼ cup fresh goat cheese

¼ cup grated Pecorino Romano cheese

1 large egg, lightly beaten

¼ cup finely chopped fresh basil leaves

1 tablespoon chopped fresh thyme leaves

Kosher salt and freshly ground black pepper

Roasted Red Pepper Tomato Sauce
   (see page 140), for serving

Grated Pecorino Romano cheese, for garnish

1. *To make the dough,* combine the flour and salt in a mixer fitted with the dough hook attachment, mixing on low speed. Add the eggs and egg yolks, one at a time, and after all have been added, mix for 1 minute. Add the 1 tablespoon oil and mix until a smooth dough is formed. If the dough seems too dry, add 1 tablespoon water; if it is too wet, add a little more flour. Remove the dough from the bowl and knead on a lightly floured work surface until elastic and smooth, 8 to 10 minutes. Form the dough into a ball and flatten slightly. Brush the top with olive oil, wrap in plastic wrap, and let rest on the counter for at least 30 minutes.

2. *To make the tapenade,* combine the olives, pine nuts, garlic, capers, anchovies, and lemon zest in a food processor and coarsely chop. With the motor running, slowly add the oil and process to a smooth paste; season with salt and pepper.

3. *To make the cheese filling,* combine the cheeses, egg, herbs, and ¼ cup of the tapenade in a medium bowl. Season to taste with salt and pepper.

4. Cut the ball of dough into 4 pieces and wrap the ones that you aren't using in plastic wrap. Press a ball of dough into a rectangle on a lightly floured surface, and roll it a few times through a pasta machine set at the widest setting. Reduce the setting and run it through a few more times, until it is about ⅛-inch thick. Place on a floured surface and keep covered. Repeat with the remaining dough.

5. Lay a sheet of pasta dough on a lightly floured work surface, and distribute heaping teaspoons of the filling on it, spacing them at least 2 inches apart. Use your fingertip or a brush to moisten the edges of the pasta sheet with egg wash. Carefully place a second sheet of pasta dough on top of the first, and press with your fingertips to separate the rows of filling. Repeat with the remaining dough and filling. Using a ravioli cutter or a pastry wheel, cut straight lines to form the ravioli squares. Press the edges closed with your fingertips to seal well.

6. Bring a large pot of salted water to a boil. Carefully drop in the ravioli and cook for about 5 minutes. Drain, and serve immediately, topped with the red pepper–tomato sauce and grated cheese.

Robert Durso and Robert "Bobby" Durso Jr.'s Osso Buco Ravioli

SERVES 4 TO 6

Basic Pasta Dough

3 cups semolina flour

¾ teaspoon kosher salt

All-purpose flour, for rolling the dough

Osso Buco Filling

2 pounds veal shanks, cut for osso buco
   (about 2 pieces)

Kosher salt and freshly ground black pepper

All-purpose flour, for dredging

2 tablespoons pure olive oil

1 small onion, finely diced

1 carrot, finely diced

1 celery stalk, finely diced

1 tablespoon tomato paste

½ cup dry white wine

2 to 3 cups low-sodium beef stock

¼ cup freshly grated Parmesan cheese

1 egg, lightly beaten with a little water,
   for egg wash

2 tablespoons unsalted butter, cold

Chopped fresh flat-leaf parsley leaves, for
   garnish

1. *To make the dough,* put the semolina flour and salt in the bowl of a mixer fitted with the paddle attachment, and mix to combine. With the mixer on medium-low speed, slowly add ¾ cup warm water and mix until the dough is smooth. Form into a ball, wrap in plastic wrap, and refrigerate for at least 1 hour and up to 24 hours.

2. *To make the filling,* preheat the oven to 350°F.

3. Season the veal shanks with salt and pepper. Dredge the shanks in flour, shaking off any excess. Heat the olive oil in a deep oven-proof pot over medium heat, add the shanks, and cook until golden brown on each side, about 5 minutes per side. Remove to a plate.

4. Add the onion, carrot, and celery to the pot and season with salt and pepper. Sauté until soft and translucent, about 8 minutes. Add the tomato paste and white wine and mix well, scraping up the browned bits in the pot.

5. Return the shanks and any juices that have collected on the plate to the pot, and add enough beef stock to almost cover the shanks. Cover, transfer to the oven, and braise until the meat begins to fall off the bone, about 2 hours. (Check the meat after an hour and add more liquid if necessary to keep the meat almost covered.) Remove from the oven and let the shanks cool in the cooking liquid.

6. Remove the shanks from the pot (reserve the braising liquid) and pull the meat from the bone. Coarsely chop the meat and transfer it to a bowl. Add ⅓ cup of the braising liquid and its vegetables to moisten the meat. Mix in the Parmesan.

7. Divide the dough into 4 pieces. Keep the pieces covered until you are ready to work with them, so they don't dry out. Roll the pieces through a pasta machine, dusting with flour as necessary, until the sheets are 1/16 inch thick.

8. Lay out the pasta sheets, dust off any excess flour, and cut them into 4-inch squares. Place a heaping tablespoon of cooled filling onto each square, gently brush the edges with the egg wash, and top with another square. Press lightly to seal, removing any air.

9. Bring a large pot of salted water to a boil.

10. Meanwhile, skim any fat from the reserved braising liquid and transfer it to a large sauté pan. Bring to a simmer over medium heat and cook until reduced to a sauce consistency, about 8 minutes. Reduce the heat to low and whisk in the butter; season with salt and pepper.

11. Gently add the ravioli to the boiling water and cook for 4 to 5 minutes. Use a slotted spoon to transfer the ravioli to a serving dish. Top with the sauce, and garnish with chopped parsley.

CHICKEN POT PIE

ON THIS EPISODE OF THROWDOWN!...

I dove fork-first into a delicious chicken pot pie. Austin, Texas, Casserole Queens Crystal Cook and Sandy Pollock really know how to dress up this creamy classic comfort food and turn pot pies into a party. ○ Friends Crystal and Sandy have an online business specializing in delivering home-cooked meals to your door. They operate with a fun and retro style—and it's not only the old-time favorites they serve. ○ Crystal and Sandy know that very few families sit down to dinner these days as they used to, and to reinforce that nostalgia, they even dress up in 1950s-style clothes, complete with funky frilly aprons, to deliver their casseroles. Sandy, a graduate of my alma mater, the French Culinary Institute, convinced her good friend Crystal to abandon corporate America and join her in this endeavor back in 2006. They've been happily and successfully bringing their brand of '50s homemaker cuisine to the citizens of Austin ever since.

"It really is a true saying that no one loses on <u>Throwdown!</u> Even though Bobby's dish reigned supreme with the judges, our pot pie still managed to win over the hearts of foodies from around the globe. Seriously, we are still floored by the amount of e-mails and support that we receive on a daily basis from people not only here in the States, but from the U.K. and Canada too! We are grateful to Bobby and Food Network for highlighting our small, two-person operation and our unique business model. The food industry can be very intimidating, and it warms our hearts to think that we are able to inspire other entrepreneurs to discover a new way to obtain their dreams."

—SANDY POLLOCK AND CRYSTAL COOK

Names: Sandy Pollock and Crystal Cook
Hometown: Austin, Texas
Website: www.casserolequeens.com
Phone: (512) 905-6967

The Casserole Queens make more than twenty different types of one-pan wonders, but the one they are most proud of is their chicken pot pie. Underneath its buttery puff pastry crust is a filling of chicken, shallots, carrots, potatoes, and red bell peppers with a wine-enriched cream sauce. These local media darlings thought that they were going to be featured in a Food Network special called "Home Cooked," while I planned to get things cooking with a chicken pot pie Throwdown. My mission was to get hip on everything there was to know about this American classic.

I have been making pot pies basically since I began cooking, and I've been serving a variation of a chicken pot pie at my restaurant Bar Americain since it opened in 2005. There are a few things that set mine apart from the classic version. First of all, I smoke my chicken before roasting it on a rotisserie. I also add sweet potatoes to my biscuit crust for their touch of sweetness and great color. Carrots, pearl onions, peas, and cremini mushrooms are all cooked in a creamy chicken gravy, neither too thick nor too thin, that gets a slightly spicy kick from just a touch of chipotle chiles.

The *Throwdown!* team trekked down to Austin, where I surprised Crystal and Sandy at their '50s-style sock hop. Crystal was so nervous that she had to make a bathroom run, but both quickly regained their composure and accepted my challenge. Hot out of the oven, it was time to sample the pot pies. The Texas crowd was loving my dish, but would I get any of that love from the judges?

Cookbook author Rebecca Rather and Daniel Northcutt set about judging our chicken pot pies on their crusts, filling, and overall comfort factor. They tasted mine first, noting how much they loved its presentation and flaky brown crust. They immediately picked up on the smokiness of the chicken. Their only criticism was that they would have preferred a creamier sauce. Rebecca and Daniel also loved the Casserole Queens' dish: the crust, its rich filling, and the creamy texture. It was a close one—very close—but in the end, they chose my chicken pot pie as the winning contender.

WINNER!

Bobby Flay's
Smoked Chicken Pot Pie with
Sweet Potato Crust
SERVES 6 TO 8

Sweet Potato Crust

1 pound (3¾ cups) all-purpose flour, plus more
for rolling

1½ teaspoons kosher salt

½ teaspoon freshly ground black pepper

1 cup (2 sticks) unsalted butter, cut into pieces,
cold

1 large egg

½ cup whole milk

1 cup sweet potato puree (from 1 large sweet
potato, roasted, peeled, and pureed in a food
processor)

Filling

4 tablespoons (½ stick) unsalted butter

1 medium Spanish onion, finely diced

3 cloves garlic, finely chopped

¼ cup all-purpose flour

4 cups whole milk, or more if needed, hot

12 ounces cremini mushrooms, quartered and
sautéed until golden brown

2 turnips, peeled, cut into medium dice,
blanched, and drained

2 carrots, peeled, cut into matchsticks, blanched
and drained

½ cup frozen red pearl onions, blanched and
drained

½ cup frozen white pearl onions, blanched and
drained

1 cup frozen peas, blanched and drained

1 roasted (3-pound) chicken (see Note),
shredded

2 teaspoons pureed chipotle in adobo, or
2 teaspoons smoked sweet Spanish paprika
(see Note)

Kosher salt and freshly ground black pepper

¼ cup coarsely chopped fresh flat-leaf parsley
leaves

2 large eggs, beaten with a few tablespoons
cold water, for an egg wash

(recipe continues)

1. *To make the crust,* stir the flour, salt, and pepper together in a large bowl. Cut in the butter until the mixture resembles coarse meal. Stir the egg, milk, and sweet potato puree together in a bowl. Add the mixture to the flour, and gently mix with a rubber spatula until just combined. Transfer the mixture to a lightly floured surface, and lightly knead until the dough just comes together. Form into a round and flatten it slightly. Wrap in plastic wrap and refrigerate until chilled, at least 1 hour and up to 24 hours.

2. Preheat the oven to 375°F.

3. *To make the filling,* melt the butter in a medium saucepan over high heat. Add the onion and cook until soft, 5 minutes. Add the garlic and cook for 1 minute. Add the flour and cook, stirring occasionally, until deep golden brown. Slowly whisk in the hot milk and cook until thickened. Reduce the heat and cook for 5 minutes, whisking occasionally. If the mixture is too thick, thin it with a little extra milk.

4. Add the mushrooms, turnips, carrots, onions, peas, chicken, and chipotle, if using, to the sauce and fold gently to combine. Season the filling with salt and pepper, and stir in the parsley.

5. Divide the dough in half, and roll each half out on a lightly floured surface until ⅛ inch thick. Invert individual heatproof bowls on the pastry sheet, and using a sharp knife, cut circles around the outside of the bowls that are slightly larger than the bowls. Fill the bowls three-quarters full with the chicken filling, making sure each serving has a nice amount of chicken, vegetables, and broth. Carefully cap each bowl with a pastry round, pressing the dough around the rim to form a seal. Brush the tops with the egg wash and season with salt and pepper. Use a paring knife to make a small slit in the center of the dough. (Alternatively, roll one large crust and use it to top a family-style pot pie in a 10-inch baking dish.)

6. Place the bowls on baking sheets, and bake until the crust is golden brown and the filling is bubbly, 15 to 18 minutes for individual pies and 25 to 30 minutes for one large pot pie. Remove from the oven and let sit for 5 minutes before serving.

NOTE

If you would like to cold-smoke your chicken before roasting it, prepare a small charcoal or wood fire in a domed grill or in a stovetop cold smoker. Lay chips of soaked aromatic wood over the ashes. Arrange the chicken on the grill rack over the chips, open the top vent slightly, and cover the grill so that the smoke stays inside. Smoke for 20 minutes. Omit the chipotle.

Sandy Pollock and Crystal Cook's
World's Greatest Chicken Pot Pie

SERVES 6 TO 8

2 cups plus 1 tablespoon whole milk

1 cup heavy cream

1 sheet frozen puff pastry, thawed according to package instructions

2 tablespoons unsalted butter

¼ cup diced red bell pepper

2 medium shallots, thinly sliced

2 tablespoons all-purpose flour

½ teaspoon crushed dried tarragon

1½ teaspoons kosher salt

¼ teaspoon freshly ground black pepper

⅓ cup dry white wine

3 cups shredded roasted chicken (from one 3-pound chicken)

1 (10-ounce) package frozen baby peas, thawed

1½ cups diced carrots, blanched and drained

1½ cups diced russet or other baking potato, blanched and drained

1 large egg

1. Preheat the oven to 400°F.

2. Combine the 2 cups milk and the cream in a bowl.

3. Roll the puff pastry slightly, if necessary, so that it measures 9 × 13 inches.

4. Melt the butter in a large skillet over medium heat. Add the bell pepper and shallots, and cook, stirring frequently, until the pepper is tender, about 5 minutes. Add the flour, tarragon, salt, and black pepper, and stir to coat the vegetables with the flour. Add the wine and let it bubble for a minute. Raise the heat to medium-high, and stir in the milk mixture. Cook, stirring, until thickened and bubbly, about 5 minutes. Stir in the chicken, peas, carrots, and potatoes and simmer, stirring, until heated through, about 2 minutes.

5. Transfer the mixture to a 9 × 13-inch baking dish. Place the puff pastry over the hot chicken mixture. Beat the egg with the remaining 1 tablespoon milk, and brush the puff pastry with the egg wash. Then cut slits in the pastry to allow steam to escape. Place the baking dish on a baking sheet, and bake until the filling is bubbling and the crust is golden brown, 20 to 25 minutes. Let cool for 10 minutes before serving.

MATZOH BALL SOUP

ON THIS EPISODE OF THROWDOWN!...

A tough challenge rolled my way: matzoh ball soup, also known as "Jewish penicillin" for its soothing, restorative properties. ○ James Beard Award winner Jeff Nathan is the executive chef of New York City's Abigael's on Broadway, and his matzoh ball soup is the one I was aiming to beat. Abigael's on Broadway has set a new standard in kosher cuisine, and Jeff's innovative, ethnic-influenced cuisine appeals to diners of all ages, kosher or not. His matzoh ball soup is a twist on tradition, starting off with a positively Latin flavor: sofrito, a savory blend of onions, peppers, garlic, and spices. ○ A graduate of the Culinary Institute of America, Jeff is an expert in his field. In addition to publishing two cookbooks, he has been the chef and host of public television's *New Jewish Cuisine* since 1998. This is a man who is comfortable in front of the camera, so he was ready to answer Food Network's call to be on their show "Kitchen Crusader," about chefs who kick it up a notch.

Name: Jeff Nathan
Establishment: Abigael's on Broadway
Hometown: New York, New York
Website: www.abigaels.com
Phone: (212) 575-1407

New York City is home to the best Jewish delis in the world, and having grown up here I have eaten my fair share of matzoh ball soup. The thing is, I had never tried to make it. Why would I, when I could walk down the street and grab a quart any time of the day? I needed to clear up some matzoh ball confusion, so I called on Sharon Lebewohl, of my favorite traditional Jewish restaurant, the Second Avenue Deli.

Matzoh ball soup has two important components: the stock and the matzoh balls. Sharon's advice: Matzoh ball soup calls for a clear broth, so never boil it while the chicken and vegetables are flavoring the broth. For flavor, make the broth from chicken bones, a whole chicken, and this great secret: flanken, which most of us know as beef short ribs, if you'd like. More flavor comes from parsley, parsnips, and unpeeled onions, whose skin also gives the broth a lovely golden color. The matzoh balls, made of matzoh meal, eggs, and schmaltz (translation: rendered chicken fat), should be soft and fluffy yet slightly al dente in the center. There are two types of matzoh balls: floaters and sinkers. That's the difference between being light and airy versus leaden and going straight to the bottom of your stomach. Obviously I was aiming for the former.

Lessons in hand, I was off to the test kitchen to look for matzoh ball inspiration. I steeped a few roasted jalapeños in my broth. Fresh dill, a more traditional touch, added lots of bright flavor. We used seltzer water in our matzoh balls to make them light. (Jeff may disagree on this point, calling it an old wives' tale, but no one can argue that my matzoh balls weren't as light as air.) It was time to put our soups to the test and see which take the judges preferred.

The judges were Joan Nathan (no relation to Jeff), renowned Jewish cookbook author, and Janice Poritsky, "Grandma" from www.grandmas chickensoup.com. If there was anyone with the credentials to call this race, these women were it. Both found Jeff's broth to be beautiful and clear, and while a little spicy, it was full of great flavor. His matzoh balls were very soft, and the soup, though more Mexican than Jewish, was very colorful. Though mine had a darker broth, it was flavorful, and Joan preferred the flavor and texture of my matzoh balls. This was proving to be a tough decision, but in the end, the "doctor" paged to the winner's circle was Jeff Nathan. It was a close one, and that was enough for me. Whether you keep kosher or not, if you find yourself with a stomach that needs healing, take yourself to Abigael's on Broadway for a bowl of the tastiest penicillin you've ever had.

Bobby Flay's Matzoh Ball Soup

SERVES 4

Enriched Chicken Stock

5 pounds chicken carcasses, coarsely chopped

2 pounds chicken wings

3 tablespoons canola oil

2 medium Spanish onions, quartered
  (do not peel)

2 large celery stalks, with leaves, coarsely
  chopped

2 large carrots, coarsely chopped

2 teaspoons whole black peppercorns

10 sprigs fresh dill

12 sprigs fresh flat-leaf parsley

1 bay leaf

2 jalapeños, roasted (see Notes, page 22)

Matzoh Balls

6 tablespoons chicken fat

3 tablespoons finely chopped fresh chives

4 large eggs

¼ cup finely chopped fresh dill

2 tablespoons seltzer water

1 teaspoon sugar

1¼ teaspoons kosher salt

¼ teaspoon freshly ground black pepper

1 cup unsalted matzoh meal

1. *To make the stock,* preheat the oven to 375°F.

2. Place the chicken carcasses and wings in a large roasting pan, and toss with the oil. Roast, turning once, until deep golden brown, about 25 minutes.

3. Transfer the carcasses and wings to a large stockpot, and add the onions, celery, carrots, peppercorns, dill, parsley, and bay leaf. Pour in 3½ quarts cold water, and bring to a boil over high heat. Reduce the heat to medium-low and simmer, skimming the surface often, for 2 hours.

4. Strain the stock through a cheesecloth-lined strainer into a large saucepan, and discard the solids. Make a small slit in the side of each jalapeño with a paring knife, add them to the stock, and boil over high heat until reduced by half (to about 6 cups).

5. Discard the jalapeños, and let the stock cool to room temperature. Then refrigerate it until cold, at least 8 hours or overnight. Once it is cold, remove the layer of fat that will have risen to the top and reserve it for making the matzoh balls.

6. *To make the matzoh balls,* heat the chicken fat in a small skillet over medium heat, add the chives, and cook for 30 seconds. Set aside to cool slightly.

7. Whisk together the eggs, dill, seltzer, sugar, salt, and pepper until combined. Add the matzoh meal and chicken fat and chives and stir to combine. Cover well and refrigerate for at least 8 hours and up to 24 hours.

8. Bring a large pot of salted water to a boil. Form the mixture into 8 equal-size balls. Add to the boiling water, reduce the heat, cover, and simmer until very tender, about 1 hour and 20 minutes. Remove with a slotted spoon to a bowl.

9. *To serve,* bring the chicken stock to a simmer, add the matzoh balls, and cook until just heated through, about 5 minutes.

WINNER!

Jeff Nathan's
Sephardic Chicken Soup
with Sofrito and Herbed Matzoh Balls
SERVES 10 TO 12

Matzoh Balls

8 large eggs

½ cup rendered chicken fat (see Sources, page 269)

⅓ cup chopped fresh flat-leaf parsley leaves

2 teaspoons canola oil

2 teaspoons extra virgin olive oil

2 teaspoons garlic powder

2 tablespoons kosher salt

1 teaspoon freshly ground black pepper

2 cups matzoh meal

2¼ teaspoons baking powder

Chicken Broth

1 (3½- to 4-pound) chicken, cut into 8 pieces

4 quarts homemade chicken stock (see page 220)

Sofrito

2 tablespoons extra virgin olive oil

1 small onion, cut into ¼-inch dice

½ cup quartered cherry or grape tomatoes

½ cup ¼-inch-diced red bell pepper

½ cup ¼-inch-diced green bell pepper

2 tablespoons chopped fresh cilantro leaves

4 cloves garlic, minced

Small pinch of saffron threads

1 teaspoon hot red pepper sauce (optional)

Rendered chicken fat, for serving

1. *To make the matzoh balls,* whisk the eggs, chicken fat, parsley, ¼ cup water, the canola and olive oils, garlic powder, salt, and pepper in a medium bowl. In a separate bowl, whisk the matzoh meal with the baking powder. Fold the dry mixture into the wet and gently mix until combined. Cover with plastic wrap, pressed tightly against the batter, and refrigerate for at least 1 hour or overnight.

2. *To make the broth,* combine the chicken pieces and stock and bring to a boil in a large pot, over medium-high heat, skimming off the foam that rises to the surface. Reduce the heat to medium-low and simmer, partially covered, until the chicken is cooked through, about 30 minutes.

3. Remove the chicken pieces from the broth. Discard the skin. Shred the meat into bite-size pieces and set aside. Return the bones to the broth and simmer, partially covered, for 15 to 20 minutes to further develop the broth's flavor. Strain the broth, discarding the bones, and return it to the pot.

4. Bring a large pot of salted water to a simmer over high heat. Moisten your hands lightly with water and form the matzoh mixture into 24 walnut-size balls. Carefully drop the matzoh balls into the water. Reduce the heat to medium and partially cover. Simmer gently until the matzoh balls are cooked through, about 40 minutes. Using a skimmer or slotted spoon, transfer the matzoh balls to a large bowl of cold water.

(recipe continues)

5. *To make the sofrito,* heat the olive oil in a medium skillet over medium heat. Add the onion, tomatoes, red and green bell peppers, cilantro, garlic, and saffron. Cook, stirring occasionally, until the vegetables are tender but not browned, about 8 minutes. Add the hot sauce, if using.

6. Return the broth to a simmer. Stir the sofrito and the shredded chicken into the broth. Add the matzoh balls and simmer until they are heated through, about 5 minutes. Ladle into bowls and drizzle some additional chicken fat over the top.

SHRIMP AND GRITS

ON THIS EPISODE OF THROWDOWN!...

I took a trip down south for one of my favorite dishes, shrimp and grits. When it comes to this southern specialty, Joe Barnett is king. My challenge: to take my shrimp and grits and win the heart of the small town of Washington, Georgia. ○ As meatloaf is in the North, shrimp and grits is one of the classic dishes in the southern culinary tradition. If you aren't from the South, grits may be something of a mystery. The base of grits is corn, cooked in the same manner as Italian polenta.

"Looking back, my favorite thing was that I got to share in the experience with family, friends, and neighbors. It was like going to the biggest and best surprise party ever. I have since signed autographs for the ten checkout clerks in the parking lot of a major building supply company, posed for pictures in a gourmet market in Augusta, Georgia, and signed menus at a Japanese steak house. The effect the show and Bobby Flay had on my life can be summed up in one sentence: It's good to be the king!"
— JOE BARNETT

Name: Joe Barnett
Hometown: Washington, Georgia
Occupation: Drapery maker

Grits are made from dried corn kernels that have been ground and passed through a screen with tiny holes; the corn that goes through the screen is cornmeal and that which doesn't go through becomes grits. I like to use a medium-coarse grind of grits that I have specially ground for use in my restaurant Bar Americain.

Joe Barnett is a custom drapery designer by trade, but this amateur chef has cleaned up in many a shrimp and grits cook-off at Georgia's Jekyll Island Shrimp and Grits Festival. He has had a passion for making shrimp and grits since he was a child, and his spicy twist on the dish—along with his friendly persona and infectious laugh—has won him blue ribbons and fans alike, as well as a slot in Food Network's special "Cook-off Kings." Little did Joe know that he'd be sharing more than his signature dish . . .

Grits don't have much flavor of their own, but they pick up the flavors of whatever they are cooked with, so I began my dish by cooking them in shrimp stock. I finished them with lots of aged white cheddar cheese for a little extra creaminess and a nice bite. We then sautéed shrimp in bacon fat and topped the whole thing off with a little garlic-bacon oil and lots of green onion tips for freshness and color.

I headed to Georgia with my NYC style of shrimp and grits to challenge Joe to a Throwdown. While he turned out to be a fan of mine, even cooking from my cookbooks, he said he would have no problem taking me down on this particular dish, calling me out as a "duck out of water."

Washington's mayor, Willie Burns, and cookbook author Karin Calloway took to the judges' table. The mayor loved Joe's use of country ham and the generous amount of cheese in his grits, and couldn't get past the fact that I opted to use bacon. It seemed I didn't have enough cheese for his liking, either. Karin liked my bacon, and while she liked Joe's Creole seasoning, she said that my dish reminded her of something her grandmother would make. After a lot of back-and-forth, they finally made a decision and went with Joe's. I thought that bacon made *everything* better, but it seems that wasn't the case with these two. Oh well, I couldn't have lost to a nicer guy. Joe, hats off to you.

Bobby Flay's
Gulf Shrimp and Grits
SERVES 4

4 cups shrimp stock (see page 180), or more
   if needed

Kosher salt

1 cup stone-ground yellow cornmeal

8 ounces thick-cut double-smoked bacon, cut
   into 1-inch-long matchsticks

20 large (21- to 24-count) shrimp, shelled and
   deveined

Freshly ground black pepper

3 cloves garlic, finely chopped

2 teaspoons chopped fresh thyme leaves

1½ cups (6 ounces) grated white cheddar
   cheese

¼ cup heavy cream

2 green onions (green parts only), thinly sliced,
   for garnish

1. Bring the shrimp stock and 2 teaspoons salt to a boil in a medium saucepan over high heat. Slowly whisk in the cornmeal and bring to a boil. Reduce the heat to medium and cook, whisking every few minutes, until the grits are soft and have lost their gritty texture, 25 to 30 minutes. If the mixture becomes too thick, add a little more stock.

2. Meanwhile, cook the bacon in a medium skillet over medium heat until it is golden brown and crisp and the fat has rendered, about 8 minutes. Remove the bacon with a slotted spoon to a plate lined with paper towels.

3. Remove all but 3 tablespoons of the bacon fat from the skillet, and return it to high heat. Season the shrimp with salt and pepper. Add the shrimp, garlic, and thyme, in batches, if necessary, to the skillet and sauté until the shrimp are light golden brown on both sides and just cooked through, 1 to 2 minutes per side. Remove the shrimp to a plate. Reserve the garlic oil left in the skillet.

4. Stir the cheese and heavy cream into the cooked grits, and whisk until smooth; season with salt and pepper.

5. Divide the grits among 4 bowls, and top each with 5 shrimp. Drizzle with some of the garlic oil from the skillet, and sprinkle with the green onions.

WINNER!

Joe Barnett's
Shrimp and Grits
SERVES 4

Sauce

2 tablespoons unsalted butter

2 tablespoons all-purpose flour

1½ cups shrimp stock (see page 180)

½ cup heavy cream

1 teaspoon Worcestershire sauce

½ teaspoon hot sauce, such as Texas Pete

Grits

3 tablespoons unsalted butter

3 cups shrimp stock (see page 180)

1½ cups quick-cooking (not instant) grits,
  such as Quaker

1 tablespoon tomato paste

1½ cups heavy cream

1½ cups (6 ounces) shredded extra-sharp yellow
  cheddar cheese

Kosher salt

Shrimp

1 tablespoon Cajun seasoning, such as
  Tone's Louisiana-Style

2 teaspoons sweet paprika

1 teaspoon Italian seasoning

Freshly ground black pepper

1 pound medium-large (26- to 30-count) shrimp,
  preferably wild Georgia shrimp, peeled and
  deveined

2 tablespoons unsalted butter

1 tablespoon minced garlic

2 ounces (¼-inch-thick) sliced sugar-cured
  country ham, cubed and browned, for serving

1. *To make the sauce,* melt the butter in a small saucepan over medium heat, and stir in the flour. Cook, stirring with a wooden spatula, until the roux reaches a medium-tan color, at least 8 minutes. Slowly whisk in the stock and heavy cream. Bring to a boil, whisking, and cook until the sauce has thickened and coats the back of the spoon, about 10 minutes. Whisk in the Worcestershire sauce and hot sauce. Taste for seasoning and keep warm.

2. *To cook the grits,* combine the butter and stock in a medium saucepan and bring to a boil over medium heat. Slowly whisk in the grits and simmer, whisking frequently, for 5 minutes. Add the tomato paste, cream, and cheese. Keep whisking for another 2 to 3 minutes, until the grits become creamy. Keep warm. Season with salt to taste.

3. *To cook the shrimp,* combine the Cajun seasoning, paprika, Italian seasoning, and pepper to taste in a bowl. Season the shrimp with the seasoning mix. Melt the butter in a 12-inch skillet over medium heat. Add the minced garlic and stir for 30 seconds. Add the shrimp and cook until just cooked through, about 1½ minutes per side. Transfer the shrimp to a plate, and stir the pan drippings into the sauce.

4. To serve, place a few heaping spoonfuls of grits onto each plate, top with several sizzling shrimp, drizzle with the sauce, and top with a few cubes of country ham.

NORTH CAROLINA RIBS AND BEANS

ON THIS EPISODE OF THROWDOWN!...

It was time to break out the moist towelettes because we were heading down to barbecue country to make juicy ribs and baked beans. ○ North Carolina is nothing if not passionate about its barbecue. Most folks agree on a dry rub and a low and slow smoking to cook ribs, but there are two distinct schools when it comes to the finishing touch, the sauce: in the eastern part of the state, barbecue sauce is vinegar-based, while in the western part it's tomato-based. ○ Ed Mitchell is the chef and owner of the upscale barbecue restaurant The Pit in Raleigh, North Carolina, and his ribs and beans are the ones to beat. Though The Pit's been open only since 2007, Ed's been Pitmaster of the South for the past forty years, cooking up some of the best barbecue in the region on his self-designed smokers and supporting the area's farmers though his use of local ingredients. ○ Ed's ribs of choice are, of course, Carolina ribs. (He calls these "man ribs," thicker and meatier than the St. Louis–style ribs I prefer.) ○ His succulent, juicy, flavorful ribs are perfectly complemented by sweet Carolina baked beans. Ed prepares his canned kidney, pinto, and black beans with onions, garlic, green bell peppers, bacon, barbecue sauce, brown sugar, ginger, and a secret ingredient he unveiled at the Throwdown: good ol' moonshine. But if you can't find it in your neck of the woods, Ed says beer works *almost* as well.

Name: Ed Mitchell
Establishment: The Pit Authentic BBQ
Hometown: Raleigh, North Carolina
Website: www.thepit-raleigh.com
Phone: (919) 890-4500

Ed's method for cooking ribs is unlike anything I have ever seen. He cooks them fast and hot—and I mean *fast,* like 20-minutes-a-side fast, and *hot,* 500°F hot! He is able to do this with his special hickory and oak–stoked smoker before basting the ribs with barbecue sauce and quickly finishing them on the grill. Unfortunately, this technique just can't be replicated well enough in your home oven or backyard smoker.

I'm of the "low and slow" school of ribs. To add moisture and additional flavor to the ribs as they smoked, I made up a mop sauce of vinegar, honey, brown sugar, and cayenne pepper. So that I could represent all of Carolina, I made my finishing glaze a tomato-based barbecue sauce. Ribs accounted for, I moved on to my beans. I cooked black beans with barbecue sauce, thick molasses, and rum and flavored them with onions, garlic, naturally sweet carrots, and one of my favorite varieties of sausage, chorizo. The *Throwdown!* team was ready for Raleigh and hoping to rack up a victory. How would Ed take it when I came in to hog the spotlight?

It was an unseasonably cold and rainy day when we arrived in Raleigh, but Ed didn't mind me raining on his parade at all and gave me a warm reception. This man is confident in what he does, and we both started cooking—and then eating—with gusto. Our ribs were totally different but both delicious. But who knew that baked beans could vary so much? I had no idea that there was such a difference between the North and South when it comes to our baked beans.

It was judgment time. Melvin Simmons, owner of Durham's Backyard BBQ Pit, and J Keith BBQ's co-owner Allison Keith rated our dishes on taste, tenderness, and authenticity. Melvin and Allison raved over the chunky texture of Ed's beans and their good barbecue taste of molasses and brown sugar. And those ribs . . . they were fall-off-the-bone tender, nicely salty with a great mix of East and West barbecue flavors. Moving on to my plate, they said the ribs had a good charcoal flavor, but not enough vinegar. They wished they were more tender, with a wetter sauce. As for my beans, they were a touch too spicy and soft and definitely *not* traditional. It wasn't too much of a shock when the judges crowned Ed the winner of this Throwdown.

Postscript: Ed's ribs were amazingly delicious, but try though we might, we just couldn't replicate them in our kitchen—you need his special rig—and so their recipe is not included here. And in the end this was really a bean battle. Find out which side you fall on, North or South; either way you can't miss with these classic bean dishes.

Bobby Flay's
Honey-Rum Baked Black Beans
SERVES 8

12 ounces dried black beans, picked over and
soaked in cold water for 8 hours

1 tablespoon canola oil

8 ounces dried chorizo, cut into small dice

1 medium Spanish onion, cut into small dice

1 medium carrot, cut into small dice

4 cloves garlic, finely chopped

1 cup dark rum

¼ cup clover honey

3 tablespoons molasses

3 tablespoons light brown sugar

2 cups homemade chicken stock (see page
220) or canned low-sodium chicken broth,
plus more if needed

1 cup Mesa Grill Barbecue Sauce (see Sources,
page 269) or your favorite barbecue sauce

¼ cup plus 2 tablespoons coarsely chopped
fresh cilantro leaves

Kosher salt and freshly ground black pepper

1. Drain the beans. Place them in a large
saucepan and add cold water to cover by
2 inches. Bring to a boil over high heat, reduce
the heat to medium, partially cover the pot,
and simmer until very tender, 1 to 1½ hours.
Drain the beans and place them in a large bowl.

2. Preheat the oven to 325°F.

3. Heat the oil in a large sauté pan over high
heat. Add the chorizo and cook until golden
brown on both sides and crisp, 5 to 7 minutes.
Remove with a slotted spoon to a plate lined
with paper towels. Add the onion and carrot
to the sauté pan and cook until soft, about
5 minutes. Add the garlic and cook for
1 minute. Add the rum and cook until reduced
by half. Add this mixture to the beans.

4. Add the honey, molasses, brown sugar,
stock, barbecue sauce, and the ¼ cup cilantro
to the beans. Mix gently to combine, and
season with salt and pepper. Transfer the
mixture to a large baking dish, cover, and bake
for 30 minutes.

5. Check to see if the bean mixture is dry; if it
is, add a little more stock. Return it to the oven
and bake for another 20 to 30 minutes. Then
remove the cover and bake until golden brown
on top, 15 minutes.

6. Garnish with the remaining 2 tablespoons
cilantro, and let sit for 10 minutes before
serving.

WINNER!

Ed Mitchell's
Carolina-Style Baked Beans
SERVES 10 TO 12

8 ounces bacon, minced

1 onion, diced

3 tablespoons minced garlic

2 tablespoons minced fresh ginger, or
   1 teaspoon ground ginger

1 green bell pepper, diced

1 teaspoon dry mustard

2 (16-ounce) cans kidney beans, with juices

1 (16-ounce) can pinto beans, with juices

1 (16-ounce) can black beans, with juices

1 cup Ed's North Carolina Western BBQ Sauce
   (recipe follows)

1 cup beer

¼ cup unsulfured molasses

½ cup packed light brown sugar

Kosher salt and freshly ground black pepper

1. Cook the bacon in a skillet over medium heat until the fat renders, 5 to 7 minutes. Add the onion, garlic, ginger, and bell pepper and cook until soft, about 5 minutes. Add the dry mustard and cook for 1 minute.

2. Add all the beans and their juices, barbecue sauce, beer, molasses, brown sugar, and salt and pepper to taste. Bring the mixture to a boil. Then reduce the heat to medium-low, partially cover the skillet, and simmer, stirring occasionally, for 1½ hours. If the beans are too soupy, take the cover off the skillet and cook until enough liquid evaporates.

Ed's North Carolina Western BBQ Sauce

2 cups apple cider vinegar

½ cup honey

½ cup tomato paste

½ cup light corn syrup

4 ounces (½ cup) liquid smoke

1 tablespoon kosher salt

1 teaspoon freshly ground black pepper

½ teaspoon ground white pepper

1 teaspoon garlic powder

⅛ teaspoon dried oregano

⅛ teaspoon ground cloves

Pinch of ground cinnamon

Combine all of the ingredients in a bowl.

GERMAN CHOCOLATE CAKE

ON THIS EPISODE OF THROWDOWN!...

I followed my sweet tooth up to Harlem for a slice of German chocolate cake heaven. Will I pull off an uptown upset or will I get laughed out of town? ○ Aliyyah Baylor, of Make My Cake, is a third-generation baker. Aliyyah's grandmother Ma Smith set this sweet train in motion when she brought her southern traditions and treats up to New York City from Mississippi in the 1940s and began selling desserts from her apartment kitchen. ○ Ma Smith handed the reins over first to her daughter, and she in turn to Aliyyah, who took over the bakery from her mother twenty years ago. Harlem born and bred, Aliyyah is devoted to her neighborhood; her bakery is a short three blocks from the house in which she was raised, and Aliyyah hires from within the community. She wants the young people growing up around her to see a young black woman succeed in business and be encouraged by that success. ○ Ma Smith's southern recipes continue to thrive at Make My Cake, particularly the German chocolate cake. This dessert has special meaning for Aliyyah because it was the first cake she learned to make, at the age of eight, from "her inspiration," her grandmother. Aliyyah thought her cake had earned her a spot in a Food Network special called "Layers of Tradition," detailing the delicious art of classic American cakes.

"It was a longtime dream to partner with such a prestigious chef from the renowned network for all things foodie. It was clear we were winners from the moment we received the call to participate."
—ALIYYAH BAYLOR

Name: Aliyyah Baylor
Establishment: Make My Cake
Hometown: New York, New York
Website: www.makemycake.com
Phone: (212) 932-0833 and (212) 234-2344

German chocolate cake is so called not because it's from Germany; rather, it's named after Sam German, the man who created the chocolate used in baking the cake. So, technically the correct name should be *German's* chocolate cake. Whatever you call it, I knew that I needed to whip up an outrageous version that would stand the test of time. Pecans, chocolate, and coconut are some of my favorite ingredients in a dessert, so even though I am not known for being a baker, I was looking forward to this challenge.

I decided to pump up the chocolate flavor with a high-quality, deep, dark cocoa powder and a splash of strong brewed coffee. The classic frosting of evaporated milk, butter, brown sugar, pecans, and coconut is good but a little too sweet for my taste buds. Breaking from tradition, I made a three-milk *cajeta* frosting from a deep caramel blended with whole milk, coconut milk, and goat's milk to cut the sweetness with its slight tang. I decided to finish the four-layer cake with a rich chocolate ganache glaze along with a sprinkling of toasted coconut. When it comes to baking, I clearly believe that more is more! So I decided to serve my cake slices with a dollop of coconut whipped cream, which, besides being delicious, is also great for masking mistakes.

Aliyyah's party was a family affair with her grandmother, mother, son, and daughter in attendance. She accepted my challenge on one condition: I had to bring it! This Throwdown was definitely not going to be a cakewalk.

Aliyyah was not impressed with my riff on her classic. Hoping to change her mind, I offered her a slice and got a slice of hers in turn. I loved the pleasantly surprising crunch from chocolate chips that Aliyyah adds to her batter, and her rich, sweet, and creamy frosting reminded me of the German chocolate cake that I ate at my favorite restaurant as a child. Our cakes couldn't have been more different, and even though I could tell the crowd preferred Aliyyah's, they did their best to be kind to me. As for judges Toba Garrett, master cake designer and instructor at NYC's Institute of Culinary Education, and Norma Jean Darden of the legendary Spoonbread culinary enterprise, they loved Aliyyah's light cake layers and pecan flavors; this was the classic cake they too grew up on. My cake got high marks for its rich chocolate, balanced flavors, and how the coconut whipped cream complemented the coconut in the frosting. It could have gone either way, but in the end, they judged my cake to be the winner.

Regardless of who took this battle, Aliyyah's cake is simply wonderful. While there are many reasons to head to Harlem, a slice of German chocolate cake at Make My Cake should be at the top of your list.

WINNER!

Bobby Flay's
German Chocolate Cake
with Coconut-Pecan Cajeta Frosting
MAKES ONE 4-LAYER CAKE

Chocolate Cake

2¼ cups all-purpose flour

3 teaspoons baking powder

¾ teaspoon baking soda

¾ teaspoon fine salt

12 tablespoons (1½ sticks) unsalted butter, at room temperature, plus more for the pans

1 cup plus 2 tablespoons unsweetened Dutch-process cocoa powder

1½ cups firmly packed light muscovado sugar

1½ cups granulated sugar

1½ cups strong brewed black coffee, at room temperature

1½ cups buttermilk

3 large eggs

2 teaspoons pure vanilla extract

Frosting

1¾ cups whole milk

1¾ cups unsweetened coconut milk

1 cup goat's milk or additional whole milk

¾ cup plus 1 tablespoon granulated sugar

Seeds scraped from ½ vanilla bean

2 tablespoons light corn syrup

2 tablespoons unsalted butter, cut into small pieces, cold

½ teaspoon pure vanilla extract

⅛ teaspoon fine salt

2 teaspoons coconut rum (optional)

1¼ cups coarsely chopped pecans, toasted

1¼ cups sweetened shredded coconut

Ganache

1 cup heavy cream

8 ounces bittersweet chocolate, finely chopped

2 tablespoons light corn syrup

½ cup sweetened shredded coconut, toasted, for garnish

¼ finely chopped pecans, toasted, for garnish

Coconut Whipped Cream (recipe follows), for serving

1. *To bake the cake,* position a rack in the center of the oven and preheat the oven to 325°F. Butter two 9-inch round cake pans and line the bottoms with parchment paper.

2. Whisk the flour, baking powder, baking soda, and salt together in a medium bowl.

3. Melt the butter in a medium saucepan over medium heat. Whisk in the cocoa powder and cook for 1 minute. Remove from the heat, add the muscovado and granulated sugars, and whisk until the sugar has dissolved. Add the coffee, buttermilk, eggs, and vanilla, and continue whisking until smooth. Add the dry ingredients and whisk until just combined.

4. Divide the batter evenly between the 2 prepared cake pans, and bake until a toothpick inserted into the center comes out with a few moist crumbs attached, 40 to 45 minutes. Let the cakes cool in the pans on a wire rack for 20 minutes. Then invert the cakes onto the wire rack and let cool for at least 1 hour before frosting.

5. *To make the frosting,* combine the milk, coconut milk, and goat's milk in a small saucepan, and bring to a simmer over low heat. Keep warm while you prepare the caramel.

6. Combine the sugar and ¼ cup water in a medium saucepan over high heat, and cook without stirring until a deep amber color, 8 to 10 minutes. Slowly and carefully whisk in the warm milk mixture, and continue whisking until smooth. Add the vanilla seeds and corn syrup. Bring to a boil, reduce the heat to medium, and cook, stirring occasionally with a wooden spoon, until the sauce is reduced by half and has the consistency of a caramel sauce, about 55 minutes.

7. Remove from the heat and whisk in the butter, vanilla extract, salt, and rum (if using). Transfer the sauce to a medium bowl and stir in the pecans and shredded coconut. Let the frosting cool to room temperature, stirring it occasionally, before frosting the cake.

8. *To assemble the cake,* slice each cake in half horizontally. Place 1 cake layer on a cake round, and spread one-third of the frosting evenly over the top. Repeat to make 3 layers, and then top with the remaining cake layer, top side up.

9. *To make the ganache,* bring the cream to a simmer in a small saucepan. Put the chocolate in a medium heatproof bowl, add the hot cream and the corn syrup, and let sit for 30 seconds. Then gently whisk until smooth. Let sit at room temperature for 10 minutes before pouring over the cake.

10. Set the cake on a wire rack placed over a rimmed baking sheet. Pour the chocolate ganache over the cake, letting the excess drip off down the sides. Sprinkle the top with toasted coconut and pecans. Let sit at room temperature for at least 30 minutes and up to 4 hours before slicing.

11. Slice the cake, and top each slice with a dollop of Coconut Whipped Cream.

Coconut Whipped Cream

1½ cups heavy cream, very cold

¼ cup cream of coconut, such as Coco Lopez

2 tablespoons confectioners' sugar or granulated sugar

1 teaspoon coconut rum

½ teaspoon pure vanilla extract

Combine all the ingredients in a mixer fitted with the whisk attachment, and whisk until soft peaks form.

Aliyyah Baylor's
Make My Cake German Chocolate Cake
MAKES ONE 2-LAYER CAKE

Chocolate Cake

4 ounces sweet chocolate, such as Baker's German's Sweet Chocolate, coarsely chopped

2 cups cake flour, plus more for the pans

1 teaspoon baking soda

½ teaspoon fine salt

1 cup (2 sticks) unsalted butter, plus more for the pans, at room temperature

1½ cups granulated sugar

½ cup firmly packed dark brown sugar

1 teaspoon pure vanilla extract

4 large eggs, separated

1 cup buttermilk

1 cup mini chocolate chips, optional

Coconut Pecan Filling

1 (12-ounce) can evaporated milk

1 cup (2 sticks) unsalted butter

5 large egg yolks, lightly beaten

1 cup granulated sugar

1 cup firmly packed light brown sugar

2 teaspoons pure vanilla extract

2½ cups sweetened flaked coconut

2 cups pecans, toasted and chopped

Chocolate Frosting (see Note)

3 ounces unsweetened chocolate, coarsely chopped

3 ounces bittersweet chocolate, coarsely chopped

1 cup (2 sticks) unsalted butter, at room temperature

2 cups confectioners' sugar

2 teaspoons pure vanilla extract

1. *To make the cake,* preheat the oven to 350°F. Butter two 9-inch round cake pans. Line the bottoms with parchment paper, butter the parchment, and then dust with flour.

2. Put the chocolate and ½ cup water in small microwave-safe bowl and microwave on high power, stirring once, until the chocolate melts, 1 minute. Stir until smooth.

3. Sift the cake flour, baking soda, and salt together in a medium bowl.

4. In the bowl of an electric mixer fitted with the paddle attachment, beat the butter, granulated sugar, brown sugar, and vanilla until light and fluffy. Scrape down the sides of the bowl. Add the egg yolks, one at a time, beating well after each addition. Blend in the melted chocolate. Add the flour mixture and the buttermilk, alternating, blending until everything is combined.

5. Using a large balloon whisk or a hand mixer, beat the egg whites until stiff peaks form. Gently fold the whites into the batter. Fold in the chocolate chips, if using. Divide the batter between the prepared cake pans. Bake until a toothpick inserted into the center of the cakes comes out clean, about 40 minutes. Remove to a cooling rack and allow to cool completely, about 2 hours.

6. *To make the filling,* combine the evaporated milk, butter, egg yolks, granulated sugar, brown sugar, and vanilla in a large saucepan over low heat. When the butter melts, raise the heat to medium and simmer, stirring constantly, until thickened, about 20 minutes. Remove from the heat and stir in the coconut and pecans. Let cool completely.

7. *To make the frosting,* melt the chocolates in a medium bowl in the microwave. Let cool.

8. In the bowl of an electric mixer fitted with the paddle attachment, whip the butter until light and fluffy, about 1 minute. Gradually add the confectioners' sugar and beat on high speed until light and creamy, about 2 minutes. Add the cooled chocolate and the vanilla, and mix until light and fluffy, scraping down the sides of the bowl as needed.

9. Top 1 layer of the cake with a little less than half of the filling. Set the second cake layer on top, and cover with the rest of the filling. Frost the sides with the chocolate frosting.

NOTE

Aliyyah's frosting is a secret family recipe that she was not willing to share (we totally understand), so we created a chocolate frosting for her cake that may not be as great as the original, but we think it comes pretty darn close.

COUNTRY CAPTAIN CHICKEN

ON THIS EPISODE OF THROWDOWN!...

We traveled up and down the Eastern Seaboard looking for the mysterious dish called country captain, a stew made with chicken, vegetables, tomatoes, and curry powder. When made properly, it is the perfect combination of sweet and savory. ◎ Charleston, South Carolina, natives Matt and Ted Lee are food writers for publications such as *Travel + Leisure, Food & Wine, GQ,* and the *New York Times* as well as the proprietors of the Lee Bros. Boiled Peanuts Catalogue, your online stop for hard-to-find southern ingredients. Oh, and they also happen to have written two acclaimed cookbooks—wow. These food-loving brothers are fiercely dedicated to preserving the foodways of the American South. ◎ Matt and Ted thought that they were going to be featured on a Food Network special called "Low Country Lowdown." Its focus would have been right up their alley—shining a light on down-home dishes that only real southerners know. My mission: get the lowdown on Matt and Ted's authentic country captain and cook up my own pot of this country staple.

"Our Throwdown with Bobby was definitely the most fun we've ever had cooking. We were confident about our recipe and the little tweaks we do to amp up the flavor, like rendering country ham and bacon together. But Bobby's dish looked so elegant, and his flavors were spot-on. His coconut rice was an especially genius touch. So we were scared right up until the judges' decision."

—MATT LEE

Names: Matt and Ted Lee
Hometown: Charleston, South Carolina, and New York, New York
Website: www.boiledpeanuts.com

To find out just what country captain was, I turned to Marvin Woods, a serious Low Country cuisine expert. He told me it's a stewed chicken dish with curry. Why curry? The dish was created by the folks who settled in the Charleston-Savannah area, among them people of Indian, Asian, and French descent. Country captain is a reflection of the amazing convergence of tastes in that area.

I headed to the test kitchen, where my strategy was to make my own curry powder blend. Because country captain is a southern classic, there has to be a pork product in it, and I opted for bacon for a smoky flavor. I added onions, red bell peppers, raisins (which I later swapped out for currants) for sweetness, and toasted almonds for crunch. Like a lot of curry recipes, coconut is often used as an accoutrement to finish off the dish. I decided to incorporate that coconut flavor into the rice that is always served with this dish to absorb the flavor of the stew. I went with chicken thighs, which would remain tender when stewed (they really do have to be skinless, as the skin tends to turn flabby when braised).

I was off to the Throwdown with my three C's: coconut, curry, and currants. After blindsiding Matt and Ted Lee with my Throwdown challenge on the Hudson, we got down to some serious cooking and eating. Judges Hunter Lewis, the test kitchen director of *Saveur* magazine, and chef, restaurateur, and Low Country cooking expert Alexander Smalls came in to rate our dishes on their taste, authenticity, and balance of flavor.

My country captain was up first. Hunter and Alexander loved the sweet flavor of the rice but felt it could have been fluffier. They said my chicken was perfectly cooked and the sauce full-flavored. They moved on to Matt and Ted's dish, saying they got more curry flavor and heat. They liked the chunkier texture of their sauce but felt it could have been a little thinner in consistency. The judges really liked both of our dishes but felt the balance of flavor and the authenticity of the dish was better represented in Matt and Ted's version, awarding the win to the brothers. Matt and Ted have been friends of mine for years and are excellent cooks. I wouldn't have expected them to bring anything but their "A" game to this competition—and they did. Their country captain was amazing.

Bobby Flay's
Country Captain Chicken

SERVES 4

6 slices bacon, diced

2 tablespoons unsalted butter

1 tablespoon canola oil

1½ cups all-purpose flour

Kosher salt and freshly ground black pepper

8 bone-in, skinless chicken thighs

1 medium Spanish onion, halved and thinly
  sliced

1 large red bell pepper, halved and thinly sliced

2 cloves garlic, thinly sliced

½ serrano chile, finely diced

1 heaping tablespoon Curry Mix (recipe follows)

1 cup dry white wine

2 cups homemade chicken stock (see
  page 220)

1 (28-ounce) can plum tomatoes, drained well
  and coarsely chopped

Scant ¼ cup dried currants

1½ tablespoons chopped fresh thyme leaves

2 teaspoons honey, or more if needed

⅓ cup coarsely chopped fresh flat-leaf parsley
  leaves, plus more for garnish

Slivered almonds, lightly toasted and chopped,
  for garnish

1. Preheat the oven to 325°F.

2. Cook the bacon in a large, deep ovenproof sauté pan over medium-high heat until golden brown and crisp. Remove with a slotted spoon to a plate lined with paper towels.

3. Add the butter and oil to the rendered bacon fat in the pan, and heat over high heat, until it begins to shimmer.

4. Meanwhile, put the flour in a shallow bowl and season liberally with salt and pepper. Season the chicken on both sides with salt and pepper, dredge in the flour, and tap off any excess. Add the chicken to the sauté pan and sear on both sides until golden brown, about 4 minutes per side. Remove to a plate.

5. Add the onion and bell pepper to the pan, season with salt and pepper, and cook until soft, about 5 minutes. Add the garlic and the serrano chile, and cook for 1 minute. Stir in the curry mix and cook for 1 minute. Add the wine and boil until reduced by three-quarters. Add the chicken stock, bring to a simmer, and boil for a few minutes to reduce slightly. Stir in the tomatoes, currants, thyme, and honey, season with a little salt and pepper, and bring to a simmer.

6. Nestle the chicken thighs into the pan, and cover it with a tight-fitting lid. Braise in the oven for 35 minutes. Remove the lid, return the pan to the oven, and cook for 15 minutes.

7. Remove the chicken to a platter and tent loosely with foil to keep warm. Place the sauté pan on the stove over high heat, and bring the sauce to a boil. Cook for a few minutes to reduce slightly. Then season with salt, pepper, and honey if needed, and stir in the parsley. Spoon the sauce over the chicken and top with the bacon, almonds, and more parsley.

Curry Mix

3 tablespoons ancho chile powder

2 teaspoons ground cumin

2 teaspoons ground coriander

2 teaspoons ground fennel

2 teaspoons ground turmeric

1 teaspoon ground cardamom

1 teaspoon ground cloves

1 teaspoon ground chile de árbol

1 teaspoon freshly ground black pepper

Combine all the spices in a small bowl and mix together thoroughly.

NOTE

Serve with white rice cooked in unsweetened coconut milk and water and garnished with sliced green onion, if desired.

WINNER!

The Lee Bros. Country Captain

SERVES 4

½ cup homemade chicken stock (see page 220)
   or canned low-sodium chicken broth

½ cup dried currants or raisins

1 tablespoon curry powder

1 tablespoon garam masala

Kosher salt and freshly ground black pepper

4 ounces slab bacon or fatty country ham,
   chopped

12 skin-on, bone-in chicken thighs

Canola oil, if needed

1 large dried chile, such as guajillo or pasilla,
   split and seeded

2⅓ cups thickly sliced carrots (1¼-inch pieces)

2 cups diced yellow bell peppers

2 cups diced onion

3 cloves garlic, unpeeled

1 (28-ounce) can crushed tomatoes

2 tablespoons grated fresh ginger

4 cups cooked white rice, hot

⅔ cup slivered almonds, toasted and chopped

½ cup chopped fresh flat-leaf parsley leaves

1. Preheat the oven to 350°F.

2. Pour the stock into a small saucepan and bring to a boil over high heat. Put the currants in a small heatproof bowl and pour the hot stock over them. Set aside to plump.

3. In another small bowl, combine the curry powder, garam masala, 1½ teaspoons salt, and ½ teaspoon black pepper.

4. Scatter the bacon in a 4- to 6-quart enameled cast-iron pot or Dutch oven set over medium-high heat. Stir the pieces around occasionally until the bacon is firm and just golden brown, about 5 minutes. Using a slotted spoon, transfer the bacon to a small bowl.

5. Pour off all but 2 tablespoons of the fat in the pot, reserving the excess fat in a small bowl. Brown the chicken thighs, in batches, over medium-high heat, taking care not to crowd them in the pot, until they are golden brown, about 5 minutes per side. If the pot becomes too dry, add a little of the reserved bacon fat, 1 teaspoon at a time. Remove the chicken to a medium bowl.

6. Add 2 teaspoons of the reserved bacon fat to the pot (if there is none left, use canola oil). Add the chile and toast until very fragrant, about 30 seconds per side. Add the carrots, bell peppers, onions, and garlic, and cook until slightly softened, about 6 minutes. Add the tomatoes, curry powder mixture, ginger, and the currants and their stock. Reduce the heat to medium-low and simmer until the tomatoes have cooked down to a puree and the sauce has thickened around the vegetables, about 8 minutes.

7. Nestle the chicken thighs gently in the sauce so that the skin side faces up and is above the surface of the sauce. Tent the pot loosely with foil and transfer it to the middle rack of the oven. Bake until the country captain resembles a roiling stew around the chicken thighs, about 20 minutes.

8. Remove the foil and bake until the sauce has thickened further and the chicken skin is just beginning to crisp, about 15 minutes.

9. Remove from the oven, skim any excess fat from the surface, and season to taste with salt and pepper. Discard the chile.

10. Spoon 1 cup hot white rice into each of 4 wide, deep bowls. Use tongs to arrange 3 thighs on top. Spoon the sauce over the chicken and rice, and garnish with the reserved bacon, almonds, and parsley.

GREEN CHILE CHEESEBURGER

ON THIS EPISODE OF THROWDOWN!...

New Mexico was calling with its irresistible specialty, green chile cheeseburgers. They are juicy, smoky, spicy, and delicious, and no one does them better than Bob Olguin. I was all over the theme ingredient because chiles, well, that's my game. ○ Three essential elements—a juicy hamburger, plenty of cheese, and New Mexican green chiles—come together in one explosively tasty burger. ○ The chiles of choice are Hatch chiles (sometimes known as "Big Jims"), grown in the Chile Capital of the World, Hatch, New Mexico. But their limited growing season leaves room to experiment with some of the state's other amazingly flavored green chiles—which means any pepper, hot, mild, or in between, that has been harvested young while still green and meaty. Once a locals-only secret, these zesty burgers are slowly making their way onto southwestern-inspired menus across the country; we even serve a version called the Santa Fe Burger at Bobby's Burger Palace.

"Governor Bill Richardson named July 24, 2009, Buckhorn Tavern Day throughout the state of New Mexico! He proclaimed that the Throwdown brought state revenue in sales of green chiles way up for the year! As for the Buckhorn, our business has tripled and it hasn't slowed down. People from all over the world say that they saw the show, had frequent flyer miles, and decided to fly in just for a burger. I can't express how much the Throwdown did for me and for the Buckhorn."
　　　　—BOB OLGUIN

Name: Robert Olguin
Establishment: Manny's Buckhorn Tavern
Hometown: San Antonio, New Mexico
Website: www.bobsbuckhornburgers.com
Phone: (575) 835-4423

New Mexico is called the Land of Enchantment, and Bob Olguin, owner of the Buckhorn Tavern in San Antonio, thinks the green chile cheeseburger is one of the reasons why. His version has brought the Buckhorn quite a bit of local and national attention; *GQ* even named it the seventh best burger in the country in 2005—and that ranking wasn't for the best green chile burger, but for *all* burgers in this burger-loving land. Bob's third-generation family restaurant was first opened by his grandfather back in 1918. Bob's father, Manny, moved the restaurant to its present location in 1943, operating it under the name Manny's Buckhorn Tavern until his passing in 1998, when Bob took his place in line. The Olguin legacy comes complete with the Buckhorn's famous green chile cheeseburger, which has been on the Buckhorn Tavern's menu since its inception—meaning I'm going up against more than ninety years of mastery.

Hungry for the test kitchen, I started off with a burger made from 80/20 ground chuck (that's 80 percent lean, 20 percent fat) because I think it makes the tastiest, juiciest burgers. I dressed thin strips (or *rajas*) of poblano, Hatch, and serrano chiles in olive oil, red wine vinegar, salt, pepper, and fresh cilantro. I went with Mexican Chihuahua cheese, which is similar to Monterey Jack, and topped the burger with pickled red onions and blue corn chips for crunch. We were New Mexico–bound!

Bob was busy holding court for the "Burger Nation" film crew at a local chile festival when I made my surprise entrance. I cooked my burgers on a grill; Bob prefers to use a griddle on top of his grill so he can control the heat a little better. Bob uses 70/30 ground meat—talk about juicy—and American cheese on top. He cooks his chiles twice, first roasting them whole, then chopping and cooking them again on the griddle with a little granulated garlic, which he says brings out extra heat in the chile.

Chile researcher and expert Stephanie Walker and Maria's New Mexican Kitchen owner Al Lucero judged our cheeseburgers on their green chile flavor, authenticity, and overall taste. Right off the bat they commented on my blue corn chips and the sesame-seed buns I used. Stephanie and Al were both pleased with my chile topping, saying it was just *picante* enough to make it good yet not overwhelm the flavor of the burger. Turning to Bob's burger, they said his traditional vegetables (lettuce, tomatoes, red onion, and pickles) were more typical of a green chile burger, and they also felt his burger had more green chile heat. Bob's was chosen as the more authentic green chile cheeseburger and thus the winner of this Throwdown.

I loved my burger, and it would have been nice to win, but I'd never be sore over losing to a guy as nice as Bob. I got a trip to New Mexico, the chance to use green chiles, and the opportunity to taste the Buckhorn Tavern's rightly famous green chile cheeseburger. I may have lost the battle, but I know I came out on top.

Bobby Flay's
Green Chile Cheeseburgers
SERVES 4

Green Chile Relish

1 medium poblano chile, roasted (see Notes, page 22) and thinly sliced

2 Hatch chiles, roasted (see Notes, page 22) and thinly sliced

1 serrano chile, roasted (see Notes, page 22) and thinly sliced

¼ cup red wine vinegar

1 tablespoon honey

2 tablespoons extra virgin olive oil

3 tablespoons chopped fresh cilantro leaves

Kosher salt and freshly ground black pepper

Burgers

1 tablespoon canola oil

1½ pounds ground beef (80 percent lean)

Kosher salt and freshly ground black pepper

4 sesame-seed hamburger buns, split and lightly toasted

Queso Sauce (recipe follows)

Pickled Red Onion (recipe follows)

12 blue or yellow corn tortilla chips, coarsely crushed

1. *To make the green chile relish,* combine the chiles, vinegar, honey, olive oil, and cilantro in a bowl, and season with salt and pepper. Let sit at room temperature for at least 30 minutes before serving.

2. *To cook the burgers,* heat your griddle or a large sauté pan over high heat. Add the oil and heat until it begins to shimmer.

3. Shape the ground beef with your hands into 4 round patties, each about 1½ inches thick, and season each burger on both sides with salt and pepper. Cook the burgers until golden brown on both sides and cooked to medium, about 8 minutes.

4. Place the burgers on the buns and top each with a few tablespoons of the Queso Sauce, Green Chile Relish, Pickled Red Onion, and chips.

Queso Sauce

1 tablespoon unsalted butter

1 tablespoon all-purpose flour

1 cup whole milk, plus more if needed

12 ounces Chihuahua or Monterey Jack cheese, coarsely grated

¼ cup freshly grated Parmesan cheese

Kosher salt and freshly ground black pepper

Melt the butter in a small saucepan over medium heat. Whisk in the flour and cook for 1 minute. Add the milk, raise the heat to high, and cook, whisking constantly, until slightly thickened, about 5 minutes. Remove from the heat and whisk in the Chihuahua cheese until melted. If the mixture is too thick, thin with additional milk. Add the Parmesan and season with salt and pepper. Serve warm.

Pickled Red Onion

1½ cups red wine vinegar

2 tablespoons sugar

1 tablespoon kosher salt

1 medium red onion, peeled, halved, and thinly sliced

1. Combine the vinegar, ¼ cup water, the sugar, and the salt in a small saucepan and bring to a boil. Remove from the heat and let cool for 10 minutes.

2. Put the onions in a medium heatproof bowl, pour the vinegar over them, cover, and refrigerate for at least 4 and up to 48 hours.

WINNER!

Robert Olguin's
Buckhorn Burger
SERVES 4

2 pounds ground beef (70% lean)

Kosher salt and freshly ground black pepper

1 medium red onion, chopped

8 slices American cheese

1 cup roasted and diced New Mexico green chiles (available frozen)

1 teaspoon granulated garlic

24 dill pickle slices

8 leaves iceberg lettuce

2 tomatoes, sliced

4 large hamburger buns, toasted on both sides

Yellow mustard, for serving

1. Heat a griddle to medium-high.

2. Shape the beef into 4 large patties, each about 6 inches across and ½ inch thick. Season with salt and pepper. Grill the burgers for 2 to 3 minutes per side for medium-rare, or to your desired doneness.

3. When the patties are almost fully cooked, put the onions on the griddle in 4 mounds, and top each with 2 slices of cheese. It is very important that the cheese melts over the onions.

4. Put the green chiles on the griddle and mix in the granulated garlic. When the chiles are hot, use your spatula to put them on top of the onions and cheese, to help the cheese finish melting.

5. Put the pickles, lettuce, and tomato slices on the bottom halves of the buns. Top each with a burger, and then use your spatula to add a mound of onion, cheese, and chiles to each burger. Spread mustard over the top bun, and place it on top of the wonderful green chile patty.

STEAK FAJITAS

ON THIS EPISODE OF THROWDOWN!...

We are breaking out the sizzle platter and cooking up some steak fajitas with Father Leo, a Catholic priest with unexpected talents. He may be tighter with the Man upstairs, so do my fajitas even have a prayer?

"My first reaction was, who is this guy standing in front of the crowd and why does he look like Bobby Flay?! Then reality struck and I realized it <u>was</u> Bobby Flay. His presence was such a shocker that I prayed like I never prayed before!

"Since the Throwdown, our website has received an average of 1.5 to 2 million hits each month. I've been asked to give presentations to groups across the country and been featured on national television and radio and in newspapers and magazines. But the most impressive reactions have come in the countless e-mails from people telling me how this one show inspired them to spend more time together and to celebrate the blessings of the food on the table with the blessings of the people around the table."

—FATHER LEO PATALINGHUG

Name: Father Leo Patalinghug
Hometown: Emmitsburg, Maryland
Website: www.gracebeforemeals.com

Father Leo Patalinghug's
Funky Fusion Fajitas

Father Leo credits his interest in food to his Filipino heritage and the broad array of cuisines he was exposed to as a child, but it was during his days as a seminary student in Rome that he really fell in love with the kitchen. Ten years later, he is still cooking. In addition to being director of the pastoral field education program at Mount St. Mary's Seminary in Emmitsburg, Maryland, Father Leo has published his own cookbook, *Grace Before Meals: Recipes for Family Life,* and stars in a Web series of the same name that averages more than 10,000 hits a month! It's that Web series that brought Food Network to Father Leo (or so he thought), as part of a new show called "Edible Airways," profiling cooks who host their own cooking shows via the Internet or local television. In honor of his star turn, Father Leo threw a fajitas party at Mount St. Mary's for parishioners, friends, and family. With an Asian-inspired marinade of soy sauce, ginger, garlic, and vinegar, steak fajitas is one of Father Leo's signature dishes.

My mission: to create a steak fajita that is a religious dining experience. Like Father Leo's, my fajitas are a fusion of southwestern flavors and Asian components. My Asian inspiration comes from red curry paste—an amazing blend of spices, red chiles, garlic, and lemongrass—which I mix with lime juice to make the marinade. I love using skirt or flank steak because of its incredible flavor and chewy texture. The marinade helps tenderize this sometimes tough cut, as do taking care not to overcook it and then thinly slicing it against the grain. Instead of charring my red peppers and onions, I decided to pickle the peppers and barbecue the onions on the grill. Typically fajitas are served with guacamole and sour cream; I came up with the idea to puree my avocado for a single condiment with the taste of guacamole and the texture of sour cream.

Definitely surprised by my arrival, Father Leo had faith in his ability and accepted the Throwdown summons without hesitation. He should be confident—he's a great cook and his technique and seasonings were spot-on. While we both incorporated Asian flavors into our dishes, the flavors of the two couldn't have been more different. The crowd seemed to be divided as to which was their favorite fajita, so as always, we turned to the judges for a decision.

Food columnist Nancy Luse and Vinnie Gordon, a mentor for high school students interested in the culinary arts, judged our entries on taste, texture, and innovation. They loved Father Leo's marinade and said the beef was so tender, it melted in their mouths. As for my fajitas, they loved the light texture of the avocado crema and the pronounced flavors of the peppers and onions, though they would have preferred the vegetables to have been cooked longer and a bit less crispy. It wasn't an easy call, but there can only be one winner in a Throwdown, and this one went to Father Leo.

Father Leo did a lot of praying during the judges' deliberation, but I don't think that he needed it. His fajitas were delicious, perfectly cooked and seasoned, and made with lots of love.

Bobby Flay's
Red Curry–Marinated Skirt Steak Fajitas

SERVES 4 TO 6

¼ cup red curry paste

½ cup canola oil, plus more for the onions

¼ cup plus 3 tablespoons fresh lime juice

1½ pounds skirt steak, cut crosswise in half or thirds

¼ cup clover honey

Kosher salt and freshly ground black pepper

2 Vidalia onions, cut into ¼-inch-thick slices

Bobby Flay Steak Rub (see Sources, page 269) or your favorite rub

Mesa Grill Barbecue Sauce (see Sources, page 269) or your favorite barbecue sauce

12 (6-inch) flour tortillas

Pickled Roasted Peppers (recipe follows)

Avocado Crema (recipe follows)

Fresh cilantro leaves, for garnish

1. Combine the curry paste, canola oil, and the ¼ cup lime juice in a food processor, and process until smooth. Place the steak in a large baking dish and add half of this marinade. Turn the meat to coat it; then cover the dish and refrigerate for at least 4 and up to 12 hours.

2. Whisk the honey and the remaining 3 tablespoons lime juice together in a bowl. Set aside.

3. Heat a grill to high, or a cast-iron pan or griddle over high heat. Remove the steak from the marinade and season with salt and pepper on both sides. Grill the steak until slightly charred on both sides and cooked to medium-rare, about 10 minutes total. Remove from the grill and let rest for 10 minutes.

4. Meanwhile, lower the heat under your grill to medium.

5. Brush the onion slices with canola oil and season with salt and pepper. Season one side of the onion slices with steak rub and grill them, rub side down, until light golden brown, 2 minutes. Flip them over, brush with barbecue sauce, and grill until just cooked through, about 4 minutes more. Separate into rings.

6. Wrap the tortillas in foil and warm them on the grill for 5 minutes.

7. Thinly slice the steak across the grain. Place the slices on a platter, and immediately drizzle with the honey-lime dressing. Lay the warm tortillas on a flat surface and arrange a few slices of the beef down the center of each. Top with onion slices, pickled peppers, a dollop of avocado crema, and some cilantro. Then roll up and eat.

(recipe continues)

Pickled Roasted Peppers

1 cup white wine vinegar

½ cup apple cider vinegar

1 clove garlic, thinly sliced

2 tablespoons sugar

1 tablespoon kosher salt

2 red bell peppers, roasted (see Notes, page 22) and thinly sliced

2 yellow bell peppers, roasted (see Notes, page 22) and thinly sliced

1 tablespoon finely chopped fresh oregano leaves

1. Combine the vinegars, garlic, sugar, and salt in a small saucepan over high heat. Boil until the sugar has dissolved. Remove from the heat and let cool to room temperature.

2. Put the peppers and oregano in a medium bowl, add the vinegar mixture, and stir to combine. Cover and refrigerate for at least 4 hours and up to 2 days.

Avocado Crema

2 ripe Hass avocados, peeled, pitted, and chopped

Juice of 1 lime

2 tablespoons rice vinegar

1 teaspoon honey

¼ cup chopped fresh cilantro leaves

Kosher salt and freshly ground black pepper

Combine the avocados, lime juice, vinegar, honey, and ¼ cup water in a blender, and puree until smooth. Add the cilantro, season with salt and pepper, and blend for a few seconds just to incorporate.

WINNER!

Father Leo Patalinghug's Funky Fusion Fajitas

SERVES 6

¼ cup dry white wine

¼ cup soy sauce

¼ cup red wine vinegar

¼ cup plus 2 tablespoons olive oil

2 tablespoons ketchup

1 cup firmly packed dark brown sugar

3 cloves garlic, minced

1 tablespoon ground ginger

Kosher salt and freshly ground black pepper

1 teaspoon red pepper flakes

1 teaspoon garlic powder

1 (1¼-pound) flank steak

½ red onion, sliced into ½-inch-thick half-moons

1 green bell pepper, sliced into ¼-inch-wide
   strips

1 yellow or red bell pepper, sliced into
   ¼-inch-wide strips

4 green onions (white and green parts), sliced
   into ¼-inch pieces

12 (8-inch) flour tortillas, warmed

Guacamole

Screamin' Sour Cream (recipe follows)

1. Combine the wine, soy sauce, vinegar, the ¼ cup olive oil, the ketchup, brown sugar, 2 of the garlic cloves, the ginger, 2 teaspoons salt, 1 teaspoon black pepper, the red pepper flakes, and the garlic powder in a large bowl, and whisk together. Remove about ½ cup and set it aside for serving.
2. Tenderize the steak by piercing it all over with a fork. Place the steak in a resealable plastic bag, pour the rest of the marinade into the bag, and seal. Refrigerate the steak for at least 2 and up to 4 hours.

3. Remove the steak from the refrigerator 30 minutes before grilling.
4. Heat the grill to medium-high.
5. Remove the steak from the marinade, discarding the marinade, and season with salt and pepper. Grill for about 6 minutes per side for medium-rare, or to your desired doneness. Let the meat rest for 10 minutes while you cook the vegetables.
6. Heat the remaining 2 tablespoons olive oil in a large sauté pan over medium-high heat. Add the onion, bell peppers, green onions, remaining 1 clove garlic, a tablespoon or so of the reserved marinade, and salt and pepper to taste. Cook, tossing occasionally, until the vegetables are crisp-tender, about 8 minutes.
7. Slice the steak into thin pieces across the grain. Spread each tortilla with some guacamole and top with 4 to 6 slices of meat, some vegetables, some sour cream, and a drizzle of the reserved marinade if desired. Say a "Grace Before Meals" and enjoy the feast!

Screamin' Sour Cream

½ cup sour cream

2 tablespoons hot sauce

½ teaspoon kosher salt

½ teaspoon freshly ground black pepper

1 teaspoon garlic powder

Whisk all the ingredients together in a small bowl. Cover and refrigerate for at least 30 minutes.

BARBECUE CHICKEN AND POTATO SALAD

ON THIS EPISODE OF THROWDOWN!...

We are standing at attention for barbecue chicken and potato salad, and who better to take on with this all-American meal than bona fide Army man Brad Turner? ○ Sgt. First Class Brad Turner of the U.S. Army is posted in Fort Lee, Virginia. He thinks Food Network is joining his ranks to film a special on the armed forces: "Red, White, and BBQ." It makes perfect sense that Food Network would want him on the job. More than just a man in uniform, Sergeant Turner is also an accomplished chef who has traveled the world to cook his first-class cuisine for our men and women in uniform. ○ One thing that Sergeant Turner has learned on his culinary tour of duty is how to satisfy the troops' hunger for good old American food. This Throwdown-bound menu fits the bill. His Sunshine Barbecue Chicken and Roasted Red Potato Salad has his recruits giving him a twenty-one-gun salute. His savory barbecue sauce begins with a trinity of onions, garlic, and bell peppers cooked until soft with olive oil and sesame oil, before being blended with mustard, brown sugar, sesame seeds, and ginger. Brad's potato salad reminds me of the picnic fare of my youth; its down-home ingredients include mayonnaise, mustard, pickle relish, and hard-cooked eggs.

Name: Brad Turner
Hometown: Fort Lee, Virginia
Occupation: Sergeant First Class, United States Army

I head to the test kitchen anxious to try out a new technique for my barbecue chicken and to polish up a potato salad that I haven't broken out in a long time—a Mesa Grill classic. I start by marinating the chicken in buttermilk to tenderize the meat, give it a nice tangy flavor, and help it to keep moist on the grill. I've also decided on a rub (sixteen spices, anyone?) to add additional flavor and help create a really great outside crust that grabs onto the barbecue sauce, making it cling to the crisp skin. A key phrase to remember when grilling chicken is "low and slow." Low heat allows the fat to render and the skin to turn crisp; by the time the skin is crisp, the chicken is cooked through. My spicy barbecue sauce starts with a base of onions, garlic, red chiles, and ketchup and gets an extra shot of flavor from a good dose of bourbon. My mayonnaise-based potato salad is totally inspired by the Southwest and is flavored with some of my favorite ingredients—garlic, red onions, and red and green chiles.

Stephanie, Miriam, and I arrived on base, suited up in protective gear, and were taken by a military escort to see Sergeant Turner. While the crowd seemed to be enjoying my chicken, the majority of the troops remained loyal to their leader and fellow Army man. But we all know that the Throwdown title isn't decided by the audience, so Brigadier General Jesse Cross and restaurant owner Frances Daniel were on hand to critique our chicken on taste, overall balance of flavor, and wow factor. Both judges loved my chicken and felt that it was cooked to perfection

and deliciously flavored. They agreed that Sergeant Turner's chicken was perfectly cooked as well, and they liked the sweetness of his sauce as well as the egg and pickle relish accents in his potato salad. Even with all of their praise for both of us, we knew there could be only one winner. This battle, it was me.

Sergeant Turner was incredibly hospitable, and I'm not sure that I have ever met a nicer man. I was proud of our dishes and pleased with the final results, but if you've seen this episode, you might have noticed that I was eating *his* chicken during the whole competition. Really, I couldn't get enough. I'm not sure how we won this one, but a big salute to Sergeant Turner all the same.

Brad Turner's Sunshine Barbecue Chicken

WINNER!

Bobby Flay's
Bourbon Barbecue Chicken
with Sixteen-Spice Rub

SERVES 4

1 quart buttermilk

Hot sauce, such as Tabasco

3 bone-in, skin-on chicken breast halves

3 bone-in, skin-on chicken thighs

3 bone-in, skin-on chicken drumsticks

6 tablespoons canola oil

1 medium Spanish onion, coarsely chopped

3 cloves garlic, coarsely chopped

½ cup plus 2 tablespoons bourbon

1¼ cups ketchup

1 heaping tablespoon Dijon mustard

1 tablespoon red wine vinegar

1 tablespoon Worcestershire sauce

2 canned chipotle chiles in adobo, chopped

2 tablespoons dark brown sugar

2 tablespoons ancho chile powder

1 tablespoon smoked sweet Spanish paprika

¼ teaspoon chile de árbol

1 tablespoon honey

1 tablespoon molasses

Kosher salt and freshly ground black pepper

Generous ½ cup Mesa Grill 16 Spice Poultry
    Rub (see Sources, page 269) or your favorite
    poultry rub

Mesa Grill Potato Salad (recipe follows), for
    serving

1. Pour the buttermilk into a large baking dish, add a few dashes of hot sauce, and stir to combine. Add the chicken and turn to coat. Cover and refrigerate for at least 2 hours or up to overnight.

2. Heat 2 tablespoons of the oil in a heavy-bottomed medium saucepan over medium-high heat. Add the onion and cook until soft, 3 to 4 minutes. Add the garlic and cook for 1 minute. Add the ½ cup bourbon and cook until completely reduced. Add the ketchup and ½ cup water, bring to a boil, and simmer for 5 minutes. Add the mustard, vinegar, Worcestershire, chipotle, brown sugar, ancho chile powder, paprika, chile de árbol, honey, and molasses. Simmer, stirring occasionally, until thickened, 10 minutes.

3. Transfer the mixture to a food processor and puree until smooth; season with salt and pepper. Pour into a bowl, add the remaining 2 tablespoons bourbon, and cool to room temperature.

4. Heat a grill to medium heat. Brush the chicken with the remaining 4 tablespoons oil, and season on both sides with salt and pepper. Rub the skin side with some of the spice rub. Grill slowly, closing the lid of the grill and turning the chicken as needed, until the chicken is golden brown on both sides and the fat has rendered, 20 to 25 minutes. During the last 10 minutes of grilling, begin brushing the chicken liberally with the barbecue sauce.

5. Serve the chicken with Mesa Grill Potato Salad.

Mesa Grill Potato Salad

12 (about 3 pounds) small new potatoes

1 cup mayonnaise

2 tablespoons Dijon mustard

2 tablespoons fresh lime juice

2 tablespoons ancho chile powder

½ teaspoon cayenne pepper

1 large ripe beefsteak tomato, seeded and chopped

⅓ cup chopped fresh cilantro leaves

1 jalapeño, finely diced

3 green onions (white and green parts), chopped

1 medium red onion, halved and thinly sliced

4 cloves garlic, finely chopped

Kosher salt and freshly ground black pepper

1. Put the potatoes in a large pot and add cold water to cover by 1 inch; salt the water. Bring to a boil over high heat and cook until tender when pierced with a knife, 12 to 15 minutes. Drain well. Let cool slightly and then cut into ¼-inch-thick slices. Place in a large bowl.

2. Stir together all the remaining ingredients, except the salt and pepper, in a medium bowl, and pour the mixture over the potatoes. Mix gently until combined. Season with salt and pepper to taste.

Brad Turner's
Sunshine Barbecue Chicken

SERVES 4

1 (3½- to 4-pound) chicken, cut into 8 pieces

Kosher salt and freshly ground black pepper

1½ teaspoons garlic powder

1½ teaspoons Italian seasoning

1 small onion, cut into medium dice

1 small bunch green onions (white and green parts), sliced about ¼ inch thick

1 small yellow or orange bell pepper, cut into medium dice

4 celery stalks, cut into medium dice

3 cloves garlic, minced

¼ cup extra virgin olive oil

2 tablespoons toasted sesame oil

1 cup yellow mustard

1 cup loosely packed light brown sugar

2 tablespoons white sesame seeds

1 teaspoon ground ginger

Roasted Red Potato Salad (recipe follows), for serving

1. Preheat the oven to 450°F.

2. Season the chicken pieces with salt and pepper, the garlic powder, and the Italian seasoning. Refrigerate while you make the sauce.

3. Combine the onion, green onions, bell pepper, celery, and garlic on a rimmed baking sheet. Drizzle with the olive and sesame oils, season with salt and pepper, and toss. Roast until tender, about 10 minutes. Set aside to cool slightly.

4. Reduce the oven temperature to 350°F.

5. Whisk the mustard, brown sugar, sesame seeds, and ginger together in a medium bowl. Stir in the warm vegetables and allow to sit for at least 30 minutes before using. Set half the sauce aside for serving.

6. Heat a grill to medium-high. Grill the chicken pieces, flipping them once, until nicely marked, about 5 minutes per side.

7. Transfer the chicken to a rimmed baking sheet, baste well with half of the sauce, and bake, basting frequently, until a meat thermometer inserted into the meat reads 165°F, about 15 minutes. Serve with the reserved sauce and the potato salad.

Roasted Red Potato Salad

2 pounds medium-small red potatoes, quartered

2 tablespoons extra virgin olive oil

Kosher salt and freshly ground black pepper

¼ teaspoon cayenne pepper, plus more for garnish

½ teaspoon garlic powder

⅓ cup mayonnaise

2 tablespoons yellow mustard

2 tablespoons sweet pickle relish

4 hard-cooked eggs, chopped

1. Preheat the oven to 375°F.

2. Put the potatoes on a baking sheet and drizzle with the olive oil. Season with salt and pepper to taste, the cayenne pepper, and the garlic powder. Roast until tender, about 35 minutes. Set aside to cool slightly.

3. Combine the mayonnaise, mustard, relish, and 3 of the chopped eggs in a large bowl. Toss the potatoes with the dressing. Garnish with the remaining chopped egg, and a pinch of cayenne pepper for good measure.

LOBSTER CLUB SANDWICH

ON THIS EPISODE OF THROWDOWN!...

I went up to Rockland, Maine, for some heaven between bread: lobster club sandwiches. **O** Mainer Lynn Archer knows the ropes when it comes to lobster. Starting at the age of ten, Lynn and her six siblings would often rise before dawn to join their fisherman father and reel in the catch of the day. Her great-grandmother taught her to cook and instilled in her a "made-from-scratch" motto that, combined with Lynn's passion for cooking, helped her to create one of the most popular restaurants in Maine, Rockland's Brass Compass Café. **O** Hailed as the "king of clubs" by the *New York Times*, Lynn's lobster club sandwich is about as all-American as you can get: fresh Maine lobster, perfectly toasted homemade white bread, smoky bacon, beefsteak tomatoes, and crispy green-leaf lettuce. This is an attention-grabbing sandwich, and it certainly got ours. Lynn thought she had been called by Food Network to take part in a special called "Taste of Summer."

"When one of my waitstaff said, 'Food Network is on the line,' I replied, 'Take a message. They should know enough not to call a restaurant at lunchtime!'"
    —LYNN ARCHER

Name: Lynn Archer
Establishment: Brass Compass Café
Hometown: Rockland, Maine
Phone: (207) 596-5960

Of course the most important part of a lobster club is the lobster, and using the freshest lobster you can find is key; frozen just won't do in this sandwich. The ideal size is about 2 pounds; smaller ones don't really yield a lot of meat and larger ones can have meat that's a little tough. Having steamed my lobster and separated its meat from the shell, I was ready for its salad phase. I turned to Spain for my inspiration, adding a little saffron, vinegar, honey, and garlic to the mayonnaise I used to bind the sweet hunks of lobster meat.

I knew that I was going to have to bake my bread from scratch if I wanted to compete against Lynn. I decided on a French classic, brioche, and because I love spice in my food, I folded in a little pureed chipotle in adobo for flavor and a beautiful color. I mounded the lobster salad high on the bread and finished it off with crispy Serrano ham instead of bacon, to follow my Spanish theme, and a final handful of peppery watercress.

I showed up at Lynn's "Taste of Summer" party, and though she seemed surprised to see me, she barely blinked when I challenged her to a lobster club Throwdown. She was actually worried for me! And as I began to assemble my lobster salad, I understood why: the home crowd slowly started to turn on me. It seems that ingredients such as saffron, garlic, and celery are all looked down upon when it comes to lobster salad in those parts. Lynn thinks those ingredients all have their place in other recipes, but not in a lobster salad.

Lynn tried my sandwich and while she thought it was good, she said she couldn't really taste the lobster. One bite of Lynn's sandwich and I had to agree with her and the rest of the crowd; really great, fresh Maine lobster needs nothing more than a little bit of mayonnaise and some salt and pepper.

Judges Sam Hayward, a well-known restaurateur, and Annie Mahle, a cookbook author and chef, were grading our lobster clubs on taste, our bread, and whether or not they inspired thoughts of "must have seconds." Lynn's sandwich was up first. Annie and Sam loved its big chunks of lobster and homemade bread as well as the nice, slightly smoky bacon flavor, which they felt didn't overwhelm that of the lobster. They felt her club was straightforward and simple, and that is what Maine cooking is all about. Moving on to my sandwich, the judges felt that my lobster was chopped finer, and while they couldn't figure out the Serrano ham, they loved it—whatever it was. They also took notice of my herbs. So overall, I did pretty well, but as for the winner, that was Lynn, all the way.

Looking back, I don't think there was one moment that Lynn didn't think she could win this competition—I love that! She is a woman who is confident in her ability as a cook and delivers an amazing dish; and *that* is what *Throwdown!* is all about.

Bobby Flay's
Lobster Club with Crispy Serrano Ham and Watercress

MAKES 4 SANDWICHES

¼ cup pure olive oil

8 thin slices Serrano ham

¼ cup red wine vinegar

Large pinch of saffron threads

1 cup mayonnaise

1 tablespoon honey

2 cloves garlic, mashed to a paste

Kosher salt and freshly ground black pepper

½ cup finely diced celery

¼ cup finely diced red onion

1½ pounds fresh cooked lobster meat, chopped

1 tablespoon finely chopped fresh tarragon
   leaves

8 slices brioche, preferably chipotle brioche,
   lightly toasted

2 bunches fresh watercress

1. Heat the oil in a large sauté pan over high heat until it begins to shimmer. Carefully add 4 slices of the ham and cook until crispy on both sides, about 40 seconds per side. Remove to a plate lined with paper towels. Repeat with the remaining ham.

2. Bring the vinegar to a boil in a small saucepan, add the saffron, remove from the heat, and let steep for 10 minutes. Strain, and let cool.

3. Whisk the mayonnaise, honey, vinegar, and garlic together in a large bowl, and season with salt and pepper. Add the celery, onion, and lobster meat, and gently fold to combine. Add the tarragon, and season with salt and pepper.

4. Top 4 slices of the bread with the lobster salad, crispy Serrano ham, and watercress. Top the sandwiches with the remaining slices of bread.

WINNER!

Lynn Archer's
King of Clubs
MAKES 4 SANDWICHES

4 cups cooked Maine lobster meat, in
   big chunks

About 1 cup mayonnaise

12 (½-inch-thick) slices good-quality white
   bread

1 head green leaf lettuce

2 ripe red tomatoes, sliced

12 slices thick-cut bacon, cooked until crisp

1. Gently toss the lobster meat with 2 to 3 tablespoons of the mayonnaise in a large bowl.

2. Lightly toast the bread, and spread each piece with about 1 tablespoon mayonnaise, or to taste. Add 1 or 2 leaves crisp green-leaf lettuce, 2 or 3 slices red ripe tomato, and 3 slices crisp bacon to 4 slices of the bread. Top with the next slice of bread; then heap up lots of lobster salad. Top it off with the last slice of bread and toothpick it together. Halve and serve.

PUMPKIN PIE

ON THIS EPISODE OF THROWDOWN!...

I stormed onto a Connecticut pumpkin patch to challenge Michele Albano to a pumpkin pie Throwdown. But would she give thanks when I showed up? ○ Michele always dreamed of owning her own pie shop, and one day, while watching a show on Food Network, she realized she had everything she needed to do it. Shortly after that, she opened Michele's Pies in Norwalk, Connecticut. Michele now sells between thirty and forty different kinds of pies throughout the year, from fruit to nut, cream to savory. It was her bestselling autumn pumpkin pie that put her on my *Throwdown!* radar. ○ Michele thought she was taking part in a Food Network special on the perfect Thanksgiving meal, called "Thanksgiving in a Twist." Her contribution to the show would be her amazing pumpkin pie with a maple streusel topping. My mission was to elevate this classic holiday dessert to new heights by adding some of my favorite flavors and textures into the mix.

CASE FILE: 7.4

"When I began my pie business, I could only imagine how cool it would be to go up against Bobby Flay in a pie Throwdown. Never did I think for one minute that it was going to be a reality. Even though we did not win, I felt that we won just to be on his show. Since we aired two weeks before Thanksgiving, we knew we had a crazy and wild whirlwind ahead, and boy has it been that way ever since! Every time I think about the experience, I have a hard time wiping the smile off of my face!"
—MICHELE ALBANO

Name: Michele Albano
Establishment: Michele's Pies
Hometown: Norwalk, Connecticut
Website: www.michelespies.com
Phone: (203) 354-7144

I headed to the test kitchen to open a can of Throwdown. Michele is a firm believer in using only fresh pumpkin for her signature pie. But in my opinion, there is no shame in using canned pumpkin; I think it is one of the few consistent canned products in the market. My strategy was to make a really intense filling chock-full of flavor from molasses, cloves, cinnamon, ginger, and vanilla. I also wanted my pie to have a really creamy texture, and so I used lots of eggs, milk, and heavy cream. Even though Michele would be bringing a crust made from her grandmother's secret recipe, I decided to keep it simple with a graham cracker crust. Though nontraditional, a graham cracker crust just screams "autumn," and most important for this baking-challenged chef, it is easy. To finish off my pie, I topped each slice with a light and airy bourbon-maple whipped cream and a cinnamon-oat streusel, giving it a great contrast of textures.

It was a picture-perfect fall day when we set off for the Jones Family Farm in Shelton, Connecticut, to visit Michele. I have to say that I had never before seen a reaction from one of my competitors like Michele's; she was unflappable. Almost immediately, Michele and the crowd frowned on my decision to make a graham cracker crust. I knew there had been a chance that I would take some heat for that, but I learned a long time ago to do what you do best. My choice of canned pumpkin was next to get boos from the audience. I was starting to feel a little defeated even before I began.

Michele and I switched pies for a taste test, and she could tell immediately that I hadn't used fresh pumpkin, finding the texture dense and lacking that fresh pumpkin flavor. And while I have been a fan of canned pumpkin for years, I was beginning to have second thoughts about not taking the extra time and energy to use fresh pumpkin puree. Stephanie and Miriam agreed. The final call would be up to our pastry-savvy judges, James Beard Award–winning cookbook author Dorie Greenspan and chef/co-owner of Metro Bis Restaurant outside Hartford, Connecticut, Christopher Prosperi, who dug into our pies to assess their crust, filling, and overall flavor. Both loved Michele's flavorful, balanced filling and the pie's salty, sweet streusel, but neither felt her crust stood up to the filling. On the other hand, the judges loved my graham cracker crust. They both thought my filling had more spice in it and were enamored of my flavored whipped cream. My pie brought back memories of childhood Thanksgivings and was pronounced the Throwdown winner.

Any time I win a Throwdown that involves baking, I am a little surprised. I was pleased with the win, but I still have to say that Michele's pie was one of the best pumpkin pies I have ever eaten. It has everything that I look for in a dessert—a creamy texture, big bold balanced flavors, and great contrast of textures.

WINNER!

Bobby Flay's
Pumpkin Pie with Cinnamon Crunch and Bourbon-Maple Whipped Cream

MAKES 1 (10-INCH) PIE

Cinnamon Crunch

½ cup all-purpose flour

½ cup quick-cooking rolled oats

½ cup light muscovado sugar

1 teaspoon ground cinnamon

7 tablespoons unsalted butter, cut into small cubes, cold

Crust

2 cups graham cracker crumbs

8 tablespoons (1 stick) unsalted butter, melted

⅛ teaspoon ground cinnamon

1 large egg, lightly beaten

Filling

3 large eggs

3 large egg yolks

¾ cup dark muscovado sugar

¼ cup granulated sugar

2 tablespoons molasses

1½ cups canned pumpkin puree

1¼ teaspoons ground cinnamon, plus more for the top

1 teaspoon ground ginger

½ teaspoon ground nutmeg

¼ teaspoon ground cloves

½ teaspoon fine salt

1 cup heavy cream

½ cup whole milk

½ vanilla bean, split lengthwise, seeds scraped out and reserved, or 2 teaspoons pure vanilla extract

3 tablespoons unsalted butter, melted

Bourbon-Maple Whipped Cream (recipe follows), for serving

(recipe continues)

1. *To make the cinnamon crunch,* preheat the oven to 350°F.

2. Combine the flour, oats, muscovado sugar, and cinnamon in a food processor, and process a few times to combine. Add the butter and pulse until combined. Pat the mixture evenly into a 4-inch square on a parchment-lined baking sheet. Bake until golden brown and crisp, about 15 minutes. Remove and let cool. Transfer to a cutting board and chop into small pieces. Keep the oven on.

3. *To make the crust,* combine the graham cracker crumbs, butter, and cinnamon in a bowl and mix until combined. Press evenly onto the bottom and sides of a 10-inch pie plate. Brush with the beaten egg. Bake until light golden brown and firm, about 12 minutes. Remove from the oven and let cool on a wire rack.

4. Reduce the oven temperature to 300°F.

5. *To make the filling,* whisk the eggs, egg yolks, both sugars, and the molasses together in a medium bowl. Mix in the pumpkin puree, cinnamon, ginger, nutmeg, cloves, and salt. Whisk in the heavy cream, milk, and vanilla seeds or extract. Strain the mixture through a coarse strainer into a bowl. Whisk in the butter.

6. Place the pie plate on a baking sheet, pour the pumpkin mixture into the shell, and sprinkle additional cinnamon over the top. Bake until the filling is set around edges but the center still jiggles slightly when shaken, 45 to 60 minutes. Transfer to a wire rack and cool to room temperature, about 2 hours.

7. Cut the pie into slices and top each with a large dollop of whipped cream and some of the cinnamon crunch.

Bourbon-Maple Whipped Cream

1¼ cups heavy cream, very cold

½ vanilla bean, split lengthwise, seeds scraped out and reserved

2 tablespoons Grade B maple syrup

1 to 2 tablespoons bourbon, to taste

Combine the cream, vanilla seeds, maple syrup, and bourbon in a large chilled bowl, and whip until soft peaks form.

Michele Albano's
Maple Pumpkin Pie with Pecan Streusel

MAKES 1 (9-INCH) PIE

Pie Crust

1¼ cups all-purpose flour, plus more for dusting

½ teaspoon fine salt

½ cup solid vegetable shortening, very cold

1 to 2 tablespoons heavy cream, for brushing

Pecan Streusel

¾ cup pecans, toasted and chopped

¼ cup firmly packed dark brown sugar

2 tablespoons all-purpose flour

½ teaspoon ground cinnamon

2 tablespoons unsalted butter, diced, cold

Filling

2 cups pumpkin puree, preferably fresh

2 tablespoons all-purpose flour

⅓ cup firmly packed dark brown sugar

½ teaspoon ground nutmeg

½ teaspoon ground cinnamon

½ teaspoon fine salt

1¼ cups heavy cream

1 cup Grade B maple syrup

3 large eggs, beaten

Maple Whipped Cream (recipe follows), for serving

1. *To make the crust,* combine the flour and salt in a medium bowl and mix well. Break up the shortening and toss it with the flour mixture to coat. Using a pastry blender or your fingertips, mix the ingredients together until the dough forms coarse crumbs. Add 3 to 4 tablespoons ice-cold water, 1 tablespoon at a time, until the dough easily forms a ball that can hold itself together. Cover in plastic wrap and refrigerate for at least 30 minutes and as long as overnight.

2. While the dough is resting, *make the streusel:* Toss the pecans with the brown sugar, flour, and cinnamon in a medium bowl. Add the butter, and using a pastry blender or your fingertips, work in until you have small clumps. Set aside.

3. Preheat the oven to 425°F.

4. Sprinkle flour generously over a hard surface and roll the dough out with a rolling pin until it forms an 11-inch round. Fold the round in half, place it in a 9-inch pie plate, and then unfold the dough to completely cover the pie plate with a bit of an overhang. Tuck the overhang under to make a double-thick rim, and then use your fingers to crimp the edges of the pie shell. Brush the heavy cream over the crimped edges, and refrigerate until the filling is complete.

5. *To make the filling,* mix the pumpkin, flour, brown sugar, nutmeg, cinnamon, and salt together with an electric mixer on medium speed until smooth, scraping the sides of the bowl well. Add the heavy cream and maple syrup, scraping the bowl several times while mixing. Mix in the beaten eggs.

(recipe continues)

6. Pour the filling mixture into the pie shell, and bake for 15 minutes. Then lower the oven temperature to 350°F and bake until the filling is almost firm, about 30 minutes. Remove the pie from the oven and sprinkle the pecan streusel over the top, covering the pie completely. Return the pie to the oven and bake until the filling is just a bit wobbly in the middle and the pecan streusel is golden, 10 to 15 minutes. The total baking time should be 55 to 60 minutes.

7. Cool the pie on a wire rack. The pie is best served at either at room temperature or cold. Before serving, garnish the pie with the Maple Whipped Cream.

Maple Whipped Cream

2 cups heavy cream

⅓ cup confectioners' sugar

1 teaspoon pure vanilla extract

½ cup Grade B maple syrup, or to taste

1. Place the metal bowl of an electric mixer in the freezer to chill for at least 15 minutes.

2. Combine the cream, confectioners' sugar, and vanilla in the chilled bowl, and beat on high speed until the mixture thickens. Add the maple syrup and beat on high speed until the cream holds firm peaks.

Sources

Mesa Grill Barbecue Sauce, Bobby Flay Steak Rub, Mesa Grill 16 Spice Poultry Rub, and Bobby Flay Hot Sauce
www.bobbyflay.com

Specialty items
Red curry paste, spices, vanilla beans, and vanilla extract
www.kalustyans.com
www.melissas.com

Fresh seafood
www.gortonsfreshseafood.com

Fish, shrimp, lobster, meat, and chicken stocks
www.clubsauce.com

Duck
www.dartagnan.com

Cheeses
www.murrayscheese.com

Rendered chicken fat
www.aviglatt.com

Cast-iron pans/grill pans
Bobby Flay line at
www.kohls.com

Credits

Pages 2, 4, 5 (left and middle), 8, 11, 22, 23, 27, 28, 31, 33, 37, 38, 41, 42, 45, 46, 49, 51 (left), 55, 56, 59, 60, 63, 65, 69, 70, 75, 77, 81, 82, 85, 87, 91, 92, 95, 98, 101, 102, 107, 108, 111, 113, 117, 118, 121, 122, 127, 128, 130 (right), 133, 136, 137, 141, 142, 144, 147 (bottom), 151, 152, 155, 156, 159, 160, 163 (right), 164, 167, 169, 175, 177, 181, 182, 185 (left), 187, 191, 192, 194, 196, 201, 202, 204 (right), 207, 209 (left), 211, 215, 217, 220, 222, 225, 226, 230 (left), 231, 235, 237, 240, 243, 247, 248, 250, 251, 255, 257, 261, 262 (right), 265, 268: photographs copyright © 2010 Ben Fink

Pages 5 (far right), 15, 17 (right), 19, 20, 39, 40, 43, 44, 61, 62, 67, 71, 83, 84, 94, 99, 103, 119, 120, 124, 125, 129, 130 (left), 138, 139, 143, 147 (top), 157, 161, 166, 170, 171, 172, 198, 199, 213, 214, 216, 218, 219, 232, 233, 239, 260, 262 (right), 264, 267: still shots from episodes of *Throwdown! with Bobby Flay,* produced by Rock Shrimp Productions for the Food Network

Pages 16, 17 (left), 18: photographs courtesy of Connie Santandrea

Pages 24, 25: photographs courtesy of Lyle Ruybalid

Pages 29, 30: photographs courtesy of Eric Dominijanni

Pages 34, 35, 36: photographs courtesy of Patricia Schnatter

Pages 47, 48, 51 (right): photographs courtesy of Heather Bohm-Tallman

Pages 52, 53: photographs courtesy of Michael Arciprete

Pages 57, 58: photographs courtesy of Jim Collucci and Harry Cason

Page 66: photograph courtesy of Sean Kavanagh-Dowsett

Page 72: photograph courtesy of Alan Rosen

Pages 76–77: recipe courtesy of *Junior's Cheesecake Cookbook: 50 To-Die-For Recipes for New York-Style Cheesecake* by Alan Rosen and Beth Allen

Pages 78, 79: photographs courtesy of Frank Pena

Pages 88, 89: photographs courtesy of Joseph M. Cascio

Pages 104, 105: photographs courtesy of Phillip Hernandez

Pages 109, 110: photographs courtesy of Debbie Ali

Pages 114: photograph courtesy of P. J. Walter

Pages 134, 135: photographs courtesy of Bob Bernstein

Pages 148, 149: photographs courtesy of Roberto Ayala

Pages 153, 154: photographs courtesy of Joanne Correia

Pages 162, 163 (left): photographs courtesy of Billy Rhodes

Pages 169–170: recipe courtesy of chef Ilse Parra and Caracas Arepa Bar co-owners Maribel Araujo and Aristides Barrios

Pages 178, 179: photographs courtesy of George E. Mouledoux Jr.

Pages 183, 185 (right): photographs courtesy of Stephen L. Reynolds

Pages 188, 189: photographs courtesy of Teresa Salomon

Pages 193, 197: photographs courtesy of Rebecca Earl

Pages 203, 204 (left): photographs courtesy of Michael Schultz

Pages 208, 209 (right): photographs courtesy of Justin Gerena

Pages 223, 224: photographs courtesy of Sparky Newsome

Pages 228, 229, 230 (right): photographs courtesy of Greg Hatem

Page 231: recipe courtesy of executive chef Lauren Smaxwell and The Pit owner Ed Mitchell

Page 238: photograph courtesy of E. V. Day

Page 244: photograph courtesy of Debbie Olguin

Pages 249, 252: photographs courtesy of Joseph Hansbrough

Page 254: photograph courtesy of Linda M. Dodich

Pages 259, 262 (left), 266: photographs courtesy of Julie M. Fernandez

Page 263: photograph courtesy of Michele Albano and Kelly Stuart

Index